HOW TO CONTROL HUMANS

Exposing the Ancient System of Slavery Plaguing Us All, and How to Defeat It.

DANIEL GRAY

How to Control Humans • Exposing the Ancient System of Slavery Plaguing Us All, and How to Defeat It

How to Control Humans / Daniel Gray
Fisrt Edition

CONTENTS

Chapter ONE

THE RISE OF THE SEA PEOPLE

"You have to beat the king to be the king.
No one is going to hand you a gold medal."

~ Donovan Bailey ~

ANCIENT REIGN OF TERROR

God-Kings were the norm for ancient humans for thousands of years. They would build massive ziggurats, to be the centers of their cities. These ziggurats housed royalty, and their religious leaders. The common folk lived surrounding these giant edifices, and were meant to live in awe of them. The system we live under mimics this structural setup.

The common refrain for every local civilization was worship the local god, or die. It was a brutal system of control. One most people accepted, for safety and sustenance. A big problem with this system, was that quite often, the god-king, drunk on his own arrogance, would declare his own dominance over another god-king. Deadly campaigns of conquest ensued. The victors would declare dominance over loser's god, and people would in turn begin worshiping the ascendant deity. The loser deity would lose followers, and their temples were raided and destroyed.

All of this may sound familiar to you if spent any time at church. The Israelites also had a holy ziggurat, the first of which was built by King Solomon approximately in 1000 B.C. While recounting the brutality of other ancient god-kings would be more historically accurate. Biblical accounts of glorious war, gives a sense of what a victorious god can do for his followers.

The Israelites in the bible had a different belief system than the other peoples of the time. Firstly, they only had one god; Yahweh. All other peoples were polytheistic. The second difference was that if the Israelites lost in battle, or suffered some other calamity, it wasn't the fault of their god, it was their own faults for not following Yahweh's instructions.

Hearing these stories in fiery sermons are quite moving. I can recall many sermons about the walls of Jericho falling. If it's true, it's amazing. But the preachers all like to skip over the fact that all the men, women, and children were murdered. In fact, it was ordained, in the book of Deuteronomy, that the Israelites needed to exterminate the Hittites, Amorites, Perizzites, Hivites, Jebusites, and Canaanites, as they would contaminate Israel.

Rape, enslavement, and genocide were commonplace during the Bronze age, and writings, mythological or not, understood this as a fact of life. All throughout the first five books of the bible the authors recount the details of the genocide, plundering, and rape of various peoples. Biblical scholars like to discount many of the stories as myth, as there's no historical data supporting them.

Proving or disproving biblical accounts are irrelevant to this book. I just want to point out what was accepted, during this time period, as evidence of supremacy. Which makes the confederation of Sea Peoples all the more puzzling. They arose out of no where and began to relentlessly attack the ruling kingdoms at the time. All of this during a time of relative peace and stability. Most historians attribute the collapse of the bronze age to the Sea Peoples. They indiscriminately attacked and destroyed entire civilizations, to the glory of nothing.

The Sea Peoples relentless attacked the great empires of the time. The attacked the Egyptians, Libyans, Assyrians, the Hittites, and anything that moved in the fertile crescent. Many cities were sacked and left uninhabited. Some razed cities still exist in ruin until this day, and archaeologists are still studying them. There is very little known about the Sea People's. The most famous recounting of them was from Ramesses III. He constructed a monument, in Medinet Habu, to the Battle of Djahy, fought in 1178 B.C. It's instructive because it was the longest hieroglyphic inscription that we know of. Keep in mind, he is a god-king, and what he's saying is likely propaganda to calm the fears of the population.

"The foreign countries conspired in their islands. All at once the lands were removed and scattered in the fray. No land could resist their arms, from Hatti, Kode, Carchemish, Arzawa, and Alashiya on – being cut off at one time. A camp was set up in Amurru. They desolated its people and its land was like that which had never existed. They were coming forward toward Egypt, while the flame was prepared for them. Their confederation was the Peleset, Tjeker, Shekelesh, Denen, and Weshesh, lands united. They laid their hands upon the lands as far as the circuit of the earth, their hearts were confident and trusting as they said 'Our plans will succeed!'"

Many folks attempt to find logic and reason behind the attacks. Some attempt to try and figure out the cultures of the people who could've potentially comprised the Sea Peoples. This is also irrelevant to this book. What's important is pattern recognition and the correlations to the current times. There is a clear pattern here, but first I'd like to point out something suspicious about the biblical recounting of the time.

Bible believers like to say that the twelve generations from Moses to Solomon was about 480 years. While biblical scholars attribute only 25 years to a generation, and agree on the likely date of the Exodus to be about 1290 B.C.

A longer time period seems a lot more reasonable to conquer an entire region. This is at odds with the reality of the Sea Peoples. In fact, while Rameses III 'won' against the Sea People, their relentless attacks caused the entire empire to collapse in less than 80 years later. The last Pharaoh of Egypt was Ramesses XI. About 100 years later, Solomon built the first temple in Israel.

It's literally quite suspicious that the time period between Moses and Solomon is meant to have happened directly during the relentless reign of terror by the Sea Peoples. Another Egyptian Pharaoh, Merenptah, had battles with the Sea Peoples in the year 1209 B.C. In typical god-king language, Merenptah writes in his funerary temple at Thebes:

"The princes prostrate themselves, saying, "Peace!" Not one of Nine Bows dares raise his head; Tehenu is plundered while Hatti is peaceful, Canaan is seized by every evil, Ashkelon is carried off and Gezer is seized, Yenoam is made as that which never existed, Israel is wasted without seed, Khor is made a widow of Egypt, All the lands are at peace. Everyone who travels has been subdued by the King of Upper and Lower Egypt."

Here, he is talking of the confederation known as the Sea Peoples, destroying other helpless nations. Same as Ramesses III, he declares victory and glory. It's telling because he speaks of the destruction of Israel, precisely when Israel is meant to have been kicking ass all throughout the region. In fact, this is the first known mention of the word 'Israel.' The Sea Peoples are an enigma, they rampaged all across known civilization with no apparent goal in mind. And it appears to me, that the Israelites of the time simply claimed credit for the Sea Peoples' triumphs, as the Sea People didn't care about godly bragging rights.

So who were the Sea Peoples? It really doesn't matter. Their origins, their beliefs, what happened after their raids succeeded are all irrelevant. What we should notice is that they were what we call nowadays; terrorists. And like most modern terrorism, they had a guiding hand. I call them "The Controllers." They operate in secret, manipulating behind the scenes, rarely taking any risks; asymmetrical warfare.

I can't say for certain who the Controllers were, but what happened directly after the collapse of bronze age is also known. We call it the Greek Dark Ages. It lasted from 1100 B.C. to 750 B.C. The Controllers thrive in chaos, disparity, and war. They despise the truth, science, and history. There was a mist of confusion all throughout this period, in Greece. It was intentional. I suspect the Greeks were advancing in knowledge the same as other humans. While other civilizations had made a number of scientific advancements, I believe that some Greeks figured out a way to control humans.

A big part of the control is the need to suppress or destroy knowledge. The control can only work with constant terror and misinformation. You can be forgiven for not knowing the four hundred year dark age in Greece. Because when we speak of the dark ages, we are usually speaking of the almost thousand year calamity after the decaying ruins of the Roman Empire. I believe they are the same movement, by the same people. And we are in a time similar to then. First the Egyptian Empire, then the Roman Empire, and now the United States. If this system of control succeeds, humans could be in for thousands of years of darkness. You will know them by their lies.

MY PERSONAL QUEST FOR THE TRUTH

Most of my life, I struggled with a variety of types of panic attacks. And almost all of them have at least an online article dedicated to them. There was one the confused me to no end. I would have a panic attack every time I tried to lie. There is no name for it either. 'Liephobia?' This made life exceedingly challenging for me.

Ten years ago, after six months of deep meditation 12-16 hours per day, I was free of the other types of phobias. When it came to lying, I accepted that I've only wanted to tell the truth, and promised myself to only tell the truth and follow all of the laws. And since I spent so much time disconnected from my body, I promised to accept all of my emotions as the truth. Some of the emotional directions seemed random and counterproductive. In hindsight, it was the best decision of my life.

Not long after that decision, I felt the need to unburden myself. I had a lifetime of shame that I didn't want inside of me. In 2012, I wrote "Violent Tremors: Journey to Overcome the Legacy of Slavery." I spend most of 2012 crying and typing; it was agony. I tried getting it published and got no takers. It wasn't well written, and it was over 600 pages long. I tried to share it because that's what I felt like I should do. But I was happy that I got no takers.

In 2014, I uploaded to Amazon. For years I was terrified people would read my book and see what a despicable monster that I was. Looking back, I can see how cathartic it truly was. It became necessary to revisit "Violent Tremors" to write this book. I read the last part of my book and became overwhelmed. I'll share it with you now.

I'M FREE

"For a long while I had been focused on two things. The first was a child that I was introduced to by Rachel Hott, the NLP instructor, in a therapy session. The second was a book that I wrote in my mind, which connected my life to everything I thought I knew about the world. The end of the book was to be the solution the all the problems in my life. This is how I solve problems sometimes.

"The child proved to be far more fruitful. The child rarely spoke to me. But after spending years sitting beside him, he trusted me enough to let him be me. It felt horrible being him, but knew that he was important so I allowed it. The impossibility of the book helped distract from the pain.

"One day, the child gave me love to feel. It made my entire shitty life worth it. When the love went away I stopped thinking about the book and made my life's purpose being the child. I knew that I couldn't force him to do anything, so I found a quiet place and waited. I thought love was the greatest thing in the world and I wanted to be ready for it if it ever happened again.

"Something just as amazing as love happened on that beach in DR. The only way I can describe it is 'the greater me.' I felt one with the universe. I want to say that this feeling was greater than love, but I honestly can't remember the difference between the two. This state seemed spiritual, but I think I just tapped into how the brain really works. What I loved about this state was all the ones that weren't really me faded away. The other ones couldn't survive in the presence of the greater me. If life hadn't caught up to me, I don't think I would've ever left that beach.

"Returning to New York, I had a hard time returning to that amazing state. There was too much noise, distractions, and abusive people. I had come to a crossroads. There were two paths that I could pursue; love or oneness. The madness in my family, lack of opportunity, and financial hardship lead me to believe I should sell all I had and find a place that would allow me to sit quietly for the rest of my life. But Gale wouldn't allow me to fire her. I guess I didn't really choose; I let Gale choose. I sat on Eastern Parkway wondering what I should do. I was sure that once I stopped trembling with fear the magic would just happen.

"I thought it would be a good idea to write the book that I'd been thinking about for the past couple of years. The aim of the book was to tie together a bunch of biblical stories, historical stories, and my life stories with the inner battles that I had faced. I was supposed to conclude that I was the asshole who did everything to oppress me. That I was the one that rebelled by causing problems in my body. I was the one who suffered. I was the one who started an uprising. I was the one who found the little one and protected him. I was the battered child. I was the only one able to approach the greater me and I was the great me.

"It all seemed simple in my mind. I was all the characters in all of the stories. It all repeats again and again, and despite what I believe I'm not at all unique; I've happened before. This child is the gateway to something amazing and the image I would try to portray is me sitting by the side of this child defending any attack that comes. He is battered, broken, bloody, and immortal. I protect him so he can heal…

"…I tried sharing more ideas with more people when it hit me; 'I should write I book of ideas!' I was happy on the inside when I decided to write this book instead of the other one. This book was meant to be nothing more than the ideas that the other book would've been based on. Also, at the end of the book, I was supposed to be transformed. The book itself transformed and so did I.

"I think that I'm different now. I'm a little hesitant to test as I don't want to force myself to fake it. Writing this book proved to be extremely difficult at times. Throughout the process of me writing this book, it felt like there was a gentle breeze in the center of my chest. Sometimes that breeze blossomed into an explosion of a beautiful emotion. I don't know what that means or even why it happens. Maybe it's the child telling me that he's happy. I feel the breeze right now. At least it feels like a breeze. I planned to end this book with the beginning of the book that I don't want to write. I don't need to. I think I've achieved my purpose. I finally feel free."

I'M THE ONE WHO SERVES

In a way, it seems like I foretold a book that I was going to write; this book. The me that I was had no clue what I know now. Also, this isn't precisely what I was thinking almost ten years ago. The words that I used were striking, and not what I think it meant when I wrote it. For over twenty years, I've questioned my own sanity. Even up to this day, I have to check 'am I crazy?'

I did lots of therapy, and regularly went to ASCA (Adult Survivors of Child Abuse) meetings, and deeply studied Neuro-Linguistic Programming (NLP.) In the last ten years, I changed the name of the greater me to the Creator. As I remember when it was that I was created. This was also in the Violent Tremors. I believed that I had solved an impossible physics problem in my late 20's.

"I stood there with glee as I had solved an impossible problem. There were a number of logic consequences from my line of thinking. 'I wonder what humans look like from different directions? I suppose from one perspective we look like empty space and another we appear to be energy beings. We are energy beings. Something about us is passing out of existence and not returning. Humans are complex and there are a number of energies produced by us and passing through us constantly. Right. If there were a way to put that energy back we could live forever. It may not be beyond our reach. But in order to do that we need to figure out how to unburn a match. Exactly, even the simple act of lighting a match causes the same reaction. I don't get it. What we call fire is nothing more than motion in a specific direction. If a match is unburned will it be the same as before? Probably not.'

"'Amazing! I think I figured out something important. Yeah, so what's next? Obviously, I need to work out the math. How can you do that? Most of this is all made up. I know. I have to make it all work; same as Einstein! Sweet! Wait, so how long do you think it will take for you to figure out the math? Hmmm, maybe another ten years. This is so excit…'

"Even though I never admitted to myself why I focused so intensely on this impossible problem; I knew. I thought that it would be great to have something else impossible to think about. I was wrong. As soon as I completed that final thought I clasped my hands against my temples and squeezed with all my might. I began screeching at the top of my lungs in agony. If felt as if my head was going to explode. I had sharp pains all over my body. 'Open your eyes and see if anyone can help.' I heard a voice in my head say.

"I continued screaming while my eyes tracked white people walking around me. 'Why won't they help?' I heard a voice say. To their credit the ones that walked by me looked me over to make sure I wasn't hurt as they walked by. I later found out that Madison Square Park was frequented by heroin users.

"When I realized no one would or could help I began to panic even more. That is when I could comprehend all the voices inside screaming unintelligibly all at once. It appeared to be a power struggle between many opposing factions. While the pain didn't stop I forced myself to stop screaming. Then I struggled agonizingly as took a few steps backwards and sat down on the bench behind me. I closed my eyes, placed my hands on my knees, and was determined to work out a peaceful resolution.

"'Alright I understand; you want children. We need a woman first right? Okay, okay I understand; nothing serious right now. When do you think is the right time? Okay, first we need to deal with these emotional blocks. No? That's fine. I understand. What's stopping us from healing ourselves? Okay, so we need money? How much money do we need, a million dollars maybe? No? Oh, that's too much. It will be too distracting? So what's a good amount? Alright, we'll make ten thousand per month in cash flow. So we need to find the right way to invest what we have to make 10K monthly without working. What's that? No more chess? I used chess to hide and no more hiding? I understand. But what if I just taught chess solely for the money? I have a fairly successful career you know. No? Okay, I understand. How should I go about making this money? You want to perform? Okay I understand.'

"'Wait; there are many objections to that. How about we leave performing until after we are healed? Great! So how am I to make this money? Alright, alright I'll figure it out. It would be nice to study something new. Hmmm, no more random studying? How do I figure out how to make this money? Okay, I can only study the things that are related to goals that I'm setting now. I promise no more hiding. So in summation, I will quit studying and teaching chess, I will stop finding new things to study, I will make ten thousand per month in cash flow, when I no longer have to work I will spend my time, energy, and money on healing myself, then I'm free to perform and settle down with a girl. After all of this happens then I can have a child. Great it's settled!'

"My panicked breathing subsided along with the pain. All of the unintelligible yelling had subsided. I was at peace internally. I sat bewildered and dumbfounded. Over the course of a few minutes my entire life had completely changed. I was amazed at the process and the speed in which things transpired. I was also aware that I had traded one impossible problem for another of a different sort. Yet, that wasn't the most astounding realization that I had.

"'Intersting. What's interesting? You don't know what I find interesting? No. Does anyone here know what I find interesting? No. What's interesting? Wow, even more interesting. What's interesting! Where's the one who was completely focused on the problem that we just solved? Why do you want to talk to him?! He's an asshole! Fuck him! He's hardheaded. Hello? Are you there? Yes. I'm here. I wan… '

"After a couple of words I had a strong sense that he was suppressed in mid-sentence. I knew that he was still there, but I got a sense of him being engulfed by blackness. 'Interesting. What the fuck is so interesting! What happened to him just now? Fuck him! We don't need him anymore! Does anyone think that problem we solved is at all important? I thought you were going to do what you promised! No! You aren't going to do what you said! You should know that I'm honest. I will do as I said I would. I'm just curious. No one thinks that what we were doing was important? Do you think it's important? Actually, no I don't care about it at all. That's why I'm curious; we were excited about it a few minutes ago. Fuck that stupid problem! It could all be bullshit!'

"'Interesting. What the fuck is so interesting!! Yeah jerk what's so interesting? Hello? Which one is the real me and what do you want? I'm the real me you asshole! Me too! What the fuck kind of stupid question is that? Obviously we are all me! Incorrect, I suspect none of us communicating is the real me. Fucking asshole! He's not going to do what he said he would do! Rest assured that I must comply with the existence I was created for. This ordeal has agitated each of you enough to become distinctly audible.

The fact that none of you understands what I understand further exemplifies what I have concluded. Go on.'

"'First, let's look at what happened previously. We had been consumed with constant learning and solving impossible problems. Solving a problem that had morphed from many other problems spanning almost fifteen years apparently caused us to have a mental breakdown. Duh, we all noticed that. Go on. I'm aware that this very process has happened to us multiple times. But the speed at which it happened this time made me notice something. What? I'm not the me that I was a few minutes ago! In fact I'm a brand new me! I still remember what the old me knew, but I have a different purpose. The moment that I could hear you all screaming the me that I am was dispatched with a single purpose; find out what each of you wants and help you get it.'

"'So! What's so interesting about that? Upon realizing my newness I wished to communicate with the me that I was. I wasn't allowed. Thus far, what I've noticed is that each of you has your own agenda and will stop at nothing to achieve it; regardless of how it affects the rest of us. What's more, we've been aware for some time that some of you are images of whole other people. So what's your point? Which of you has the power to suppress the me that we used to be?' I waited a few moments for a response. I didn't hear anything. 'Do you see now? If any of you had power to overtake the me that I was, it would've happened long ago. Better still, there is one here that I'm sure comes from within me; my biological nature.'

"'Up until this point, I had no idea that I had a desire for children. There was a sharp pain in my groin associated with this desire. I had ignored and suppressed this desire. A few moments ago, that raw desire was powerful and present. For some reason, now he seems content to wait for an impossible set of circumstances to take place. Who among us has the strength to calm such a powerful force? We did it together! I wish that were true. The fact is, each of you distinctly wishes for your own ends. Now we are stuck with a seemingly unworkable compromise.'

"'I wonder if I had become a new person at each impasse in my life? I wonder if other people experience that same things generally or specifically? I wonder if this is common or is something wrong with me? This is something that we may or may not wish to answer. But, given the me that I am, I'm compelled to find out what each of you wants and help you get it. Understanding that none of us communicating has the power to change a thing, then logically the real me is hiding. The me that gave me control and has the power suppress any of us. This is the me that I wish to communicate with. Hello? What do you want?' I sat still for a few minutes, with my eyes closed waiting for a response; there was none. I had a sense that everyone else understood what I had already realized, and they all waited patiently for the real me to speak up; he didn't.

"'If we don't leave now, then we won't be early.' A voice told me. I looked down at my watch and I had about five minutes to be six minutes early. I used to set my watch six minutes ahead. This was a little trick to make sure that I was always early. Also, it was used to break any train of thought that I had and focused on arriving on time. Part of me was furious that my watch was set six minutes ahead. Five minutes and seven minutes ahead didn't bother me at all. Six minutes ahead always started a lengthy tirade about how ridiculous it was to use six minutes. Looking at my watch always successfully brought me back to reality.

"'Yes, I should get going. I'm always early.' I began walking feeling fortunate that I had learned NLP and regularly spent time communicating with each part of me. That major mental breakdown could've turned out differently. I then had a new purpose in life. I didn't take any more language partners and didn't renew any of my chess teaching gigs. I honestly didn't care much for the grand compromise. The greatest thing that I realized was that I wasn't the real me. This led ultimately to a greater purpose and a problem even more impossible. What does the real me really want?[1]"

I've since given names to some of the main ones that aren't me. I usually name them for the purpose I understand that they do. They all know me as the One Who Serves.

Chapter TWO

THE KNOWLEDGE OF THE ANCIENTS

"If, like me, you're interested in history, Egypt is a place of wonders. It's the land of many civilizations, including Greek, Roman, Christian, and Muslim."

~ Michael Portillo ~

THE POWER OF SOUND

Understanding that the patterns have been repeating for thousands of years is important. The Controllers thrive when there's economic disparity. They infect a populace with lies and rumors. They use subterfuge and terrorism to have everyone focused in the wrong direction. Since the Egyptian empire was the last bastion of the Bronze Age, we'll focus on what made them such a super power of the time. Yes, I figured out the ancient technologies of our ancestors. And I'm going to share it here.

Firstly, I'd like to say that I may not have 'figured it out,' as much as I might be remembering it. The truth is important to me. But the truth of the past is quite simple, and once you've heard the truth the lies become even more pronounced. Understanding who we were is vital to breaking the mist of lies surrounding the past.

I suspect that there is an ancient text, that the Controllers guard with their lives. It's like a human spell-book. In it, there is an immutable command "All knowledge and history started with us!" The Controllers can, in all likelihood, trace their lineages back to the time just before the Greek Dark Ages. They had successfully supplanted the god-kings of old, but they had the same arrogance and blood-lust.

The knowledge of the past was suppressed through assassinations, oppression, and propaganda. In modern times, it's mostly suppressed with money and conspiracy theories. Before I go into technical detail of how things were done in the past, I'd like to tell you how I got there. By watching the television program "Ancient Aliens."

I know, the show is bullshit. I am who I am. I'm obsessed with the truth. Whenever I'd see a clip of Ancient Aliens pop up in my YouTube feed, I became livid. If I was angry, I was supposed to be angry, it was the truth. Every episode pissed me off to no end. I couldn't believe how often and freely that these horrible people would regurgitate giant lies!

Over the last decade, I watched almost every episode of that horrible show. I did it because I had to. A few times, I would watch YouTube videos exposing some of the lies that they told, to calm me down. Sometimes I would watch Action Bronson watch Ancient Aliens. During that period, I had started smoking weed. I made sure to get giggly weed so I could watch that wretched show while Action Bronson got high and watched that show. After a while, the weed didn't help anymore. The lies infuriated me so. I reasoned that someone is purposely promoting giant lies, and sharing those lies on the History Channel. The History Channel!!!

Eventually, I began watching the show and pausing whenever I thought I heard a lie, and began researching whatever they were talking about to confirm that they in fact are lying directly into the camera. It was soothing to ad infinitum disprove every lie. The answers, to ancient technology, came to me recently. It wasn't Ancient Aliens, it was us. The answer is obvious, because they've been saying it for thousands of years. The ancient peoples used the power of sound to fuel their civilizations. Scientifically speaking they used acoustic propulsion and thermo-acoustics.

ACOUSTIC PROPULSION AND THE STIRLING ENGINE

Acoustic propulsion, or moving things with sound, is a simple concept in physics. A YouTube search will yield a plethora of individuals play a tone, making plastic soda bottles rotate in the air. Ancient humans didn't have plastic bottles, so they likely used clay jars. The neck of the jar simply needs to be narrower than the body of the jar. If you blow air over the neck, a tone is produced. If you play the tone that the jar resonates with, there will be a small amount of force emanating from the jar.

The Ancient Egyptians didn't have the tools we had. So they likely attached the clay jars to something like the Sabu disc. This artifact was found in the tomb of Prince Sabu(3000 BC.) It was an odd thing to be buried with Royalty. Only the most valuable of things are found buried in royal tombs. And no one had any clue what this thing does. For our purposes, the Egyptians fastened two to three clay jars on top of the Sabu disc, and fixed the bottom with whatever work needed to get done. By generating a sound that resonates the jars, you'll create rotational motion. With this, you can grind, sand, buff, bore, drill, and with gears you can have simple machines. All of this would be slow going, as acoustic propulsion doesn't generate much force.

In order to power such a device, you'd need to generate a tone that would last for hours. Where did they get that tone? There are many traditions alive today where large groups of people chant a single tone for hours. They were the power source of the ancients. They made religion out of science. It's likely that ancient scientists exploited human ignorance for their own personal gains. But, little did they know, that chanting a tone could be therapeutic.

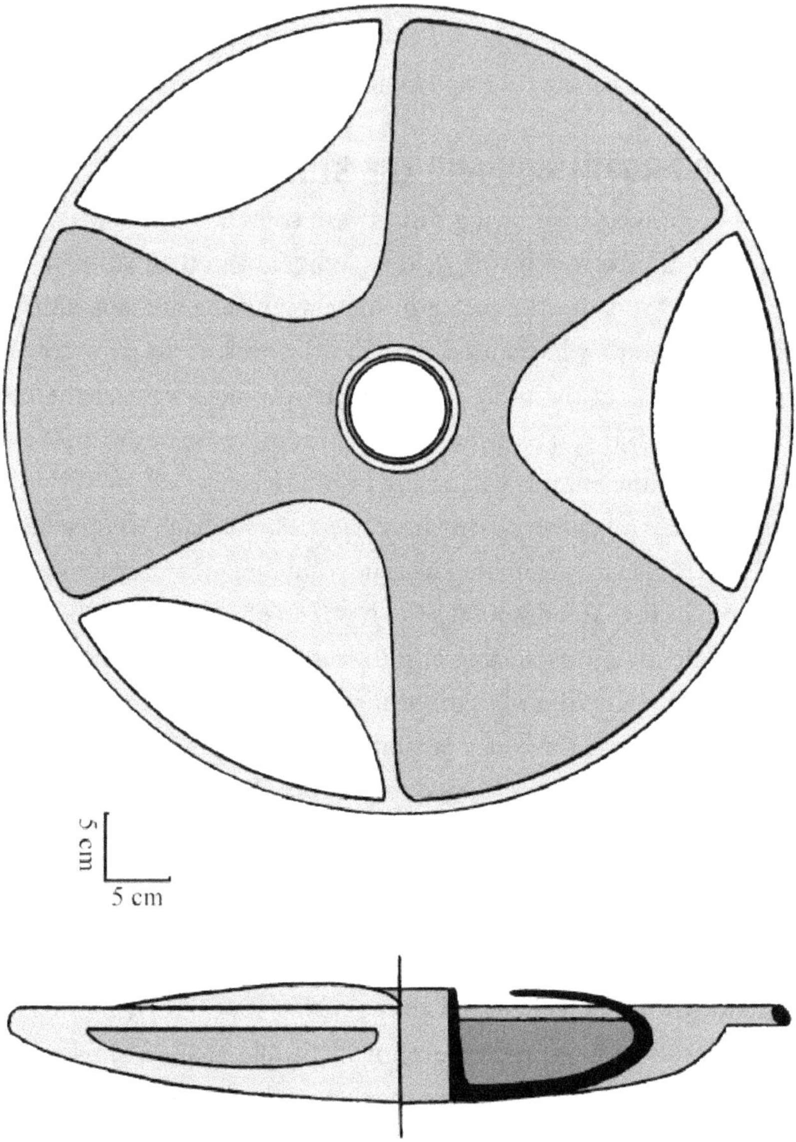
5 cm
5 cm

While acoustic propulsion explains much of the ancient technology, How did the Ellora Caves get built? They were built well into the Iron age, long after the collapse of the Egyptian Empire and after the Greek Dark Ages. They also used the power of sound. They used what we call today a Stirling engine. The science of it is called thermo-acoustics. Meaning, with heat, you can create sound waves. By using a Stirling engine, you can create complex machines used the materials of the time. Yes, ancient people had complex machines using heat.

Ancient humans carved a glorious temple out of a mountain and it still stands today. It certainly wasn't aliens. It was us. If you want to learn more, just do a video search on Stirling engines. And imagine to yourself, could such a device drill and sand if we wanted to?

I suspect the scientists who knew this knowledge kept them as secrets for their own personal power. It was simple for the controllers to erase the memory of the science. Those with the forbidden knowledge were assassinated. For now, let's only focus on Egypt. What was the point of the Pyramids?

THE PYRAMINDS WERE MUSICAL INSTRUMENTS

I believe the ancient Egyptians built the Pyramids in order to create long sustained tones, in order to do work using acoustic propulsion. Not all the Pyramids had this specific function, which aids the confusion and conspiracy theories. Lets just focus on one, the Great Pyramid of Giza.

Firstly, the only solid blocks in the entire thing are the granite blocks shown at 10, the so called King's Chamber. They likely managed it by floating the blocks, with animal skin balloons, along the Nile, and then up the air tight causeway. But the rest is what we nowadays call concrete. In fact, Professor Joseph Davidovits, of the Geopolymer Institute, demonstrated the process the Egyptians likely used in 2002. They created an imitation pyramid with a mixture of things that were available to the ancient Egyptians and water. With wooden molds, they created the very same structures the Egyptians did. Ancient people understood what concrete was.

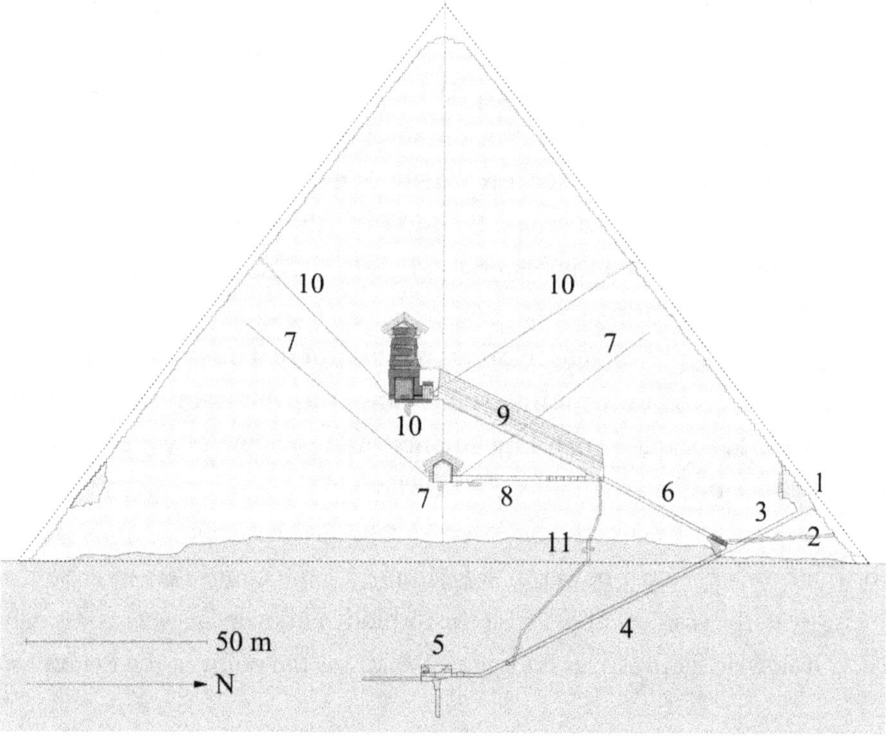

Great Pyramid S-N Diagram.svg. Flanker. Creative Commons Image

There were four different materials that make up the Pyramid at Giza. There's the granite, which can hold an electrical charge, the yellow limestone, which is semi-conductive, the outer white limestone, which was not conductive, and the golden cap, which is highly conductive. How does any of this make a sound?

There are a myriad of technologies at work here. Atmospheric electricity is one of them. This is something that we all should know about. Our planet is a gigantic magnet. Though not a very powerful one. Imagine taking your refrigerator magnet and making it planet sized. That's about how powerful the Earth's magnet field is. The ground is negative, and the ionosphere, 31 miles from the surface, is positive. There is a constant flow of electricity from positive to negative. It's so faint, that no one on the surface notices. But the higher up you go the higher the voltage will be.

Yes, there is a company trying to harvest atmospheric electricity right now. The Ion Power Group is pushing atmospheric energy as a renewable energy source. The only real drawback, which is a big drawback, is lightning would destroy their equipment.

With an electrically insulated Pyramid, a conductive gold top, and semi-conductive interior, a continuous electric current would pass from the base of the pyramid to the top. Some electrons would get stored in the King's Chamber, and it would get warm. But what about the problem the Ion Power Group has with lighting? If there is an electric current, in the largest structure on the Earth at the time, in the middle of a rain forest, wouldn't lighting be a huge problem?

In fact, thinking of all of the massive ziggurats, what happened when they got struck by lightning? Since the Earth is a giant magnet. As water vapor condenses and form clouds, ice particles bump into each other and knock electrons loose from the particles. Then the different charged ice particles separate in the same fashion as the Earth. The tops of clouds are positive and the bottom of clouds are negative. As these clouds pass over tall structures there's a chance that a bolt of lighting will strike it.

There's evidence that the Pyramid of Medium, a Pyramid in Teotihuacan, and also the Great Pyramid had been involved in an explosion. Ancient Aliens would like for you to believe something about alien power stations and mercury. What about the old fashioned, 'tall things get hit by lightning?' If lighting strikes a thing, and there is nothing to contain the charge, then you will have a plasma explosion. The Pyramid at Giza is the second structure built on the same solid granite site. The base of the Pyramid is older than the Pyramid itself. The first one likely exploded from consecutive lightning strikes. What did the ancient Egyptians do to combat this? Nothing, lightning was the point.

If the causeway were sealed airtight and filled with water, when the Nile flooded it would create a stream of water due to atmospheric pressure differences. With an airtight seal over 1 and 2 in the image above, water can be directed

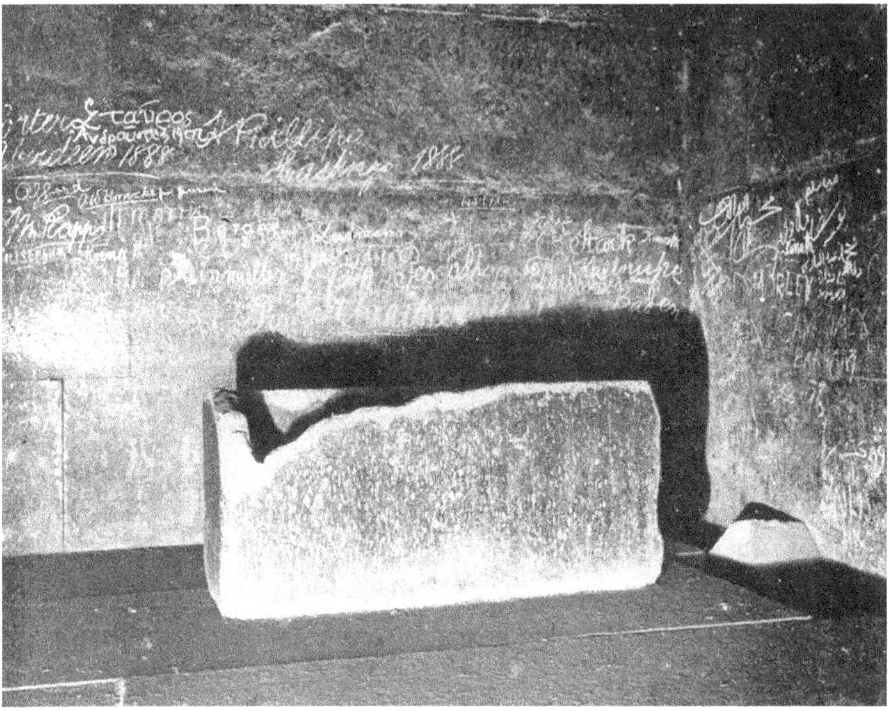

into different parts of the instrument. By blocking 1, water would be forced up through 2, and slowly flood until reaching chamber 10. How would they know the instrument is flooded enough? The shafts of seven would click as the pressure of the rising water forces the air out. What's in chamber 10? That's the so called King's Chamber. A granite container. If chamber 10 is flooded, and the water is released, then what's left is water inside the granite container.

If 1 is left unblocked, the water will drain down through 11 and 4, and into chamber 5. The design of the chamber would create a thumping effect on the granite that surrounds it. The rhythmic striking will knock electrons loose from the granite base, that traverse the semi-conductive limestone into the granite in chamber 10. Making it hotter. All of this will create an electro-magnetic field that would increase the chances of getting struck by lighting. Given that the Nile is flooded, it is likely rainy season in the middle of a rain forest. A lightning strike, thousands of years ago, was almost a given.

What happens if lightning strikes the Pyramid at Giza? The electricity would get stored in the gigantic granite blocks in 10. Making them incredibly hot. The heat will cause the water in the granite container to boil making a temperature differential inside of chamber 10. That temperature difference creates concussion waves, or a tone. Just outside chamber 10 is an acoustic sync, and chamber 9 is a resonance chamber. I suspect chamber 10 had a wooden structure to direct condensed water back into the granite container in order to sustain the tone as long as possible without the need to constantly flood the instrument.

In this way, the Egyptians could create a sustained tone for long periods in order to get work done, with acoustic propulsion. I probably could write a lengthy book just about these technologies. It isn't important for this book. It's vital to realize that the Ancient Aliens program is intentional propaganda. They are throwing up smoke screens, because the Controllers don't want people to realize that humans had any advanced technology before them.

ANCIENT TECHNOLOGY WOULD DESTROY THE MODERN SYSTEM

Controlling the narrative surrounding human history isn't the only reason to suppress ancient knowledge. It would be convenient to say, that the Controllers simply didn't understand how the science worked. But that's highly unlikely. Under their control knowledge, science, and history are all suppressed and attacked. The knowledge that I just shared with you is incompatible with their system of control, and needed to be constantly attacked and systematically silenced.

Take acoustic propulsion for instance. We can right now make an acoustic propulsion device that produces electrical current when a tone is played. In fact, with enough of these devices, connected to a DC converter and sent into batteries, you could power your home with only sound.

The controllers of the system want people to be completely dependent on them for all things. The idea that people can use sound to power anything would make you an instant enemy of the controllers. Their lies about there not being enough wouldn't work. When you upgrade to a Stirling engine, things are even worst.

The only Stirling engines on the market are science experiments and giant industrial ones that are made for organizations like NASA. The market will never provide ones slightly large. Why? Because you could just power your entire life with candles. Do a search for Free Piston Stirling Engine generating electricity. You'll see the small science class ones. If you bought a dozen of these things, you would generate significant current. To power your home? No. But it would be enough to slowly power batteries, which could power your entire life. Most people don't use electricity all day. So yes, there is an amount of Stirling engines, and candles, such that you could power entire life, using ordinary car batteries.

I suspect that the Controllers developed human technology, and needed to decimate anything that interfered with that technology. The main crux of their control are lies. One day I hope they turn on the instrument in Giza. It would be a trumpet signaling the end of the thousands of years of lies and suppression.

Chapter THREE

CONTROL THROUGH THE DIET

"A bad system will beat a good person every time."

~ W. Edwards Deming ~

MY CHILDHOOD FRIEND CHARU

Charu Malik Robinson
January 3, 1977 – October 13, 2020
Rest in Peace Friend

People usually focus on the good characteristics of a person who's passed away. To say that Charu was a good person is almost cliche. We were in the same class in Junior High School. He was always on the honor roll, he always did his homework, and almost never missed a moment of school. I believe it was close to the end of the ninth grade when the school had a special ceremony just for him. They filled the auditorium up with all of the special progress classes and gave a ceremony for the only person who never missed any classes and was never late. Although, he called in sick for a few days after the award. I think he may have been surprised by the award as well. All the guys on the chess team were upset about it. "If they wouldn't have said nuffin he wouldn't have missed any school at all!" Micheal Johnson exclaimed.

I on the other hand was always late. And usually missed one to two days of school per week. At least until the ninth grade. If you ask anyone who knew me at the time, they would tell "I'm surprised that Daniel made it." I was certain that I was going to die. I longed for it, and had a list of people that I planned to take with me. I was bored with school, yes it was easy, but I was in a lot of pain and hated being alive.

The year the Raging Rooks won the National Championships, I was removed from the chess team because I was never in school. It hurt not going, and it especially hurt when all the news cameras showed up and interviewed my friends. During that time, I had turned my life around dramatically. I tried being 'good.' But the incessant trauma persisted. I was supposed to held back in the eighth grade, in fact Mr. Balfour spoke to me alone in his room to lecture me about how he had to hold me back.

"With the amount of latenesses that you had in one month I'm supposed to hold you back! That's not even counting the absences! I don't even know how you have good grades at all! I feel a little bad that I kept you off the chess team, but that was your own fault!" Mr. Balfour was a tough as nails Italian guy. Or at least that's what I think his ethnicity was. "Maurice begged me to let you go to the Nationals, but I couldn't do it. I thought you'd get the message and look at this. Legally you are supposed to repeat the 8th grade! What the hell is going on with you?!"

A few weeks earlier, I had a life changing vision. The vision itself is unimportant. I know now, it was me, rescuing me from self-destruction. I've escaped death many times in my life. I was a child and I was trying to change.

I don't remember exactly what I told Mr. Balfour, I just remember hold back tears as I spoke to him about my life. Tears that are streaming down my face right now. I remember promising him "I'll never be late again."

"Bah!" He threw his hands up in the air. "If you were anybody else, I would hold you back. How the hell did you miss so much school and pass all of your classes? You're lucky I'm retiring kid. Don't think you're getting off scot-free. I'm going to check in on you and see if keep your word!" He stared at my attendance card while shaking his head. "I'll deal with this. Get outta here." He waved me away. He was kind to me, and I didn't deserve it. To this day, I'm almost always early.

I was always jealous of Charu. He was tall, handsome, intelligent, funny, and his mom always took care of him. As a child, although he didn't admit it, he would take care of his friends as well. He would share his food with Brian because he was usually hungry. And for a while he would pay me to come over to his house to tell him jokes. We were all poor, I would've told jokes for free. "Talent!" he would exclaim. That was his catch phrase.

I was jealous that he got into Dalton for high school. I wound up going to my zone school, even though I passed the specialized test to get into Brooklyn Tech. For a long time, I thought my mother kept me out of that school on purpose. After I confronted her about it a few years ago, she told me it was Mr. Fishkin. Even though I had good grades and passed the test, he unilaterally blocked me. My mom said, that he said, that I wasn't Brooklyn Tech material. I admit, I wasn't always the best student. But I really did try my best in the ninth grade.

Charu was nearly the opposite of me. He always did the right things. The path that the teachers drilled in our heads again and again, Charu did it all as a matter of course. He wasn't perfect, and he had many ups and downs. In all, if there were ever a role-model of a person who grew up in the nightmare of Harlem, NYC, in the 80's, he was it.

I have to admit, I wasn't a very good friend to Charu. These last ten years, I basically spent alone. In retrospect, I'd call it meditating. I'd been so disconnected from myself for so long, I made it a point to listen to and trust the feelings that I had. Early on in my hermitage, Charu seemed to be having a hard time. Kasaun had reached out on Skype and tried to get us to meet up. I wanted to be alone, and expressed that. For ten years, I barely spoke to anyone.

Finding work proved to be difficult since I promised myself that I would only tell the truth, and not accept abuse. I made over a quarter of a million dollars in 2011. By 2017, I was working for Chess NYC, making less than $25k, and substituting for another chess teacher, and team teaching with Charu! We greeted each other as childhood friends would. Then we got to work. During the class, he would randomly fall asleep for no reason. I would tap him on the shoulder to wake him up. "You alright man?" I asked. "Yeah man, we're trying to figure it out. I don't know what's wrong with me. Sometimes I would just doze off. This ..it is killing me!" He said, not cursing as there were kids around.

He the made light of it by telling me of all the awkward places he would just pass out for no reason. He could tell that I was concerned. I guess that's why he joked about it. After the class, he said to me "You know what? You're a really good chess teacher." "Thanks," I said. "No seriously, really good. Why don't you work at Success Academy? You're way better than the bums they be hiring." He chided. "I didn't get passed the phone interview." I told him.

Then he recounted the story of how he started working there. He said it took him two years, and they were really strict with their hiring process. He was really pitching me to sign up, because they have a signing bonus if you recruit new teachers. "You know with your math degree and the chess, you'd be making six figures within five years." He implored while leaning towards me. I was a bit ashamed to admit it at the time, but Charu was my friend. "I can't lie Charu." I told him about my panic attacks and my pledge to myself.

I think one of the answers I had given was "This is the best job with the highest pay that I can get right now." He burst out laughing and proceeded to demonstrate how I could get around not being able to lie. His voice, face, and posture changed. He gave complete sentences without saying a word. While he was demonstrating I became sick to my stomach. That is the person that I had been pretending to be for most of my life. I felt a deep sadness while watching him teach me how to interview. I knew that I wouldn't be able to do it, and decided to not interview for anymore chess jobs.

In fact, I was fired from that job only a few weeks later. The owner of the company regularly skirted labor laws, and ignored my requests to change. Even though I was technically making $25 per hour, in reality I was making between ten and fifteen per hour. One Friday, he underpaid me by a couple hundred dollars. Then told me "I'm looking out for you! You're going to pay less in taxes." When I refused and demanded the money owed, I was fired by email on Sunday morning.

It hurt a lot. In the last ten years, I was passed over in most interviews, and often fired. People say that they want folks around them to tell the truth. That's a lie. Every employer that I've had in the last ten years expects you to accept some amount of lies or abuse in exchange for money. When I refuse, it's almost always a scorched earth policy. I not only didn't get the final pay for almost three months, Micheal Propper even claimed to the Unemployment Insurance board that I was a terrible worker and that he gave me multiple warnings of something. There was an investigation and I eventually won. But it took weeks of financial hardship before I got my first small unemployment check.

It was time to wrap up, Charu and I put the class in order, and packed up the chess sets. There was a closet outside the room, on another floor, where the chess sets were stored. We both hobbled down the steps like old men. We joked together about how we both had become elderly. We continued chatting as old friends would. Once the pieces were stored, we both hobbled down the steps quickly and both rushed to the bathroom on the first floor. We both laughed and joked about how often we had to pee. Once we washed our hands and made it out of the bathroom, Charu stopped me from leaving the school. "Wait a minute. We might have the same thing." He puzzled with a serious look on his face.

I listed all the things wrong with me, and all the things that I had been going through. One by one he would shake his head 'yes.' "Oh my god! We got the same thing! You don't understand. I've been struggling with this for so long. This is the first time I met anyone with the exact same thing. Like nobody knows what's wrong with me." We both stood there, at the doors to the school, recounting decades long struggles, the things that we tried that didn't work, and the various doctor visits and surgeries. We both gazed at each other trying to find the answers in each other's eyes. Nothing that we tried worked.

"Listen, if you find anything out let me know. Okay?" He said as if we were going to say goodbye. "Alright," I said flippantly, recognizing the end of the conversation. He took a breath and shook his head. "No, seriously" He put his hand on my right shoulder, "if you find out anything. Anything! Please! Let me know. I'm scared." I became distressed at his sudden and acute seriousness. "I will," I said "I'm scared too."

We continued chatting and walked to street vendor. He ordered a gyro and ate it in front of me. I wanted him to buy me one too. He would've if I had asked. I was hungry to the point of starving. All I had was two dollars and I was holding on to it for some reason. I was too ashamed to ask him to buy me food. There was a special bus that took him right to his apartment in the Bronx from the Upper East Side. He complained about the price but said it was super convenient. He hustled to his bus, and that was the last time that I saw him.

I remember that day because I remember giving in and buying two slices of pizza. There is a slope on the Upper East Side in Manhattan. It was a struggle for me every time I walked it. I slowly plodded up the incline, gasping for breath while eating the only food that I'd have for a while. I don't know how many times in my life that I was sure that I was going to die. In 2017, I had no faith that I was going to make it. Again, I'm still here. But Charu is not. As of right now, I'm in the best shape I've been for more than twenty years.

THE SOLUTION WAS WITHIN

By the 2020 presidential election, I'd firmly accepted a personal truth. That my body is alive, and it isn't me. I have nominal control over it, and am a passenger like the other ones inside of me. Though I was essentially alone, and spoke to no one, I found solace in the me that isn't me.

In NLP, you learn to connect with and communicate with various selves inside of you. I'd come to realize that NLP is somewhat limited. My selves weren't an ethereal substance that sometimes interacted with who I am. They are real and sometimes completely take over. It's the same for everyone else as well. Most people have been so angry that they blacked out. I've been that angry, and was that angry by election day. The difference is, I don't black out usually. I remain and the self I call Rage is present with me. I allow him to move our body.

I sat in my chair, where I was usually, instead of meditating, I was focused on who would win. For four days no one dared call the election. It was Saturday when the news outlets finally called it for Biden. I was prepared to leave the country and never return if he had lost. When it was confirmed that he won, I stood up and allowed every inch of my body to well up in Rage. I had made up my mind to run for mayor of NYC. I was fed up with what kept happening to me, and wanted to at least get on the ballot and shout about the lawlessness from the mountaintop.

It didn't matter that I was essentially a hermit for the previous ten years. It didn't matter that I was terrified. It didn't matter that I didn't have a job or money beyond the stimulus check that I had received. I had to, because I'm the One Who Serves. I promised to protect myself from abuse. I promised to always tell the truth and follow the laws. I promised that I would trust my feelings. I was welling over with rage and had to comply.

There was only one way that I could back out of something one of the ones inside of me wanted; safety. In the ASCA handbook, the first chapter is entitled "Safety First." For people like me, it seems like whatever we try we end up in the same abusive situation. The only veto that exists for me is if I feel unsafe. I was scared, and I was alone, but I didn't have any safety concerns.

I pumped my fist in the air, and said "Now it's Time!" Just then, it felt as is someone pushed me back into my seat, and I became hyper aware of a giant mass in my gut. 'Did my stomach just sit me down?' I thought. I hadn't eaten anything, or pooped, for at least two weeks prior. I was a bit concerned, but when I sensed the mound inside of me I began to freak out. Then I had flashbacks of the times that I spoke to doctors concerning a mass of fecal matter in my large intestines.

The first time was when I started having health problems. I was a freshman at Vassar college, and I would occasionally wake up in the middle of the night and my throat would be completely closed. I would also have coughing fits often, until I would throw up. The doctor did a host of tests, and found nothing. On the chart, there was a mass in my gut. I asked what that was, and he waved his hand dismissively. "Don't worry about that! Everybody has that." I listened and spent many months trying many different medications that didn't work.

The next time I remembered, was a recent visit to Dr. Osmani. I had become poor enough to qualify for Medicaid. He showed me that the mass in my gut had gotten much larger and lectured me on the health problems that might come from it. He was the only doctor that didn't dismiss it. When I asked what I could do about it. He began lecturing me about my diet. I tuned him out. Firstly, because I couldn't afford the rich foods he was telling me eat. Secondly, I used to eat that way when I had lots of money, and it didn't change a thing.

When the one who controls my digestive system directed my focus, I listened. I didn't move much from that spot. I meditated for at least twelve hours per day trying to divine what was happening. When I wasn't meditating, I was looking on the internet for help understanding what was happening. A few weeks later, I stumbled upon a study that entitled "Coca-Cola May be the Best Cure for Stomach Blockages."

A few years prior, I had totally cut out sugary drinks from my diet. But there were many pages and videos about how Coke was a miracle cure for blockages. On the internet, people said they drank Coke for six weeks and up until they were able to eat and poop again. No part of me was against drinking Coke, but I had become sick of drinking the stuff close to the sixth week of not eating or passing fecal matter. Then something strange happened.

I could feel the ileum, part of small intestines connected to the large intestines, celebrating. It was like it was having a party. I had fecal matter spilling from my large intestines into the small intestines. It was an amazingly pleasurable experience when it was finally gone. Sometimes I take things too far. I got excited and started drinking an inordinate amount of Coke. I read somewhere that the active ingredient making things happen was the acid in the Coke. That information was wrong.

I ended up in the ER, for the last time, in agony. I begged the doctor to take the giant hunk of food out of me. He wouldn't even show me the x-ray of it. He said "I don't want to do anything invasive. I just want you to be regular." After a few hours at the ER my bowels calmed down, and he prescribed me two different laxatives. I then went overboard with a variety of laxatives until my stomach told me to stop. I haven't used laxatives after I was told to stop.

At some point in January, after not eating or pooping much for more than two months, I scheduled myself for a colonic. My body didn't like the process, but I felt like I had solved the problem. I scheduled myself for a few more colonics and also bought an enema bucket. I gave myself an enema, mixed with probiotics, every morning. My body resisted a little, but I ignored the minimal resistance. I was just happy to finally be making progress.

I started eating again, but it was different. I spent so much time connected to my digestive system, he was still with me. So I allowed him to become me. The one who controls my digestive system is like a cat. He doesn't communicate much. All I could ever really get out of him was yes, no, and wait. When he would become me, it felt like I was tiger hunting for a meal. I allowed him to eat whatever he wanted. What he wanted was double portions of everything. If extra gravy was an option, I had to take it. I stuffed myself every meal. Most of my life, I didn't even know if I was hungry or not. Sometimes I'd forget to eat for a few days. It was glorious and delightful to see him enjoy the food so much.

One day, at a Mexican restaurant, a short, fat, and drunk Mexican began talking to me. It was a pleasant conversation. He even bought me a delicious spicy Mexican candy. The conversation took a turn when we both began having a water off. We were challenging each other to see who drinks the most water. He won with "I drink 5 gallons over water everyday!" I felt a strong revulsion on the inside. My body was telling me to stop drinking as much water as I used to.

I listened, and only drink when my body tells me. But I searched the internet on drinking too much water. There I stumbled into the one meal a day internet. As I had been eating one giant meal per day, I thought my body lead me to the salvation that I sought. Only one problem, sometimes my body didn't want me to eat for one to two days.

On one of those occasions, out of frustration, I demanded that I eat. Store by store, and restaurant by restaurant, I stared at different things to eat and all I got was no. Until I asked if he wanted to eat marshmallows. It was a resounding yes. I was hesitant and almost called safety, as one of the times I was hospitalized the entire staff kept telling me that I was pre-diabetic. It was a weak safety and I acquiesced. When I got home, I devoured every single one. It was as if giving a baby their first marshmallow. I didn't know what to do.

"My god, he's a fucking kid." I thought. But I wasn't eating, and rules is rules. I'm the One Who Serves. Instead of deli marshmallows, I went to the local Rite Aid to get the good stuff. While there I felt an overwhelming urge to devour the caramel popcorn that I was eying. I let him have it. He was like an animal who caught his favorite prey. "God, he's a kid." I complained more. I remained in the background shaking my head, as he stuffed my face with that all that deliciousness. I ate everything, all at once. I was full from marshmallows and caramel popcorn. Then I drank some water, as I was thirsty.

It was a pleasurable experience, but I was skeptical of doing that again. I tried to return to meditating when I had a sharp pain in my gut. "What the fuck is that!" I screamed in my mind. I forgot that he was like a cat. The agony persisted, so I had to start asking yes or no questions. "Should I go the the ER?" 'No.' "Should I be afraid?" 'No.' "Is there something that I can do?" 'Wait.'

There were strong contractions in my stomach that lasted for days. Every question was a 'no' or a 'wait.' I became frustrated and started telling him what I was going to do. "I'm gonna take all these laxatives!" 'No.' "I'm gonna do this enema!" 'No.' I had two different types of fiber, I was really about to take lots of it daily and do water enemas daily. I made up my mind and I didn't even try to talk to him. 'No!!' He screamed. It was after it was clear what I was about to do when he made it clear what was happening. There was a mighty contraction, my eyes widened and I screamed on the inside "Is that a fucking mouth!!"

WE ARE ENERGY BEINGS

Since must of us are living in the grips of incessant lies, I'll try and be short and sweet. Only precise facts. The first of which will expose a lifetime of lies and control. **The human body is made up of 15 trillion living cells, on average. The power source for each and every cell is SUGAR!** Cells consume sugar and oxygen, and after the energy is released, the waste products are water and carbon dioxide. Meaning, every time you breath out, you're making water in trillions of cells. We don't need to drink massive amounts of water. If you aren't thirsty, why are you drinking it?

When you consume anything with sugar in it, the sugar gets absorbed in the stomach and pumped directly into the blood stream. That's where it's supposed to go. The blood stream is how the trillions of cells get the sugar they need. What happens if there's too much sugar in the blood stream? The pancreas secrets insulin, which is a signal to the fat cells to absorb the excess sugar. The insulin dissipates within 5-6 minutes. But the affect it had on the fat cells lasts at least an hour and a half. Meaning, the fat cells will only absorb sugar for an hour and a half after they get the insulin signal.

Fat cells aren't evil, and they don't need to be fought. They're alive and serve a vital function of storing energy for when you need it in the future. If there's no insulin in the veins, and the body has need of sugar, fat cells will freely release the sugar into the blood stream.

Starches, fats, and alcohol are all delicious because the body can break each of these down into the sugar our cells need. Starches will break down directly into glucose, which gets stored in fat cells. Fats are concentrated sugars, they take time to break down. Extra fat is stored in the veins as plaque. Excess alcohol is stored in the liver and is also broken down into glucose.

The other thing all 15 trillion cells needs are replacement parts. The body creates the replacement parts itself with the nutrients that we consume. Almost 99% of the human body is made up of oxygen, carbon, hydrogen, and nitrogen. The other 1% is a long list and we really don't need to know about them. Because the body knows what it needs. Most of our nutrients come from consuming other living cells.

Though our DNA is different, most cells are made of the exact same ingredients. When we consume other living cells, those nutrients are digested and pumped into the blood stream. Where other cells can replicate or repair themselves. How often does this happen? Every 7-15 years almost the entire human body is replaced with new cells. The eyes, teeth, and the brain remain until death. For our purposes, it's important to know that your digestive system is complete replaced every 5 days.

How are nutrients regulated in the blood stream? The large intestines. As far as I can tell, I'm the only one saying this. Everyone else keeps saying that we don't use the large intestines anymore. They're wrong, mine is on all the time. Excess nutrients are compacted and stored in the large intestines. And when the body has need of nutrients it breaks pieces off of the stored fecal matter, and allows bacteria to consume it. The bacteria breaks the matter down to its base elements, and natural gas is released. The large intestines has a complicated job of delivering nutrients, into the blood stream, at the right amount the cells of the body need them.

I know I'm just stating things, because I know no matter how much information I throw at you, some of you will resist because a lifetime of lies. I could literally make a whole book out of just this. But I really want you to see the lies for what they are. You will be as angry and terrified as I am.

Athletes have a tradition of something called carb-loading. It's where they consume large amounts of bread and pasta before a high-endurance event. When you consume carbohydrates in this way, all at once, the excess sugar is stored in fat near the muscles, rather than long term fat storage; ei butt and stomach. You can get the exact same effect, in shorter amount of time, and less stress by eating candy. All the exact things will happen, there is no difference. The literal only difference, in the body, is that carbohydrates take longer to digest than sugar.

For the last few months, I've been periodically sugar loading. Currently, I buy bulk candy from Amazon with EBT. I want to tell you something, that I hope you never forget. I realized that **most of the times that I felt hungry, I really just needed sugar.** Here's what I do. I get candy that I like. No nutrients at all! No nuts, eggs, milk, or anything else that isn't clearly sugar. I eat it until I'm full. If I feel the urge to drink some water, I'll drink it.

I don't really go full sugar often, but if you're just starting out, you should know the limits of your body. I would load up on sugar for two or more days. I would only eat candy, until I'm full, and then drink some water. You see I didn't tell you any amounts, right? You keep eating until your tongue tells you to stop. The sweet receptors on your tongue will turn off and you will lose any cravings to eat anything that will break down into glucose. In fact, for 2-3 days the only craving that you'll have is to drink some water occasionally. When you're tongue stops you, your body will be fully powered.

What happens next might surprise you, so I'll give you a heads up now. If you have stored up nutrients in your large intestines, like I did, then your large intestines will go into overdrive breaking chunks of fecal matter off the hunk of nutrients stored in what they call the traverse colon. When you are full sugar, the fecal matter will move to the left, and fill up what they call the ascending colon. Here the bacteria will feast on the fecal matter, nutrients will be absorbed into the blood stream, and the natural gas will come out as a burp.

If it hurts too much, and you wish to stop, or slow down, the bio-reactor, eat some of your favorite nutrients; nuts, jerky, chicken, etc. Depending on how much you eat, the large intestines will measure what the body needs and change accordingly. If you eat too much, everything in the ascending colon will come rushing out, as if you consumed a laxative. If you eat a moderate amount, fecal matter will move from the ascending colon to the sigmoid colon, where the bacteria can still consume the fecal matter. Nutrients will be absorbed into the blood stream and the natural gas will come out as a fart. When the large intestines are active, I can feel it's motions in the base of my jaw, close to the front, behind my teeth. It's connected there for some reason.

I've consumed a significant part of the food stored in my large intestines. My health has radically improved. I used to have skin blotches, strong allergies, alopecia, acid reflux, heart palpitations, and my knees seems like they were ready to give out. I had all manner of knee-brace, for every weather condition. In 2020, I was looking into cool canes and walkers to buy, and help me get around.

Clearly, I'm not a doctor, and everything I said shouldn't be misconstrued as medical advice. I'm also hesitant to try and correlate my dead friends unknown cause of death, with what I believe that I discovered through meditation. Before you dismiss what I've said, recount what I suggested. Eat something you know is delicious(candy) until your full, and drink some water if you're thirsty. If the pain in your gut becomes unbearable, eat some of your favorite nutrients until your full. I can feel the animosity that will directed towards me as I'm writing this. Because we've all been actually trapped in the Matrix. Let's look at some of the lies.

SYSTEM OF FOOD LIES

The first of the lies are calories. Do you know what a calorie is? It's a unit of heat emanating from a substance that is burned. They are measured in a device called a calorimeter. Do you find it off that a lump of coal could have all the calories you need for the day? There is no reason to measure food in calories, because there's no fire in the body.

Having a number, of an arbitrary measurement, distracts the mind. You'll trust a number rather that trusting your body on how much food you need. This is on purpose by the way. You see, on top of calories, there's a giant food pyramid. It's confusing and complicated. You literally need to go to school in order to understand it. It's this way intentionally, so that you can continuously eat, and think that you're doing the right thing.

Our diets are designed so that there's always insulin in the veins. Many Americans consume something with sugar, starch, or fats every 2-4 hours. In addition to this, we consume pick-me-ups to get us through the day: soda, coffee, alcohol, candy, desserts. Most people don't realize it, but if you keep consuming small amounts of sugar, the fat cells will be constantly absorbing sugar the entire day. If the fat cells aren't able to deliver sugar when needed, you'll need to consume more sugar.

But the system is constantly drilling into our heads all the things that we need to avoid. Cut the carbs, cut the sugar, cut the fats. That is a lie, designed to get you to continue to consume. Fats, sugars, and carbs are exactly what the body needs. Shaming you into hating the very thing you need is sinister, and literally what they always do. What's the saying "Don't eat too many sweets, cuz you'll spoil your diner!" Sugar is the dinner the body wants and needs.

The system always gives a false choice, and two waring sides. Meat-eater or Vegetarian is the food choice everyone is supposed to make. It's a false choice that's detrimental to all of our bodies. There are two things that the body needs, glucose and nutrients. If you have enough sugar, how much nutrients do you think that you need? Well, the fastest the human body replaces itself is every seven years. So you'll need (Your body weight)/(7 * 365.) That will give you the weight of nutrients the body needs per day. For me it's much less than a pound of nutrients.

This may seem shocking, but I'd rather you be infuriated. Is there a class of people who regularly eats that much nutrients? Yes! The uber rich! I've been to many $10k per plate fundraisers. It's always like a sample of food. But in reality, they are the Controllers, and made sure to make it expensive to eat correctly and cheap to eat yourself into the grave. Yes, the rich eat small amounts of nutrients, but how do they get their sugar? Wine and cheese anyone? Wine will break down into sugar and cheese is full of fat. It's amazing how little I eat now, it's like I have the entire day to myself.

What's the endgame for the Controllers? On the surface, it's quite simple. The Controllers always give farmers power over the rest of the populace. Farmers, in each individual system, have some amount of homogeneity. Also, the controllers have a significant stake in the farming industry. People over consuming nutrients, makes the highly efficient body inefficient and often broken. The controllers can extract lots of value from your suffering. You have to eat their food, and if you're suffering they have remedies to help you cope, but never cure.

That seems bad, but these are just side effects of the real purpose of the food lies. There was a time, in the not so distant past, that walking up a small flight of stairs would have me winded. What was happening? I was trying to exert myself a little, and I didn't have enough sugar in my veins for energy. That is the ultimate goal.

If you think that you're 'out of shape.' Try something for me. Find a flight of stairs and run up as much as you can until you feel faint. Don't push yourself, this is just a test. Catch your breath, then fill yourself up on sugar. It may take two days, but once you've done it make sure you haven't eaten any sugar for a few hours, and try the same patch of steps. You won't be gasping for air. Why? Because you won't be hungry and you're body will understand that you'll be running on fat. When you exert yourself in that state, you'll actually be able to feel the fat turn on. There should be a marked difference.

What's so special about that? Why would the controllers want you to think that you're 'out of shape?' What does society tell you to do to get in shape? They tell you that you need to exercise! The training is always grueling, and its up to you to fight through the pain. What passes for exercise here is you having too much insulin in the veins and forcing yourself to exert yourself until the adrenaline kicks in. Adrenaline forces the fat cells to release glucose into the blood stream.

If you get winded by doing simple things then you have a major problem. Why? Because we are biological computers, and the part of us the **uses half of the sugar in the body is the brain!** Get it now? The Controllers want your brain to be sugar deficient. They want your mind to be not working at capacity. Some people who follow the Controllers' diet, think that they were born stupid. You aren't stupid, you're a super computer, and your brain isn't getting the power it needs. The power is literally glucose.

In order to complete the transformation, the controllers constantly fill their targets up with terror or rage. Why? These feelings release adrenalin. When the adrenalin kicks in, the fat cells are free to supply the body with the sugar it needs. Meaning, the only times these folks minds are at full power is in a panic or in a rage. In this state, people are open to suggestion.

I believe this is the first of human technologies the Controllers have used for thousands of years. This is how they've created know nothings, that are impossible to reason with. The did it with the Sea Peoples, they did it in Europe, and it's happening here and now. It's near impossible to reason with these people.

If you are of the alabaster persuasion, isn't this the origins or your ancestors? For thousands of years, your ancestors would over consume meat and alcohol. They would breed, fight, and die. Wasn't it only the Controllers who would eat the right amounts? There's far more we can discuss with just this alone, but I have a lot to share. We've only scratched the surface.

Chapter FOUR

CONTROL THROUGH DISTRACTION

"The ultimate tragedy is not the oppression and cruelty by the bad people but the silence over that by the good people."

~ Martin Luther King, Jr. ~

THE MODE OF MADNESS

I've had the unique experience of being completely disconnected from my emotions, and then plunging headfirst into them, with a deep understanding of NLP. Inside of us all, there are different selves. Some of these selves have specific jobs like operating the lungs, or knowing how to do double dutch. Some are difficult to communicate with, and some you can access if you're in the right setting.

A mode is different. It is still associated to a self, except they have the power to override the one I call the Focus. The Focus is the position the self who we think we are inhabits. Modes can simply combine itself with the Focus and change it's perspective. Quite often, a mode will simply turn the Focus off, if the Focus opposes that mode's wishes.

For example, Rage is a mode. The angrier you get, it affects your logic and perception. If you aren't prepared mentally for what Rage thinks is important, Rage will turn the Focus off, and when Rage is done with it's mission, the Focus will return and the Rage will slowly share what had transpired.

Love is also a mode. Most modes can be permanent, but Love could also last for an extended period. Love will bind itself to the Focus and change it. The entire perspective of the Focus may be altered, and if there's resistance, Love can shut the Focus off as well. Some modes can't mix, and some mix out of necessity. I hope you have a basic understanding of what I mean by a mode.

There is a Mode of Madness, I've encountered often throughout my life. And for many people, watching what's unfold right now in America, they are encountering it for the first time. You try to put terminology to it, but those labels are simply inadequate. Racist, sexist, anti-this, and anti-that; all meaningless. It is a mode that can be manifested in a human in the same way Rage and Love can manifest itself.

Since the religion the Controllers are utilizing right now is Christianity, we should use the Bible as reference. The story of Sodom and Gomorrah is quite famous. But it's usually retold by those who are Moded with Madness, in order to do the very same thing that the Sodomites wished upon the travelers.

"The two angels arrived at Sodom in the evening, and Lot was sitting in the gateway of the city. When he saw them, he got up to meet them and bowed down with his face to the ground. 'My lords,' he said, 'please turn aside to your servant's house. You can wash your feet and spend the night and then go on your way early in the morning.' 'No,' they answered, 'we will spend the night in the square.'

"But he insisted so strongly that they did go with him and entered his house. He prepared a meal for them, baking bread without yeast, and they ate. Before they had gone to bed, all the men from every part of the city of Sodom--both young and old--surrounded the house. They called to Lot, 'Where are the men who came to you tonight? Bring them out to us so that we can have sex with them.'" Genesis 19:1–5.

The angels were there to 'judge' the city. God found the city unworthy and sent the angels to find anyone worth saving. What was the problem? All the people were Moded with Madness. When done as a group, they see those who are 'different' as worthless and they can do what they wish to them. People try to make this story about homosexuality, because the truth of it convicts them.

If the travelers were Jews in Nazi Germany, the story would've been similar and nothing fundamentally would've changed. The angels were going to stand in the middle of the city until morning. If Jews had done that in Nazi Germany, what would have been different? Or maybe Black men during many time periods in the US, it would be the same outcome right?

The feeling of the story remains if you exchange the targets to the the target of the modern day Moded Mad Ones. I will repeat the story with trans women to make it clearer. The two trans-women arrived at Sodom in the evening, and Lot was sitting in the gateway of the city. When he saw them, he got up to meet them and bowed down with his face to the ground. "My lords," he said, "please turn aside to your servant's house. You can wash your feet and spend the night and then go on your way early in the morning." "No," they answered, "we will spend the night in the square."

But he insisted so strongly that they did go with him and entered his house. He prepared a meal for them, baking bread without yeast, and they ate. Before they had gone to bed, all the men from every part of the city of Sodom--both young and old--surrounded the house. They called to Lot, "Where are the men in dresses who came to you tonight? Bring them out to us so that we can kill them."

The tenor of the story is the same, and it exemplifies what Lot was going through. He was scared that the townspeople would harm the angels and begged them to hide in his house. He thought the travelers were unaware of the crazies. When the modern Mad Ones try to make this about homosexuality, it's a defense mechanism of the mode. When people are Moded with Madness, they often project anything that could implicate them onto another. This mode makes you feel as if what you are doing is right, and everyone else is wrong.

The Controllers have figured out how to create this mode in humans, and have successfully caused people for thousands of years to exhibit this mode. I know how they do it.

ANCIENT SYSTEM OF SLAVERY

The system that we currently live under has been replicated over and over for many thousands of years. Mouthpieces for the controllers like to call the system 'modern.' It is far from modern, trying to piece together where it first started is difficult as I've only been alive for 44 years, and the controllers are particular about obscuring their roles and suppressing true history. I'll go back as for as I can, without trying to stretch. When you point out the truth, only once, it makes all of the lies more pronounced.

In the bible, during the time of Jesus, there were three clearly defined groups; the Sadducees, the Pharisees, and the Unclean. The bible has sparse commentary about the Sadducees, I think deliberately. I'll use broad strokes that are easily checkable either in the bible or a basic internet search.

Both the Sadducees and the Pharisees were apart of the same political religious movement. They ran the entire state of Israel from the Temple. I'm not concerned about their religious beliefs or practices. Both groups were aligned when it comes to religious ideals. The difference between the two groups were that the Sadducees were rich and the Pharisees were what we call middle class. The Sadducees held all of the positions of power, and made most of the major decisions. The Pharisees all hoped to one day be a Sadducee, but most never did.

The Pharisees did most of the work in the nation, and the Sadducees received most of the benefits. On the surface it seems like a bad deal, until you consider the Unclean. It seems like a good idea to quarantine people with a contagious disease, but if you've been paying attention, you'd recognize the system that we live under. The Unclean are the people that the Pharisee can look down on and abuse. From ancient times, up until this day, the movements and the resources of the 'Unclean' are purposely limited. There is no escape from being Unclean, nor is there escape from being a Pharisee.

Let's use simple terms for these three groups, because there is always at least three. The Controllers are the ones who have absolute control over the resources. The Sadducees were the local Controllers in biblical times. Pharisees, people may want to say are middle class, but want to use a more descriptive term; the Targets. The Targets of the system always do most of the work, they do most of the sacrificing, they are always called to maintain the system, and the only real compensation that they get for their hard work is the knowledge that they are better than the class beneath them.

Finally, we have the 'Unclean.' It's best to describe them as the Controllers likely do; a Distraction. The Distraction class exists to suffer. They must be isolated, abused, and exploited. In this system, the Distractions aren't really human, making it okay to kill them as needed.

If you're anything like me, you've seen this very dynamic play out all around the world. You can see it happening in real-time on the news if you're an American. It's a system of theatrical terrorism. In order for it to work, everyone involved has to accept some fundamental lies. We will address some of the major lies within the system later. But there are a few giant ones that we need to address right away.

Firstly, the idea that resources are limited it a massive lie. There is literally more than enough for everyone. Before the end of this book, I'll demonstrate for you how resources are precisely unlimited. The next giant lie, the most people implicitly accept is that the Controllers are the best people to manage everyone's resources. They are literally the worst people to control the world's resources. They purposely limit the resources to create 'value.' They crush anything that competes with their control, and they deny anyone the ability to own or store their own resources.

The biggest lie, some of you may not accept, but, it is the basis of the entire system of control. The truth is that we are self-aware, hairless monkeys. We don't need gold, diamonds, or money. What we need is food, water, energy, and shelter. I can't say for certain how they did it in the past, but today anyone can verify where they are in the system.

As a self-aware, hairless monkey, make a list of the four things you need and ask yourself do you control any of it? How much of what you need can you store up for later? Who controls your space, food, water, and energy? Do you even have a choice with these four things? Regardless of how wealthy you are, the system has a time limit on all four of the things that you need. The system likes to praise high-income earners. But do those individuals have an agency in the system? No, they need to constantly produce or they'll be removed from the system, and become a Distraction. All anyone, except the Controllers, has is credit.

The point of the system, and they try their best with propaganda to emphasize it, is the Distractions are forever meant to crave the lives of the Targets. Only some of the Distractions can make it into Target collective. The Targets are always supposed to wish that one day, they can count themselves among the Controllers. That almost never happens, but when it does, the system likes to make a big hay out of it. Anybody can do it!

CRYING NONSENSE AND COMMITTING ATROCITIES

"The Pharisees and some of the teachers of the law who had come from Jerusalem gathered around Jesus and saw some of his disciples eating food with hands that were 'unclean', that is, unwashed. So the Pharisees and teachers of the law asked Jesus, 'Why don't your disciples live according to the tradition of the elders instead of eating their food with defiled hands?'

"He replied, 'Isaiah was right when he prophesied about you hypocrites; as it is written: 'These people honor me with their lips, but their hearts are far from me. They worship me in vain; their teachings are merely human rules.' You have let go of the commands of God and are holding on to human traditions.'" Mark 7:1–8.

There's quite a bit going on here. On the surface, it seems like a fair request. There's a pandemic going on, maybe Jesus should just wash his hands. Also, it was tradition. There's some debate on the meaning of this. Modern Christians like to make this about doing away with the old traditions and making new ones. But fundamentally, this is a major facet of our system of control.

I'm going to break it down so you can more easily recognize it. Individuals of the Target class, or people who wish to be apart of the Target class, make a seemingly reasonable demand to those in the Distraction class, and there are consequences if there isn't compliance. In the bible, the Pharisees killed Jesus.

Before we get to deep into the command, let's focus on the underlying issue. We are self-aware, hairless monkeys. The system wants you to not realize it. Like all other monkeys on this planet, when one monkey beats their chest in front of another monkey it is a declaration of dominance. All things being equal, a fight would ensue with actual monkeys.

The system retards that basic monkey principle. Though the Targets do most of the work, and rarely gets any rest, they get one thing. They get to beat their chests in front of the Distractions and get away with it. If the Distractions fight back they are punished or killed.

Once we understand this, it makes the system of control more transparent. The initial demand almost always seems reasonable, and that's what people like to focus on. In reality, the demand is always bullshit. The Targets don't care about the demand, they like the adrenaline coursing through their veins as they beat their chests in front of helpless Distractions. Fundamentally, this system of control is about lawlessness. As the laws can't be equally applied, or the control won't work.

The Distractions don't have any protections and are at the mercy of the Targets. To make matters worse, the Distractions almost always have to live under extra unwritten laws, that can change on the whims of the Targets. In addition to this, the Controllers can abuse anyone they wish within the system, and no one has the power to stop them. They usually stay in the shadows and allow others to do their dirty work.

Now let's focus on the request. It's always based on the current disposition of local humans. In the example of Jesus, the command seems reasonable but it's a lie. Leprosy was a problem, and washing your hands seems reasonable. But does washing your hands cure leprosy? No. Does it make you less contagious? No. It's understood that there were neighborhoods where the Unclean were corralled to live. But did everyone with leprosy get quarantined into the Unclean zones? No.

In Matthew 14, Jesus and his disciples were having dinner at the house of a man named Simon the Leper. Scholars agree, that he was a Pharisee. Not only was Simon not quarantined, he had a dinner party. The request is never really about the request, it is always monkeys beating their chest declaring dominance.

The Controllers play a huge part on maintaining this system. Nowadays, the Targets get commands on the internet and over the airwaves. They are a calls to arms from the Controllers. They let the Targets know who they can beat their chest in front of and what the excuse they can use to do it.

There are many examples of this all throughout our history, but also in the present! I'm just going to open up the current top news. Today is 9/4/21, yesterday three men with zip ties threatened to do a citizen's arrest on a school principal in Arizona, over mask mandates. It is the very same energy that the Pharisees of old used. It is a demand that the real rules don't apply to the Targets, and because of something innocuous I get to threaten you and demonstrate my dominance. The funny thing about this story is, only one person was arrested.

Nations and Empires have long struggled with dealing with these know-nothings: the Egyptians, the Romans, and now the United States. You have to realize that the initial demand is fine if that's something that you wish to discuss. But that's now how it really works. The demand always comes with a beating of the chest. An expression of dominance. Or called more appropriate, terrorism. At it's heart, this system of control is the pure manifestation of lawlessness.

The Target class, because they regularly break the law and get away with it, feel superior and some believe they are godlike. They become human predators looking for their next victim. How do the Controllers encourage this? In the Bible, those who publicly and passionately ceremoniously wash their hands will be rewarded within the system. Those who do not, may be stricken with the Unclean status. What's more, the Controllers likely financially supported individuals whose only job is to go around enforcing the ceremonial washing of hands.

Let's look at today. How do the Proud Boys have the funds to travel the country and 'protest?' Most people can't take off of work as much as these guys 'rally.' Who pays for food, shelter, and living expenses? There's currently an army of anti-mask protesters. How are they supporting themselves in this system? Many of these people travel the country without any visible means of income.

For some time now, I've been telling people there's no point in fighting racism, sexism, class-ism, or any other ism you wish to think up. Thanks to the failure of Donald Trump, the Target's are flailing. People aren't accepting their initial demands as reasonable. All they can see is monkeys beating their chest in front of helpless people and are getting enraged themselves.

The Controllers make this happen by limiting the resources and giving one group of monkeys more resources and weapons, and another group less resources and no means of fighting back. The Controllers reward lawlessness, and punish those who refuse to accept. It's apt that the Targets have chosen for themselves to believe that Covid is a hoax. Even Trump is trying to get them to take the vaccine, and they refuse.

What we are seeing, in real time, a potential time that the Controllers are losing control over the Targets. The real problem of leading from the shadows. Unchecked lawlessness always lead to the Mode of Madness; where everyone is an enemy. There are a couple of fixes.

The first fix is to unlimit the resources. We will get to this before the end of the book. The other is bureaucracy. We need to understand and appreciate who we are. Some monkeys need to beat their chests, and some need to get their asses whooped. If you want to claim dominance fine, but people who wish to accept your challenge should be able to fill out a form to accept that challenge.

You will need to get physical and mental health checked, fighting ability measured, maybe some avenues of remediation, and also possible alternatives to fighting. But some people are incorrigible, and need to be checked. For groups, they could play basketball, football, or group poker. Whatever the case, you can't allow monkeys going around terrorizing other monkeys and getting away with it. If you do, they become more bold and become addicted to abusing the weak and defensless. Before you know it, they will start challenging bigger targets. And they'll do it as a group.

They will always cry nonsense, it's a self-aware, hairless monkey trap. If you waste even a second on their bullshit reasons for lawlessness, then you've already lost. The things that they are violently shouting are for you. It's something that you feel a certain way about. The Mad Ones don't care one iota about the shit they are shouting. They just like the rush they get dominating others. The words that they are crying about are for your benefit, to distract and control you. If you don't beat your chest back, then you've lost the monkey battle.

CURRENCY THE ULTIMATE LIMITER

In 2015, I wrote the book "Follow the Money: Path to Our Inevitable Economic Ruin or the End of Global Poverty." I recognized a multitude of weaknesses in the system and made a good faith effort to suggest possible fixes for the system we currently live under. I was somewhat naive back then. In fact, mid book, I shed my naivety when I experienced another terrorist stop by a police officer and was punished for no reason. I was fundamentally wrong in my thinking back then. The system exists as planned and the outcomes were designed this way. It's a waste of breathe demanding the system be fixed, from the very people who designed and maintain the system as it is.

This is a system that supplanted the god-kings of old. The god-kings would demand loyalty or death. The Controllers demand the same, except instead of loyalty they want you to deny who you are in exchange for whichever currency they are using at the time, or you die slowly. They desperately want you to not notice that we are beings of this Earth. We don't need currency, we need food, water, shelter, and energy. Everyone willfully accepts that they get to control all of the resources and the rest of us bums need to constantly 'perform' for the rest of our lives to survive.

They achieve this feat with currency. I doesn't matter which currency we use, gold, fiat currency, or crypto-currency all have the same limitations and drawbacks. They all come with a variety of rules that always end up benefiting the Controllers. You can start an insurrection with currency, you can fund a war with currency, you can subjugate and entire population with currency. They've trained us to value the worthless, to distract us from what is actually happening.

There a few topics that I'd like to share with you regarding currency, that I spoke of in my book "Follow the Money." Now that I look back, it shows a conscious thought process to the supposed Invisible Hand.

The first issue with currency is that it is limited. Regardless of how much currency that exists, the fact that it's limited creates disparity. All the things that we need to survive aren't limited. There is unlimited food, water, energy, and space. But by forcing everyone to use currency creates artificial disparity. Now you they get to decide, who gets to make how much money. Since currency is limited, if one person make lots of money, then some need to make less money. And the counter argument is to share, which sounds nice but will never work in reality.

We are monkeys of this earth, we don't need a limited currency. Once you have limited currency, all things priced in that currency is subject to the bid-ask spread. We pride ourselves on our thriving markets. But our markets 'thrive' at the expense of other markets. In addition, there is an inherent danger of the bid-ask spread, prices can at any time go to zero, or to the moon. The Controllers have cut entire nations out of the system, and none have survived. The system is purposely confusing so that you don't realize that you have no agency in it. The system will crash again, and all you monkeys will be helpless against it, same as governments.

The next issue that I spoke of, in my book "Follow the Money," was reciprocity. Recently, the entire country received a history lesson about 'Black Wall Street.' I think that lesson is inadequate. It's true that the Greenwood district was burned to the ground and many people died. The 'reason' for the violence is irrelevant. Also, I don't buy that it just happened randomly. What transpired?

Former slaves began starting their own communities. They had to live under constant terrorism and, for hundreds of years, most businesses were whites only. Something happened that shook the Controllers to the core, everyone in the town became wealthy. As the same dollar continued to repeat among the populace, everyone's income increased radically. That town needed to be destroyed, and what made it happen removed. Black Wall Street was a threat to the Controllers. Money is meant to flow only towards them.

There were multiple race massacres after this. But in case you think it wasn't by design, after the Tulsa Race Massacre, public policy changed. Now blacks were allowed to spend the money in white areas, except they were given sub-par accommodations. The law of the land went from black exclusion to separate but equal.

Look at your own finances. Most people get a rate of pay every two weeks. Can you say for certain that some of that money returned to you from your previous spending? Everyone is ignorant of the very thing that they depend on. The flow of wealth can be best described with fluid dynamics. All currency is meant to flow in one direction, to the Controllers. Once there, they hoard it like their lives depended on it. Which it actually does.

THE FALL OF AN EMPIRE

I want to emphasize that the system is quite simple. Control and limit the resources that humans need, gift a class of those humans resources beyond what they deserve, deny resources to a class of humans even though they deserve more, and infect the local government with corruption. You can do all of this with the local currency.

People don't notice it because history is purposely obscured by the Controllers. Let's do a brief recap of the past. The ancient empires that endured in the bronze age where under relentless attack from outside invaders. Most fell to the constant onslaught, but Egypt endured. The Pharaohs tried to reason with the invaders, with no luck. They even tried to integrate some of them into their empire, it didn't work. They simply kept coming with mindless attacks.

Eventually the Egyptian Empire fell because of many factors, constant war, climate change, wars with other nation-states, and incessant terrorism. Most historians agree that Egypt fell because they ran out of gold. One crisis after the next depleted their financial resources. A different explanation would be that wealthy merchants and bankers exploited misunderstanding about currency and distracted the Pharaohs with constant attacks.

There are many other instances of this same thing happening around the world. It's better to focus on big events to be succinct. Jesus existed, and he had a powerful affect on life in Northern Africa and the Middle East. It's just a coincidence that all of the New Testament was written in Greek a hundred years after his death. A few hundred years after that, the Emperor Constantine convened the Council of Nicaea, held at his summer palace. Why were they meeting? To stop the fighting and wars between the Jesus factions. This one event in time likely marked the eventual end of the empire. Why? Imagine President Biden convening something similar at Camp David. Religious groups trying to kill each other for believing in different versions of Jesus. If he compromised with their violence, and declared the resulting body the official American religion, we'd no longer be America.

The ancient system of slavery is the only thing that can explain how such a thing happened. The Controllers gifted resources to whomever believed what they told them to believe, and they took resources away from those that didn't. They bribed or corrupted officials to look the other way when those that were gifted resources abused those without. It creates a sense of superiority and invincibility. It's ironic that the teachings of Jesus were used to create this chaos.

How did the Roman Empire fall? The politicians were corrupt and there was rampant poverty. They had to endure constant attacks from raiding parties from all directions. In addition to this, there was internal strive, the people were fighting over which Christianity was the right one.

Is the Catholic Church the enemy that is doing all of this? No. I believe they were shaped by the Controllers using currency. They make powers in their image and likely to control from the shadows. If you focus for one minute on the reasoning you already lost. They pit one side over the next and sometimes they pick a winner.

One example is the story of the Germanic tribe the Vandals. History is quite sparse about these peoples. But what we know for certain is they were followers of the Jesus story, and they're rallying cry was about the second commandment "Thou shalt not make unto thee any graven image." Also, the Catholics simply dropped that as a commandment. This was enough to have a war over? The Vandals attacked the Roman Empire and the Catholics. They even sacked Rome itself. All the while, destroying any images or sculptures of a god. Eventually they lost, and no longer exist as a people. I suspect they lost because they ran out of resources. The Controllers can pull the rug out from any group they wish, when they are done with them.

While I can't prove that the Vandals lost because they ran out of money, it's clear that the Roman Empire fell because they ran out of money. People were fed up with the corruption, lawlessness, and constant terrorism. There was depopulation and the coffers ran dry due to constant internal and external strife. The cause of the Vandals are now in our common language. If I deface public property, it's called vandalism.

It just so happens that right now, in this country, our budget is inflated due to constant wars and corruption. As we speak, there appears to be an ongoing insurrection. The ever changing reasoning for it is irrelevant. It is about dominance. In my twitter feed today two videos keep coming up, violence with the Proud Boys and a Wisconsin college football game. They are the same thing, but one is worst.

The Proud Boys, and other similar movements, are supported by money powers, and mostly ignored by law enforcement. Giving them a sense of superiority. I don't bother listening to what they are chanting. What they are doing is displaying their monkey dominance by publicly beating their chests and getting away with it. This is the same for many of the terrorist organizations that are currently active now. If there are no consequences for the things that they are doing, then it will only get worst.

The massive football game in Wisconsin was terrifying. People are trying to use logic to describe it. That unmasked football game with thousands of cheering people is a show of dominance. Even if it means death. It's honestly too late to reason with those Moded with Madness. They've had many generations of breaking the law, and getting away with it. They've were already gifted resources beyond what they deserve, while others had their resources denied. The problem is, as a nation, we allow some monkeys to beat their chests and they get rewarded, regardless of the circumstance. And other monkeys are denied the ability to beat their chests, and if they tried to they would be punished or killed.

What we are experiencing now are the death throws of a powerful empire. It just repeats again and again. The names of the antagonist or protagonist organizations are irrelevant. What matters is who controls the resources and who controls the money. No one ever speaks of that in the history books, as if they aren't relevant.

I'd like to share with you the final chapter of my book "Follow the Money." After attempting to impartially write about the system we live under, the terrorism from another local police officer enraged me so much, that I finished the book with a chapter entitled "How to Destroy America." It's surprisingly relevant right now.

HOW TO DESTROY AMERICA

PROLOGUE

"First, I'd like to say that this isn't how I wanted to end this book, but it was a nagging reality that I have held for many months now. Let me tell you how I thought I would end this book. I wanted to tie together the rise and fall of the British Empire, with the very same mistakes the US has done. The revolt that the British Empire experienced was a corporate revolt. In the same way the British Empire installed corporations around the world to represent its interests, the US did the very same thing after WWII. It seemed like a fitting end, especially since I started with 'Driverless Cars will Destroy America!'

"The truth is, I'm a secretive man and this entire book reflects a challenge that I had given myself well over 15 years ago. I recounted for you the moments that I received two phone book sized documents from the Federal Reserve. What I didn't tell you is that it pushed me over the edge and I had a breakdown. When I realized what the Fed had sent me, I also realized that most of the far right wing stuff that I was reading was all garbage. I had spent a number of months praying and fasting, hoping God would change me in some way. I was angry, frustrated, alone, and depressed. Whenever I was in such a state, I would think of something impossible to remain sane. I remember being curled in a ball, on the floor, when I asked myself, 'How could I destroy America?'

"For weeks, I remained on the floor curled in a ball. Sometimes I used the bathroom and returned to the floor. Rarely, I would eat. Most of the times that I got up from the floor were to check the feasibility of my plan of attack on the internet. Before this exercise, I knew literally nothing about how our government worked. After this exercise, I understood quite a bit, as most of my plans of attack simply wouldn't work. For well over a year, I wracked my brain trying to destroy the nation. After I had come up with a solution, I decided to return to civilized life. Figuring out how to destroy the country seemed to help me with my personal problems. But I still had a long way to go from there.

"Being a secretive person, I shared the plan to destroy the nation with no one. The reason I struggled with including this section was, again, my secretive nature. The reality is this: This book was written to stop my plan to destroy the US. I understood the weak points and tried to shore them up as much as possible. Clearly understanding the point of attack led me to look for historical references to bolster the plans to destroy the country, and to defeat my plan to destroy the country. I'm absolutely not a historian, and before writing this book there were many things that I was unaware of.

"Part of me was concerned that I would be picking and choosing historical events out of context. I was beyond surprised that our history lines up so completely with my plans and premises. I had no idea about Greenwood, the Civil War, Martin Luther King, the New Deal, slavery, and on and on. America has had, and continues to have, the same weaknesses that can be exploited. These weaknesses can be avoided, only if people take the threats posed seriously.

"What prompted me to finish the book this way? The police! Part of me is concerned about people taking my plans and adopting them for themselves. But I'm sick and tired of being treated as a second class citizen. I'm still angry, and I don't care what happens. If someone looks at my plans and decides to act on them, I want to make something clear. I didn't create the weaknesses that exist in America. It's not my fault that these weaknesses can be exploited. If all you can do is blame me for America's weaknesses, then I say you are lazy and stupid.

THE WEAKNESS AND MY ORIGINAL PLAN

"I believe that I was twenty-two years old when I originated this plan. The point of ingress should be obvious if you have read this book up until now. If I were planning to bring this country down, I would attack the flow of wealth in the nation. The weakest points in this flow of wealth are the very rich. But there are other choke points within the flow of wealth that can also be exploited. Back then I chose to attack the health care system.

"It is a fact that health care spending accounted for 17.4% of the US GDP in 2013. It is expected that health care spending will reach 19.6% by 2024. These numbers should be mind-numbingly alarming. These numbers are barring a health crisis or epidemic. Think about this, in a few short years, if nothing calamitous happens, twenty cents of every dollar spent in America will be spent on health care! There are many terrorists out there hoping to strike a decisive blow against the US, why not attack the health care industry?

"The health care industry itself is a financial choke point in the flow of wealth in the nation. There are others that are bit more difficult to affect, but for now let's focus on health care. Here is what you should be most concerned with. Of the money sent into the health-care industry, where is that money spent? How much of it is spent? And how quickly is it spent? The problem with so much of the nation's wealth passing through the hands of a few people, is that those people can effectively shape the course of the nation's future.

"Can you imagine that there are places in the nation where wealth passing through the health care industry will never reach? Then it isn't hyperbole saying that the Health Care Industry is making certain parts of this nation poor. This is not asking whether or not these areas have insurance. The germ of the original plan was to simply increase health care spending. I reasoned that dramatically increasing health care costs would have an immediate impact on certain areas, creating relative deflation zones.

"I didn't need to go any further with my reasoning back then. If I could find a way to get the nation to sharply increase their health care spending, it would create sharp enough imbalances to collapse the economy. I know that I haven't yet convinced some of you. I simply wanted to convey the germ of the argument. The truth is, I was incredibly naive back then. I didn't believe that race played a significant enough factor to cause any change. I've had sixteen years to ponder these matters, and I'm of a different opinion now.

DESTROYING AMERICA STEP BY STEP IDENTIFYING THE GOALS

"If I were going to destroy this country, I would need to be clear on my targets. The primary target would be the very rich. It would be my primary goal to keep them from spending any money in the US. They are in fact the weakest link in the nation's flow of wealth. Money flows to them effortlessly, and they don't have to spend most of it to survive.

"Next are the flow of wealth choke points. The one we discussed is health care, but there are many others. Creating a comprehensive attack on all of the choke points is unnecessary and risky. I would get caught easily if I tried to be too broad. Also, this is not a blueprint to follow and actually destroy America. It is my hope that people will look at this and make changes. Anyhow, the other choke points are fairly obvious.

"Lastly, there are the minority groups that I would need to hurt by the subsequent deflation. People in the nation love to openly proclaim that, 'We solved our race problems back then.' I can tell you that not much has been 'solved.' If I could, I would use women as the group, but honestly it seems too challenging to make the hated group all women.

"Tying all of these things together are the "cyclical downturns" in the economy. People call this cyclical because it happens regularly. Even though it happens regularly, doesn't mean that it's normal. What is happening is the destruction of wealth. If market forces are allowed to operate, wealth will flow in one direction until the wealth stops flowing. In the midst of one of these regular downturns, is the perfect time to strike.

CREATE A BOOGEYMAN AND THEN ATTACK

"I've been debating which groups that I wish to use to blame the attacks on. So I'll have all three. I will use a masked Mexican, an Arab, and an African American to claim responsibility for the things that my group will do. I would use current issues relevant to those specific groups as demands. It's important to recognize that I would choose things that are incredibly hard to achieve. For example, the Mexican demand could be to take down the existing wall along the US-Mexican border. I would use current events to find causes to take up.

"The point of using front people to make masked video demands, is to create a solidarity with those specific groups. People will likely disagree with our tactics, but will agree with the causes. These are the groups that will be most hurt by a decrease in the flow of wealth. Especially African Americans. The saying is, that African Americans are last hired and first fired. As long as I've been alive, this has been true. It is good fortune that white Americans openly claim that there are no race relation problems in this nation. The denials would be used to our advantage, with propaganda. One last piece is that we will likely only use white Americans to carry out any of our plans. The minorities will just be the face of the group.

"While this group will be clearly defined as a "terror" organization, mass deaths or highly valued targets won't be important. If deaths do occur, we will either denounce them or not claim responsibility. We need to make sure the minorities aren't turned off by inhumane actions. Solidarity needs to be the initial aim. Although, things may not turn out well for the minorities as a whole. Now that we have a front organization, let's implement the original plan and see what happens.

THE SKETCHY ORIGINAL PLAN

"In order to make the original plan a success, we would need an airborne, contagious virus that could be deadly without medical attention. What comes to mind is something similar to the H1N1 virus in 2009. I'm clearly not a virologist, so all I could do is wish for such a thing. If money weren't an issue, I would have my swine flu-type virus. What's unfortunate about the H1N1 virus is that a vaccine is currently available.

"At this point, I must admit that my plans would likely be exposed. This is because there are very few people in the world who could provide me with such a virus. In order for this plan to work, I would need to have incredibly deep pockets and have many friends in high places. If you assume that I'm capable of having such a virus, then the plan can go ahead.

"My group would post a video on the dark web, and spam the news media of its existence. The message will be in English, Spanish, and Arabic. It would warn of an imminent attack on the US because of (fill in the blank) reasons. If only America would do (fill in the blank), then there would be no attacks. It is important to declare intentions first and then follow through; this way, future bluffs can be taken seriously.

"If I have the means to acquire the perfect virus, then I would have a simple means of dispersal. I would have white members of my organization disperse the virus in high traffic areas in white parts of the country. I would target train stations, malls, concerts, and airports. It is necessary to get maximum exposure. Also, to keep deaths to a minimum, the authorities will be alerted within, say, 48 hours. The warning time would depend on the speed at which the virus propagates. Though deaths may occur, that isn't the goal.

"It's important to warn the authorities to try and save the infected. The first issue is that there is a limited amount of space at hospitals. The CDC can lend a helping hand, but care will literally be stretched to the limit. When I first thought this scenario up, there was no Affordable Health Care Act. Now that more people have health care coverage, the rate of health care spending won't jump as dramatically as I'd hoped. Yet it still will be an issue.

"You may be wondering why I'm attacking average white Americans? In the long term, the racial divisions will come into play. This is an attack on the very wealthy in the nation. You see, usually during an economic downturn, the wealthy put their wealth in a variety of health care stocks.

They are known as defensive assets. This is because the health care industry, as a standard, does their billing one year after health spending took place. Increasing the amount of people accessing care will spook investors who would otherwise invest in health care stocks without thinking. In fact, people may sell health care stocks in the sight of a nationwide epidemic. In the midst of an economic downturn, this type of thing could lead to a catastrophic deflationary event.

"I hope the catastrophic event doesn't happen yet, as we still have more planned. Health insurance companies will need to increase premiums or they will go out of business. Although I did intentionally attack white Americans, it will be the minorities who suffer economically. The higher premiums will affect them the most, as they make the least in the country. Again, the ACA may have put a damper on this as well. Markets are fast moving, if the government doesn't allow insurance companies to raise rates, then the government will need to step in and increase its spending on health care.

"A financial collapse would be a great outcome. But increased spending to the insurance companies is also a good outcome. The question is this, if the government sharply increases its spending, and that spending passes over minority groups, doesn't that make them more poor? The fact is, there is a limit to how much of the nation's GDP the health care industry can take up before there is a catastrophic collapse.

"I admit that this plan isn't all that great. There are far too many things that I would have to assume. But the essence of the plan still remains solid. Redirect the wealth away from certain areas, and get the government to increase its spending.

INCREASED LAW ENFORCEMENT PRESENCE

"Calling in the FBI, the National Guard, and giving the police overtime are all expected. These things are paid for by emergency funding from the State or Federal Government. Most of this is paid for by shifting money from one program or project to law enforcement. The rest will be paid by borrowing the money. Hopefully, the investigations are long-lived. What does this do? It created another choke point in the economy. It is a reality that most law enforcement aren't people of color. Either money will be redirected from other areas, or the money will simply be created. This redirection of wealth, even though slight, will have an adverse impact on communities of color.

"I'm making assumptions about this nation that some may find disagreeable. This idea that racism no longer exists works in my favor. Even now, some of you are reading this and thinking, How does increasing spending on law enforcement hurt blacks? The real question is this: How much of that increased spending will go to communities of color? Remember, the goal is to stop the people on the top from spending, and also keep wealth from entering communities of color.

"Increasing law enforcement budgets are just the beginning. I know that there is no way that law enforcement would actually attempt to patrol all of the roads, bridges, and rails. In all likelihood, they will go to communities of color and be themselves. Current laws already give law enforcement a great deal of leeway in dealing with the public. A terror threat will officially give them a license to step the abuse up a notch.

"Again, there are people reading this who think that the police are wonderful angels. My experience is much different from yours. My experience is that they are a lawless gang who can do whatever they want to you and get away with it. I expect law enforcement to overreact and cause problems in communities of color. To reiterate, this is an economic downturn, and many people have lost their jobs. Police escalation will add to the economic uncertainty.

"Consider me for a moment. I'm a man without a criminal record and I have no desire to talk to the police or help them in any way. That may come as a surprise to some people. But it is a reality. The police in communities of color are an occupying force whose primary goal is to put the residents in prison (slavery).

"You disagree? If a person gets mugged in a white neighborhood, what happens? The person who was mugged calls the police. The police go to the scene and gets a description of the perpetrator. Then they put a "be on the lookout" (BOLO) for that perpetrator, to all police in the area. In white neighborhoods, the police canvass the area asking for witnesses to help the investigation. If the BOLO doesn't work, the police are completely dependent on the information provided by the public. With that information, the mugger is more likely to be caught.

"That would be an entirely different scenario in my neighborhood. What would be different? The canvassing. The police don't even bother to canvass in my neighborhood. No one wants to talk to them. Years of mistreatment and harassment have cut the police, in my neighborhood, off from their main policing tool, the public. In my neighborhood, if they don't catch a person running away with the goods, they won't catch them.

"This is what makes a terror organization using minorities as front people so appealing. As long as we don't do anything horrific, the public will still be antagonistic to the police. The only tools that they will have available are threats of long prison sentences or large rewards. The threats of prison sentences are a great reason not to interact with police. The only real hope law enforcement has is a large reward leading to our capture. It's my hope that we left no loose ends. In any case, I expect police brutality.

IN THE MEDIA

"It is my great fortune that there exists a medium that will stoke the flames of fear for me. The news will amplify everything we do, and Fox News will make it even better. My terror organization would be a godsend for Fox, as they don't like to cover white homegrown terrorists. If I could, I would hand deliver all of my propaganda to Fox News. If I could manage to get a contagious virus, oh man, that would be the best! Fox News would do all of my work to "otherize" people of color.

"It is my hope that politicians use this moment and try to outdo each other in their response to the attacks. It is my hope that the media and politicians lash out against people of color. They usually do it without provocation. Terrorism will give them the excuse to do 'what they all know they need to do.' If politicians dare to be measured, I will hand deliver propaganda insulting those measured politicians. Or maybe to fan the flames even further, I could openly insult the most bombastic pundit or politician.

"It's important for them to be against the things that we stand for. I want them to openly oppose things that minorities hold dear. In truth, the propaganda part is where I would probably get caught. Unfortunately, it is beyond necessary to play upon the divides that already exist.

UNCLE SAM TO THE RESCUE

"It has become commonplace for the Federal Government to step in when the economy is in free fall. It will either come from Congress or the Federal Reserve. Trillions of dollars will be pumped into the economy, usually at the last moment. It is important to recognize the directionality of the money spent. Most of this money will pass by communities of color. It is a difficult task to have the nation feel the same way about people of color as they did in the '60s. But there still exists persistent animosity towards them. Again here, I assume that my propaganda worked, and that there still exists enough racism to alienate people of color from the economy.

"Dealing with so many unknowns is difficult. But let's assume that economic connections that exist now, remain exactly the same after all of my terrorism. This still will hurt people of color. The point of all of the attacks was to get the government to spend a trillion dollars. The economic divides that already exist will effectively direct that trillion dollars where the wealth already flows.

"What if half of that trillion dollars is spent on communities of color? This could be bad news, as people of color won't feel animosity towards the government. I don't believe this will happen, but it's important to think of the possibilities. It would make my task longer, not harder. The streams of wealth that already exist in this country will simply absorb the wealth and the people of color would be in the same situation. Even still, there is no way this will happen, if history is a guide.

"Now we have the dreaded relative deflation position. Almost anything is possible from such a position. It makes sense that I continue my random attacks to keep investors afraid. Then it will be time to step up the attacks.

PHYSICAL ATTACKS AGAINST OUTSPOKEN RACISTS

"There are scores of white Americans waiting for a race war. It is easy to find these anti-social individuals and attack them. This could possibly be a physical attack or a shooting. In the beginning, it would be important to keep them alive so they can talk about how angry they are. So if I were going to shoot one of these people, I would shoot them in the buttocks.

"I would create a different group to taunt and harass "patriots." Guns are so easy to come by, and no matter how armed you are, you can't really "defend" yourself fast enough against a person who's stalking you. At this point, normal terrorists would be attacking police officers. That's silly, the police are hyper vigilant. Soft targets are the way to go; it's much easier to get away with.

WHAT WILL HAPPEN?

"This is essentially the end of my plan. I'm limited by the means available, and the structures in place to stop me. The point is to antagonize and economically isolate people of color and scare the rich into not spending money. There are many ways to achieve these goals, and I have put forth a few.

"I assume that the people of color will be laid off at a higher rate than any other group during the recession. It is my hope that further terrorist activities and propaganda would increase that rate. I further assume that law enforcement will increase its antagonistic nature towards people of color. In addition to this, I assume that rich people will be far more concerned with making profits, or not losing money, than the state of the nation. I assume that my tactics will scare them enough to not spend.

"Next, the go-to move for the Federal Government has never, and will never, directly affect ordinary people. If enough people are disconnected from the economy, then the increased spending will create areas of relative deflation.

"Finally, antagonizing white supremacists could be the final straw. Why? Because they will find cause to counter-attack communities of color. Maybe mass shootings, maybe church burnings, and maybe much more. This will be the final straw for people of color as it will seem as if the police aren't protecting them. I personally don't feel safe around police. I don't think I'm alone in my feelings. People attacking communities of color are simply out of the police's hands. They can only do so much. But the sentiment will be anti-police anyhow.

"I hope to recreate the black uprisings of the past. If that happens, it doesn't make sense to continue my terrorist activities.

WON'T THE UPRISING FAIL?

"America has the strongest military in the world. There is no chance that there will be any sustained uprisings in America. Also, considering a good portion of the military are minorities, genocide is highly unlikely. If history is a good guide, what will happen is an uptick in arrests and convictions. This is my ultimate goal.

"America has progressed to the moment where she has forgotten why she's imprisoned so many people of color in the first place. The prison-industrial complex was a direct result of black uprisings in the past. Now that the uprisings have subsided dramatically, America is finally talking about reducing its inmate population.

"The eyesore that is the prison industry is a cancer that could cripple the America economy. It is a great fortune that the industry is subsidized by slave labor. Dramatically increasing the prison population will have extreme effects on the economy. The first effect is the direct cost of incarceration to the taxpayers. Next is the economic losses suffered to communities of color as more people are removed from the economy. Finally is the competitive cost to businesses that are unable to compete with slave labor.

"The prison system is another economic choke point in the nation. It is a self-perpetuating organism. The only thing it succeeds in doing is creating further economic imbalances and hurting the nation economically.

YOU DON'T BELIEVE

"Some of you reading this will deny the possibilities. In fact, some of you will deny that racism even exists. Some of you will believe that "American ingenuity" will save the day. You may even believe that there are people out there that won't allow any of this. For those of you who doubt, I want you to understand that our nation has had a plethora of economic collapses. Each economic collapse was just as mysterious as the next one.

"The economic collapses of the past are no mystery to me. They happen when wealth stops circulating. It is a rapid cascade effect that appears, to some, as a natural disaster. Unfortunately, they are far more predictable than some would like to admit.

"In all honesty, it doesn't really matter if the plan would work or not. The truth is, the inevitable is rushing towards us and no one is the wiser. Almost any significant technological advance will do all the work that I just laid out.

"Let's say we discover a way to extend human life by fifty years, but it costs a half a million dollars. That would create the same effects as having a contagious disease. Health care costs would dramatically shoot up, creating stark economic imbalances. How about this? How long before technology makes half of the jobs prisoners do obsolete? How long before this happens? Ten or Twenty years?? That would make for a hell of an economic problem.

"Finally, we have the driverless car. I in fact did end with this. The driverless car isn't a hypothetical; it's happening right now. It's mind-boggling that I'm the only one that I know that is insanely troubled at the thought of it. The driverless car will lay bare all of our stupid economic policies.[2]"

THE GIFT THAT IS TRUMP

I have to admit that I toned down the last chapter of "Follow the Money." My mother harassed me until deleting the section talking about a dictator coming to power as the country was overwhelmed in racial strife. I spoke of all of these calamities happening to one president and a dictator would rise up and crush the rebellion. I have copies of the first book somewhere, but I'm currently typing in a homeless shelter.

I've grown a great deal since I wrote that last chapter. The Controllers, as I call them now, aren't passive passengers on the roller coaster we call an economy. If they are active participants, and are coordinating, then we are all in danger. If the wealth flows in one direction, and if enough of the Controllers stops spending it would instantly collapse the economy. You should think of it like a flow of water, if they hoard the water, then most people will dying of thirst.

Looking back over these last few years, I come to realize that Trump winning the presidency was unplanned and he genuinely didn't want to win, or even thought he had a chance to win. Imagine if all the things that had happened during his presidency happened to Hillary. There are a number of players that would've been much more obscured.

Donald Trump was a lazy talentless agent of the Controllers. He spent his entire life committing crimes and getting away with it. Why? Because he was among the chosen to be above the rest. He was connected, and his crimes were likely protected by higher powers. It was thanks to his stupidity the actions of the Controllers are more apparent.

It's possible that there were investigations into his plethora of crimes, but they were likely small and targeted. For most of his life, he was untouchable. I can tell you where he fucked up. When he went in front of the CIA Memorial Wall, with his own cheer squad, began bragging about his electoral win and he even lied about the weather. It was a show of strength to experts in human technology. Every single CIA agent watching that shit show likely knew classified stories behind each nameless star. What a buffoon. The intelligence community went completely dark around that time, and they still are.

That idiot kicked and screamed about people getting access to his taxes. As one of the chosen, he's used to getting his way. And what's weird is, on the surface, it seems that he did. But he's a fucking idiot! Thousands of people have access to that moron's tax returns. I know of someone, who works for a firm, who has all of this simpleton's tax returns. They didn't convey anything to me. But through a second degree source I can confirm a 'shake my damned head' reaction. I say this as a legal matter, no one has told me a thing about that idiot's tax returns. Of course their full of crimes! Why would you try so hard for no one to look?

Here's where he fucked up. The IRS and state tax authorities all have access to all of his tax returns. And these agencies are full of the people that talentless cocksucker was publicly attacking. Also, and I can't stress this enough, there are people, at every tax collection agency, who's job it is to investigate tax crimes. The Controllers made sure that their jobs were difficult and arduous. There simply isn't enough people to investigate all the crimes taking place. What are the odds that a woman, a Jew, an African-American, a Mexican, an Asian, or an Arab is a tax investigator?

If you're talking about bureaucracy, I know from experience, you might be talking about a Jamaican. What are the chances this Jamaican watched this troglodyte shoot Adderall rocks from his nostrils, and simply filled out a form and took a look for himself? We all know what happened next, "Bumbaclot!" There's a form for that. Trust me, there's a bumbaclot form. There's guaranteed a giant investigation there. And lots of people are implicated in his tax returns.

Sure, he committed crimes in broad daylight. The thing that likely pissed the Controllers off was that he burned so many of their undercover assets. Control is a long term process. Putting compromised people in key places is primary goal of the Controllers. Trump being one of their assets also knows of this. He exposed so many tendrils of power. I was totally unaware of the pervasiveness of it. Thanks to Trump constantly calling for help, he depleted the ranks of the Controllers.

I literally could go on for a whole other book on how totally fucked this guy is. There's one more thing that I'd like to share before I explain the nail in the coffin for Trump. A few years ago, someone in my twitter time line sent a photo of one of Trump's properties in Miami. It was a condo complex that the guy was just asking for the government to investigate.

Apparently the whole thing is empty and no one goes in or out. I chided the man, and told him to stop spreading conspiracy theories. In my mind, the picture looked fake, and there's no way he's just this bad at crime. The guy went outside and took a selfie with the building in the background and tweeted "I live across the street." And before I could debase myself for not accepting how imbecilic that half-wit truly was, someone posted a well sourced article linking the building with money laundering. I still can't believe that mental munchkin really went for it. He thought he could bullshit his way through an entire presidency.

Where did he screw up the most? Women. I even wanted there to be an uprising with women, but he succeeded in doing it all by himself. Women have been oppressed for thousands of years. His arrogance, constant lying, and ham-fisted attempts to subjugate and silence women was his biggest mistake.

He exposed the compromised underlings in government and the movements and numbers of the know-nothings. No one can unsee the reality happening in front of them. The Controllers are afraid, because a subjugated woman is vital in this system of control. Let me explain.

CONTROL THE WOMEN

It's tempting to make this it's own section, but it is the same control by distraction. This by no means lessens the relevance of it. Women have been oppressed for many thousands of years. It's a main function of this system of control. I'm in a unique position to expose how and why it happens. In 2014, I wrote "Why Women Cheat: Confessions of a Pickup Artist." I have a question for you. Did you feel weird reading that sentence? If you did, why? I believe it's all connected to the same system of control. I'll walk you through how I got here.

After my breakdown in Madison Square Park, I listened. I quit my chess teaching jobs, stopped studying chess, began looking for work, and started studying how to make money and materials about women. I can be quite intense sometimes. I am who I am. By 2011, after years of struggling with panic attacks, one day a panic attack turned into an intense feeling of love. It was someone who I had dated 8 or 9 years prior. It had only lasted less than three days. On the first day, I sent a message to the young woman I had the feelings for. But by the time she responded the feelings were gone. I apologized to her, and told her the feelings were gone. I promised to never bother her again, I didn't want to abuse her.

"After reading her last letter I left my couch and sat on floor, in the corner of my spacious living room embracing my chins with my head buried in my knees. I didn't want to touch anymore of my stuff. 'I don't want to do this anymore! I understand. I don't care about this anymore! Okay. What the hell was she apologizing about? I don't know. I don't care. It doesn't matter anymore; I don't want to do this anymore. Problem Solver you can have it back! Things are getting better. I did everything you asked and I'm sick of it. What's the point if I can't feel what I want to feel! Susan(my therapist at the time) says maybe we are letting go our emotions stored up. So it took me over eight years to realize that I loved Rose?! Then it all went away after such a short while! Yes, and the fear we feel incessantly is something we probably forgot as well. I don't want to do this anymore. Switch! How do we do it? I don't know.'

"'I don't want to do this anymore! I'm not doing anything else! Switch. Have it back!' I shouted. 'I don't want to do this either. What's the point? One of you won't let me play chess. No matter how much I study I'm still a B class rating. I can't act; if I do I will forget all the lines when on stage. I can't sing. No matter how many lessons I get if feels like a toad is growing in my throat. I can't dance; my body cramps up at the thought of it. You let me get some financial success, but I feel like there is much more that I can do. I'm still limited. Most important of all, you won't let me be around the people that make me happy. What's the point? Have it back! I don't want to do this anymore. Yeah it's useless. Why bother? I give up. Me too. Does everyone feel the same way? I think so. Wait, it's better to ask if there is any objection. So is there any objection?' There was no answer.[3]"

Looking back, all those years making money and dating lots of women were a distraction that I had made for myself. I was incessantly in pain, and not realizing how much. Within twelve months I had gone from two dozen workers in the Philippines, to driving an Uber. I also accepted the truth of how I felt. I wasn't ready to be with anyone. I promised to not try and pick up any more women until I was ready. In 2014, I had become incredibly lonely and horny. This set off opposing strong emotions. The truth was that I was horny, lonely, and I didn't want anyone to touch me. So I hatched a plan to convince the one in charge of my sex organs.

I would write a book about dating, ostensibly written for men, but secretly was meant to be a display of who I am. The plan was to to go on radio and talk shows to talk about it, and let the women come to me. No part of me objected to it. The hope was I would eventually encounter someone who the one in charge of my sexual organs would say that he's ready. The plan went off without a hitch.

I got multiple bookings right away, some were horrible, and once a woman just hung up on me on air and kept going on with the show like I wasn't there. It wasn't until I had an interview with one woman, and we had a wonderful chat. After the show she thanked me, and gave me a lesson in what people are looking for. I'm paraphrasing, "Shows are looking for a man who's cocky, to brag about his sexual conquests, and who has an obvious fatal flaw. This man will fall apart around a real woman, and hopefully turns his life around when he meets this real woman."

She was a lot more detailed than this. She was a professional, and didn't expect me to be who I was. While reading the email, all of the imaginary characters that fit this role began flashing before my mind's eye. A deep depression had engulfed my entire spirit. Again, for the millionth time, the only way I can make paper is to play an imaginary character. This man doesn't exist! A man with an obvious tick, that only 'low-quality' women fall for. No man who's dating lots of women would publicly brag about having sex with a woman! You'd not have any more sex with anyone.

What's worst is, I co-wrote the book with three different women from different parts of the world. That would be insulting to them. I promised to keep their identities secret, and I did. I'll speak more about the three women now, only because the website I hired them from no longer exists. I created a job posting in 2014. In it, I asked for female writers to comment on two pickup artist strategies: how to make a woman fall in love, and how to have sex with a different woman every day. I got many replies.

The first woman who replied, offered half the time alloted, and half the money offered. Her proposal was multiple pages of well written English, and she was from Eastern Europe. I can't recall all of what she wrote, but I remember she started off with that she was waiting for this her whole life. She went on for a page or two about what a piece of shit I was, then proceeded to list all of the ways she was going to kick my ass. The last few pages she swore up and down that there's no way that a pussy like me would ever hire her to write in my book. I picked her first. She was clearly motivated and passionate about the project. She was comfortable expressing herself, and was a good writer. How could I not pick her? I gave her the regular time and pay. In the book, she called herself Lola-Red, and she was the youngest of the three writers.

The second woman that I hired was an American politically active feminist. She said as much in her pitch letter. It was well written and non-combative. She ended her response to my ad with, "I promise to be fair and only kick your ass when you needed it." At the time, I figured, Lola is definitely gonna kick my ass, and this woman is only gonna kick my ass when I needed it. I assumed she would be a little less fiery than Lola. In the book, she called herself Chan. You could probably guess her first name if you read the book. In it she recounts drop kicking a man sexually assaulting her friend.

I haven't spoken to Chan since 2014, but I'm willing to wager that she has many pictures of her chanting in a crowd of other women, wearing pussy hats. I paid Chan extra, as she was a native speaker, to edit the book and the things the other two wrote. I never changed a single word of any of the female writers. I think she did a really good job with it. Chan was at least ten years older than Lola-Red.

The last was Claudia. She was much older than the other two and had been in a committed relationship with her man for more than thirty years. She was from South America, and was the sweetest person in the world. When I hired her, I thought that she was the complete opposite of Lola, and hoped she would balance things out. It turns out, they were all different and unique in their own ways. Claudia was a bit more reserved than the other two, and I absolutely appreciated that.

After reading the email describing the perfect pickup artist radio guest I didn't do anymore interviews. Either I canceled them, or they canceled me. I had made a commitment to the truth, I refused to pretend to be a character for resources. Also, I completely lost interest in dating, and become more focused on meditating. The last time that I was with a woman was the end of February 2012. I'm content, as I don't have control of my sexuality. If or when that part of me is ready, I will not resist. If he's never ready, I'm okay with that as well.

Now what most guys are likely wondering, how can I get women to want me? It's very simple. You have to discard the lies of the system, which purposely deceives with the intent on control. Women are animals of this Earth, they are monkeys, same as the rest of us. A woman's sexuality is purposely obscured and oppressed. If you want to know what a woman wants, watch other animals and see how it works.

Recently, I've been feeding birds and squirrels every chance I can get. When the male pigeons are full, the puff their chests up and start cooing at one of the female pigeons. The female would start running, and the male would give chase. Every now and then, she'd stop and realize 'Oh is that rice!' and she'd start pecking at the food. Then she'd see the male pigeon coming at her and she'd go back to running.

This is the same function that happens between male and female humans. When a man sees a woman he likes, he goes after her, but is thoroughly unaware of what she wants. For pigeons, the females are checking the weather, the season, and if there's enough space, food, and water for chicks. Then and only then would she check the male pigeon out, and if she likes what she sees, that specific male pigeon can fertilize some eggs.

Some of you might be feeling helpless at hearing this, but don't stress, we are going to get to the food, shelter, water, and energy. What most guys fail at is thinking women care about money and job titles. It's distracting a bit, because women often talk about those things when mentioning men. It's simply not true. I don't know how many men would complain to me that their girl left them, or cheated, and their common refrain was "I brought home the bacon." In the midst of the constant complaining, I would usually cut them off and blurt out "it's your fault." They would be furious with me, a few may have wanted to fight me. They really just wanted me to commiserate, but it's your fault. It makes even more sense, now that I see the system as it is.

There are three groups, the Controllers, men, and women. Men are the targets, and women are the distraction. Men are raised up beyond what they deserve, and women are openly oppressed. Women are allowed to be sexually attractive to men, but are denied expressing what they find attractive. This is done to confuse men. The men are constantly told that woman want men that work hard. There's an unspoken rule, that the higher up the ladder you go, women are just waiting for you. Also, the media, which is also controlled, highlights 'playboys' as inspiration for men to 'achieve.' Men are supposed to be inspired to be like these rich 'playboys.'

One of the original 'playboys' is Hugh Hefner. He had a television show which highlighted the lifestyle men are supposed to want to achieve. He's always been a creepy dude in a bathrobe. The next is Donald Trump, the media portrayed him as a playboy as well. Whatever. The idea is, if you make lots of money, women will be all over you. Let's talk about what's really happening.

You are all monkeys! What do you think happens when you tell a monkey that if they do a something for ten or more years, and promise that they'll get sex when they reach the top? Then is doesn't happen. That monkey would lose his shit and rape some female monkeys. Which is what is happening right now. If fact, I would say the goal of the system is rape. The men who make it to the top, after a great deal of hardship, will realize right away, that there is no pussy at the top. All their hard work and women still don't want them. There are others at the top, who will encourage them to rape. Why? Because then those individuals will be compromised. They will become assets of the Controllers.

You don't find it suspicious that 25% of women, in the United States, are sexually assaulted, but magically there isn't budget enough to investigate? It's deliberate. The Controllers wish to protect their assets, and themselves. Of course there's resistance by men for women entering the workforce. Too many men accept the lie, that this is what women want. They may want a better life, because they are purposely excluded from the economy financially, but it has nothing to do with sex.

I spent $4k on a weekend pickup artist boot camp, do you know who was there? It was full of men, around the same age. They were all men who had reached to the top of the ladder and was confused why they weren't getting sex. These men were smart and asked for professional help. If you looked at them, you would see young attractive men. Some of you would be tempted to say "you don't need any pickup artist boot camp!" But this is a lie. The system teaches men to hate men like me, who are having lots of sex, but who are not rich and famous, and wish for you to emulate people like Donald Trump.

I can tell you what you will learn from learning from a pick-up artist. You will learn to display your feathers in a way women would find attractive. There's no magic. That was the whole point of my book "Why Women Cheat." It was me showing off who I am, and using three women that I hadn't met to help. I can tell you, that my ass remains unkicked. If you want to be sexually attractive, you need to find a way to puff your feathers. And what's nice is, you can gradually improve if you continue to work at it.

But there's an even better way to get women. Just like pigeons, if you supply all the things that she needs, women, in general, will be more amenable to your advances. Since women aren't pigeons, this is what they need food, water, shelter, and energy. If you can help all women get these things in abundance, for themselves, it would mark a new era in human history. I can't guarantee that you'll get any, you will still have to show off what you're working with. Women ultimately have the last say in who's DNA gets passed unto the next generation. If you are one of the guys helping women get unlimited energy, space, food, and water, you might be positioning yourself for a lot of future sex!

There's the added bonus that free women would completely destroy the system. When women are completely free to do as they please, they will no longer be afraid to speak about who sexually assaulted them. It's men who've reached the top of the ladder, and are too powerful to speak out against. They are lawyers, doctors, musicians, judges, millionaires, billionaires, cops, politicians, and on, and on.

Let's see how we can help anyone who wishes it to have all the things that they need.

Chapter FIVE

ESCAPING THE SYSTEM

"Let's pray that the human race never escapes from Earth to spread its iniquity elsewhere."

~ C. S. Lewis ~

POST APOCAYLPTIC LIES

There is a myth that most of the planet believes, that is utterly false. It is constantly promoted in the media, and in movies. It's such a common belief, that when politicians repeat it in the halls of Congress no one bats an eye. The notion that there isn't enough for everyone is the biggest fraud perpetrated on the entire population by the Controllers.

Our culture is rife with the post-apocalyptic notion that we are running out of the resources to live. The reality is, the system can't survive in a world where any resource is unlimited. The system is fundamentally anti-life. If you can successfully control and limit the precise things the living need to survive, then there needs to be competition for said resources. With competition, the Controllers can price the resources at anything that they wish.

I like watching great programs and movies, but understanding basic scientific principles has made some of them unbearable. The zombie genre is a good example of an artificially scarce society. In fact, zombie movies are like a projection of the basic tenets of what the Controllers want to happen in real life. The protagonists are trapped in an area, surrounded zombies hungry for brains, or in political speak, the 'others' trying to take your stuff. Supplies are limited, and hard choices need to be made.

With your permission, I'm going ruin every post-apocalyptic movie right now. Whenever I see one of these programs, I immediately say, "All they need to do is this or that." Every single one of your favorite dramas will seem foolish when you understand the lies behind artificial scarcity. What humans need to survive is food, water, energy, and shelter. All of these things exists in abundance, and without much effort.

Firstly, you have to understand that we are energy beings. The system purposely detaches us from nature and who we are. In order for me to defeat endless zombie hordes, I would need an easily defensible location, and unlimited supplies. If that exists, then we could potentially repopulate the entire planet. Since I'm in New York City, I'll assume that a zombie plague has reached here. How would I survive?

Firstly, I'd find the closest public school and hopefully be let in. If I can get inside the school, then there must be other people there. Let's just say that there are only ten of us. Similar to a zombie movie. Why do I like schools? They are built like urban fortresses. All of the windows already have metal gates covering them, and the doors are difficult to open. Also, schools in my neighborhood put chains on the doors at closing. So, I can reasonably expect that chains exists to add an extra level of security. Once safely inside now we have to worry about how we will survive.

Most schools have food stored inside. I'm going to give myself and the rest of the protagonists, four weeks of food and water. The plumbing and the electricity don't work. Now what? We are energy beings is what. We consume energy, and we also secrete energy. If the ten of us wants to survive, we have to create a closed life cycle. This is what the system denies us all.

We will need food and water, else we will be fighting over resources. All ten of us will need to urinate, all of it must be saved. What's urine composed of? It's 96% water, 2% ammonia, and 2% biological waste. That 2% of ammonia could be used for energy, but that doesn't help with food and water. Our bodies were designed to be giving. Our waste is exactly what other things on the planet wants to survive. Fortunately, there exists life that would thrive in urine; algae.

There are quite a variety of fast growing sea plants. Hopefully, the school has some in the science room. If not, that would be a top priority to get outside the school and find some. Fast growing sea plants would consume the ammonia and the biological matter and reform it into edible greens. All we'll need to do is place them in a fish tank by the windows, and the sun will power them. The plants will provide carbohydrates and nutrients, everything the body needs to survive. Also, the algae will leave behind potable water.

A great leap forward in getting out of crisis mode. But doing things this way, we'll run out of water right? Yes, we'll slowly run out of water, mostly because of evaporation. Back to panic mode? No! We live on a planet literally covered in water. All we need to do is get it. I don't believe the school will have the necessary equipment, so we'll have to go outside and fight zombies. What do we get? Dehumidifiers, magnets, coils of copper wire, and converters.

Magnets are how we generate most of the 'electricity' on planet. By rotating, or oscillating, a magnet through a coil of wire, an alternating current is generated. We will never run out of magnets or coils of wire. How is this 'electricity' generated? Also, why am I using scare quotes? Somehow the Controllers have convinced the planet that electricity is almost magic. All it is are electrons, from the copper wire, being displaced as a magnetic field oscillates through it. It just so happens that we can do work with that current of electrons.

I would make a bunch acoustic propulsion turbines, like earlier discussed, and set them up in the auditorium. I would connect each device to it's own converter, making direct current. Then I would connect the dehumidifiers up to the direct current generated. The dehumidifiers would mechanically remove water from the air, and we'll have as much water as we need. This will take some work to set up. But once set up, all we'd need to do is to generate the correct pitch in order to power the acoustic propulsion turbines.

School auditoriums have great acoustics, a grand piano, and most have additional instruments. The ten of us would chant a tone or play an instrument with the same tone. A school is a perfect choice, for this very reason. We wouldn't need all of us to power the devices. All we'd need if one person playing the piano, and striking one tone repeatedly.

Once we have taken care of the water, and have some food to eat, it's time to make our own energy. As I've said, we're energy beings. What we've done so far is to just extend the four weeks of food and water we have nearly indefinitely. Now it's time to thrive. Most of the United States is run on natural gas. We'll discuss later the expensive, destructive, and labor intensive way the Controllers decided to get our natural gas. They always choose the most inefficient and harmful way to do things. It's to convince you how hard it is. I want you to let this sink in, humans fart natural gas every day!

How can we capture this natural gas? Simple, by making bio-digesters. All we'll need is a container, with water in it, space on the top to capture the gas, and a spout to release nutrient filled water. So what's happening? We have bacteria inside of us that consumes biological waste. The bacteria will break down the fecal matter into its base elements, and releases natural gas as a by-product.

Here's where you say "With only ten people! That's not gonna make much energy!" That's true, but we don't need to stop with poop. Bacteria will consume all types of biological matter. Things that are usually just lying around in zombie movies. Books, food waste, newspapers, clothing, shoes, rotting food, dead animals, car tires, and dead zombies. All of these things are made from living cells. The bacteria would slowly break them all down. We could potentially make as many bio-digesters as we want. Potentially having unlimited energy.

Once we have enough stored energy, acoustic propulsion turbines wouldn't be needed. We can use the fuel for heating and electricity. I would use a solid oxide fuel cell(SOFC), instead of a combustion turbine, as SOFCs are twice as energy efficient as their combustion counterparts. Also, we can find or modify cars that will run on natural gas.

The waste from the bio-digesters can be used for hydroponic farming. The first crop that we'd grow are potatoes. Our entire body is run on sugar! Starch is concentrated glucose. Potatoes will take nutrients, water, and carbon-dioxide and make copious amounts of starch. We could potentially live indefinitely with only algae and potatoes. Nothing would ever go to waste, and instead of keeping people away, we would likely go out to find other survivors and grow our community.

Knowing that we can do this, whenever we want, doesn't that change the entire tenor of every post-apocalyptic movie? These things can only exist if you except the lie that there isn't enough. All that we need exists in abundance, but a handful of people limit our resources on purpose. How about we take this knowledge and apply it to reality.

SAVING THE PLANET WITH POOP

Knowing that we can make as much natural gas as much as we want to, why do you think we aren't just making it ourselves? The system of control that has us all despises ease and comfort. It loathes functionality and utility. Production can't be owned by the Targets or the Distractions. The process needs to be too difficult for ordinary folks to understand. So how do we get our natural gas now? Fracking.

Hydraulic fracturing is a complex and costly process. First, you need to drill a couple miles beneath the earth's surface. That hole is protected by steel, or steel and concrete if passing an aquifer. Once they've reached the desired depth, they begin drilling horizontally, repeating the steel casing. Then they set off small explosions to fracture the shale and release oil and gas.

Then they pump high pressured fracking mixture into the well. The mixture is mostly water and sand. The rest are toxic chemicals that are meant to kill the bacteria that created the natural gas in the first place. The want to save the 'oil' from bacteria consuming it. Cat out of the bag, oil isn't a 'fossil' fuel. This is another lie. People think oil comes from dinosaurs. That's wrong, **oil is dead algae**.

The high pressure fluid will further fracture the shale miles beneath the surface. Once the mixture is pumped out, natural gas and oil can be extracted, some wells can last for years. I don't want to waste time talking about the scammy casino like structure of oil and gas drilling. Rachel Maddow's book "Blowout" does an excellent job is this. I just want to stress, ordinary folks can't do this. I'm all for human ingenuity, but this is hard and complicated on purpose. It's all controlled by a handful of people. Also, it's killing the planet.

How about we try something different? For this to work, we will need to create a not-for-profit whose stated goal is "To Protect All Life." I'd like to call it "Nation Without Borders." This organization will help all animals on this planet get the resources it needs, including humans. Natural gas is easy to get if we work together. The system wants us divided and fighting over scraps.

Obviously, we are going to get natural gas from human waste. First I want to remind you of the control you are under. I did a quick summary of hydraulic fracturing, it's costly and harmful. Did you know that all human waste processing plants simply throws the natural gas away? Vice made a program called "You Don't Know Shit." You can watch it on HBO or YouTube. The series was right, I didn't know shit. I knew how fracturing worked because I'm interested in science. My blood began to boil when watch two grown men laugh at the smell as a gust of natural gas blew past them. Why make such a big deal out of drilling for the stuff, and then throw away the same exact stuff that's made for free? Control.

How can we do it without fracking? The Nation Without Borders would create a circular barge with a mile diameter. Such a thing would be incredibly stable in the ocean. The barge would be covered in solar panels to power it. Most jurisdictions have to pay people to take their human waste, the NWB would take the poop for free. The barge will create, process, and compress the gas into LNG. It can be completely automated, poop goes in and LNG comes out. It can be shipped anywhere in the world from there. The NWB won't hoard the LNG or jack up the price. The NWB will sell lifetime micro-contracts to any living being who wishes to own it. Each barge will be collectively owned, by the people who utilize it. Meaning for five or ten bucks any human can have an energy producing asset for themselves. Doing things in this way, the NWB can purchase as many giant barges to convert the poop of billions of people poop into natural gas.

How does the NWB profit? The organization will take a small portion of every transaction. This way the organization can operate and expand. I don't like the idea of selling ownership of the barge, because I suspect someone might have a legal maneuver short circuit the operation. I don't care one way or the other, I just want to help people have their own energy. With every contract purchased, that person will receive a rate of LNG for the rest of their lives.

What about the byproducts? Once the bacteria break the poop down, we'll have nutrients that we can use to save the planet. How? By making algae. Phytoplankton are rapidly growing organisms, and as a rule, civilizations try to avoid creating an algal bloom. This is because blooms will block the sun for the life beneath the surface, killing them. This won't be a problem if we make the algae in the deep ocean. The largest deserts on the planet aren't on the surface, they're in the ocean. And both land and ocean deserts are our fault.

There are literally millions of square miles of ocean where no life exists. I would take the nutrients that the barges create and release it in targeted areas in ocean deserts. Then I'd make sure to add some phytoplankton so that they would consume the nutrients and carbon dioxide. There's a problem, if simply allowed to grow, the algae would simply cover all surfaces of the ocean. This is why we would grow krill.

Krill are not only vital part of the ocean's food chain, but also, they are the only thing on the planet that can keep up with the exponential growth of algae. Krill lay ten thousand eggs at a time, and can break down the hydrocarbons that algae produce. They are literally called filter feeders. Algae is the earth's filter.

People constantly bang on about what we are going to do with the carbon once we remove it from the air, as if it's some big mystery. We can turn it into life! The only thing I would want is to be able to protect the algae, the krill, and any other life in the area the NWB uses to deposit nutrients. The NWB will need to claim the Ocean deserts as its own. There can be no fishing, or anything that disturbs the life in the areas that we will be cultivating.

With billions of people on the planet, there will be more than enough natural gas the power the planet many times over.

LIMITLESS WATER

One of the most glaring lies that exists, is the notion that we are running out of water. The planet is literally covered in water! We have the technology and the ability to gather as much water as we want. The reality is, that it's another layer in the system of control. Either a government or a private organization claims rights over a fresh water source, then they supply it to people who need it to survive for a fee, or compliance. Then they are surprised that their water supply is running out.

Very few people on this planet has any agency over their own water. Almost all people completely depend on the system supplying them with this vital resource. The control becomes more apparent when the water supply becomes tainted by big business, poisoned by poor governance, or simply shut off in a genocidal rage.

The NWB will seek to get life saving water to all life on this planet. While there are new technologies that have come to light that can help create fresh water, current technology will suffice. There are two ways simple ways to get water; dehumidifiers and reverse osmosis.

Again, this can and will be done in the ocean. Using the refrigeration process, we can condense water out of the air. Being in the ocean, there is a constant supply of pure water just above the surface of the waters. If you have a decent sense of smell, you can literally smell the water in the air around any body of water. It's simple, a fan blows air past the cold part of the refrigeration process, and water will condense and drip into a container. The cold air then passes over the warm end of the refrigeration process warming the air to its original temperature.

If we want, we can make large boats, or barges, covered in solar panels to power the device. This will condense water at a specific rate, based on how much sunlight there is. Also, when it rains, this floating machine can catch the rainwater. As always, the NWB will sell lifetime contracts for each boat or barge. Meaning, anyone in the world who wants a regular rate of water can buy it from us and have it delivered to where they'd want it.

Reverse Osmosis, on the other hand, is energy intensive. I wouldn't bother with solar power for this. Instead, we would use solid-oxide fuel cells. Since the NWB will sell natural gas contracts from poop bio-digesters, people can spend their energy in order to make water directly from the ocean, or with waste water. Since humans around the world are incessantly polluting the waterways with their waste water, the NWB will initially focus on waste water. So reverse osmosis boats will be situated off the shores of every populated area, and take in waste water and give fresh water in return. The NWB will also sell lifetime contracts from reverse osmosis ships. In addition to the contract, the buyer needs to regularly supply energy, and in return they will get a rate of water. The leftover sludge is something that the NWB will use later.

Before I end this basic argument that water is unlimited, I'd like to talk about ammonia. It is a vital part of what we call modern farming. The Haber-Bosch process has multiple steps and consumes a great deal of 'fossil' fuels. This process is obsolete because there exists multiple direct ammonia synthesis processes today. All we'd need is water, air, and electricity. The dumb part is, the Haber process was obsolete the day big business implemented it. Why? Because we're energy beings. We make ammonia as a waste product.

It's not uncommon to see that we are literally doing the worst thing possible to make what we need and at the same time destroying the free stuff. There is three times the amount of energy, in wastewater ammonia, than energy it takes for us to destroy the ammonia in wastewater. The NWB will extract that ammonia as payment. We can use it as an energy source with an ammonia fuel cell. Or we can sell an ammonia extraction factory collectively, and each owner will need to supply the waste water and energy to power the boat, and in return, they'll receive a rate of ammonia.

The NWB will only sell water and energy contract to living beings. I'd like to protect life, not any self interested organizations. If all humans have access to energy and water, it would radically change the shape of the world. Here's how.

MAKING OUR OWN CURRENCY

In my book, "Follow the Money," I tried to make sense of a complex financial system, and attempted to create complex solutions. In "Follow the Money," I hinted at the possibility that if the people who control all of the wealth, decided to collectively stop spending locally, then we all might be in trouble. Why? Because money purposely flows to them and they don't have to spend the money. If they do coordinate, and I now believe they do, then they can crash any economy that they wish.

Our entire economy runs on paper currency. Ostensibly, if people work, the economy is supposed to work. But in reality, if any location is cash starved, then no one can work. This is the third time, in recent memory, that congress has a question in front of them. Raise taxes on the rich and pay people to work, or not. Talking heads on the news can't seem to understand why people would be against government spending going towards the poorest in the nation. It's simple, you starve these people for paper, load them with debt, and then you have a giant slave force. Poverty is the point.

The counter argument is correct, there is no amount of tax that will be enough. In time, we will be back in the same position, because no one has any agency in this system. The Controllers will simply jack up the prices, and everyone will be poor again. I'd rather not dwell too much on paper. I could talk at length about it and also crypto-currencies. For now, it's a waste of space. Let's talk about what we can do.

Thus far, the NWB will be shipping LNG and fresh water all around the world. Only living beings will be able to purchase water and gas contracts. The next thing folks will need is storage. The NWB will need to control and operate it's own storage. We will lease out space to individuals and organizations, public and private. Being able to store your energy, water, or anything else means that you can trade with the stored goods.

For example, if you went to a local deli, here in NYC, and asked for a bacon, egg, and cheese on a roll, would the owner refuse an amount of LNG in exchange? They use LNG to light, heat, and cool the store. Also, the grill is powered by LNG. Delis would certainly take LNG as payment, and all that would happen is the LNG would be transfered to their storage account. Do you see what just happened? We created a currency, that's completely within your control, and you can get more if you want to. Most importantly, you wouldn't need work a single minute for it. LNG is stored work! For the first time, you'll have agency in the world.

In addition to this, the deli owner can trade LNG with other businesses, and even pay their employees with it as well. Considering everyone in NYC uses LNG for power. In fact, many of the food factories here in NYC consume a great deal of energy, and water. They use water like a broom to clean their factories. There are many bread factories here in NYC. A significant portion of their expenses are both LNG and water. Most would likely take both as payment for bread.

Of course, there will be a markup of some kind to pay the workers and for profits. The thing that happened is we officially cut the middle man out of the picture. Prices for goods and services will stabilize, and will likely never go up. Business have the right to refuse to accept LNG or water, if their storage is full. In any case, there would be no reason for giant price fluctuations.

Finally, public organizations can run completely on energy. If the government wishes to tax the LNG and the water, then they will get a percentage from everyone. Running the government on energy and water instantly unlimits everything. For example, what's the difference between the worst performing public school and the most well endowed private school? Resources right? By unfair rules, some get more than others.

If the school takes energy as payment, the first thing that can happen is that schools can be open 24/7. Not just for kids, but for the entire community. The reason that they close by five or six every day, is because it costs too much energy to heat, cool, and light large buildings like that. With abundant energy, instead of closing, schools can rent out space to the community when the kids leave. There will instantly be thousands of indoor gyms that the community can use. There will be thousands of theater spaces, with good acoustics and hundreds of seats, that will be available for use. In addition, every school will have hundreds of available rooms, that the public can utilize, and purchase with energy and water.

There are tons of things that people can do in those available spaces: chess, dance, debate, choir, church, cooking, sewing, and anything else the community deems important. These are the things that are already available in 'rich' schools. When in reality, they are simply resource rich. Even the 'poorest' school will become 'rich' overnight. With so many people utilizing the school, school administrations can even pay some of them energy to come during day, when the kids are there.

Just doing these things will completely liberate us all from this oppressive system. I'm honestly afraid, the Controllers purposely put the scariest and most evil people in charge of the 'limited' energy resources. The idea that every human can gather and store their own energy is a threat to every strongman on the planet. It's amazing that the Controllers convinced the world that energy is limited. It's a giant fucking lie, in order to control us all.

UNLIMITED ENERGY

When I tell people that energy is unlimited, they roll their eyes at me. For some reason it's a given that we are imminently running out of energy. I understand where they're coming from. If energy were truly unlimited, what is the entire planet fighting over? They are fighting over who has direct control over obsolete technology. It is a scam, we don't need them or their 'energy.' First let's understand what infinite really means.

No one has ever truly measured infinity, because it would literally take forever. In mathematics, we have a simple way to prove a thing in infinite. You ask a simple question. Can you add one more? Numbers are infinite because you can always add one more. There's no need to count. In fact, if you accept that infinity exists, then you can add one to infinity, proving there are some infinities that are larger than others. Now onto producing energy.

Currently, the best and most efficient power source on this planet is nuclear fission. There are a few concerns about it. The first is waste. Modern nuclear power not only consumes the waste of older nuclear plants. But also, they can breed their own fissile materials. Meaning, they can create indefinite nuclear reactions with the same materials. We could go completely without waste, but I'd like nuclear plants that use carbon-14 as a moderator. This will be a waste product the NWB will use later. In addition, I may be partial to nuclear reactions that produce helium as a byproduct. You'll see why later.

Other concerns about explosions and radiation, these are easily addressed. Nuclear power is literally the cleanest technology on the planet. More people die every year from every other power generation, including solar power. Also, modern nuclear reactors are walk away safe, meaning there's zero chance of explosion. But of course, no one wants one in their backyards. In fact, federal law prohibits nuclear plants from being within five miles of any populated areas. That's easy, I want to put my nuclear power in the ocean!

What is nuclear power? To put it simply, it generates continuous heat for multiple years at a time. Some can stay hot up to thirty years without any additional input. What do we usually do with this heat? We boil water, and that spins a turbine generating a current. For our purposes, I'd like to put nuclear power in the ocean, and chain multiple Stirling engines together, ending in a condenser, to get additional current. What will we do with all of this current? Make liquid fuel!

The best energy storage device on the planet has been carbon, for millions of years. The NWB will make liquid hydrocarbons and ship it all around the world. We can make any fuel that we wish; gasoline, diesel, propane, jet fuel, or ammonia. For simplicity's sake, we'll just make jet fuel for now. We have the technology to make jet fuel from carbon-dioxide and water. Those ingredients can be extracted from the air, or directly from the ocean. If we do that, then the jet fuel will be carbon neutral. I don't mind pulling the water and carbon-dioxide from the air. But pulling it from the ocean might adversely affect sea life.

In the beginning, we'll use the water and carbon we gather from elsewhere. Lots of people are going to have more water than they need from the reverse osmosis boats. We'll discuss where we'll get the carbon from later. But what's important to realize is this. If you buy a contract with the NWB for a nuclear powered boat, and you supply the water and carbon-di-oxide, then you'll receive a liquid hydrocarbon, like jet fuel. Where you can store it, trade it, or use it for yourself.

Back to infinity. There are over a hundred million square miles of ocean. Even though we literally can't have an infinite amount of nuclear powered boats in the ocean. We can get infinite energy. The question is simple, can we make one more? If we built about ten thousand of these boats, it could easily power the entire planet. Can build one more? Yes! This means energy is precisely unlimited. When we talk about having unlimited space, you'll see that we can literally always add one more.

UNLIMITED FOOD

How we make food now is literally killing the planet and starving billions of humans. It's all a system of control. People loyal to the ruling faction, are the only ones allowed to be farmers, and all others are magically excluded. In addition to this travesty, in America, we pay farmers to use our poop as fertilizer. If you watch Vice's "You Don't Know Shit," until the end you'll see the entire sanitation process was designed to create fertilizer for farms. It's infuriating that these folks get so many subsidies, are constantly demanding more, and forever complaining that everyone else is lazy and mooching off of the government. The farmers here purposely have a larger say in the government than the rest of us. This is because the Controllers have a large stake in the farm industry. Or more precisely, they have agricultural monopolies.

I could fill a book on how terrible the farming system we live under is. It's pointless. I would like to point out that I'm not upset about them using our poop for fertilizer. That's precisely what it is. The issue I have is that they destroy the urine, then have a convoluted process of making ammonia to feed the plants. Many Americans are nutrient deficient because of it. In order to have your body operate properly, you need to take multivitamins daily. Why so often, because those nutrients get flushed down the toilet and destroyed. Our farming is killing the planet, and starving billions of humans. All for the sake of control and profits. There's a better way if we work together.

With unlimited energy, unlimited food is quite easy. All we need to do is create a personal nutrient cycle. Firstly, we will make giant worm boats. On these boats, we'll feed worms our food waste and industrial waste. As always, the NWB will sell micro contracts out to all who want a piece of these boats. The difference is, any organization who wishes to own a part may do so. Doing things this way gives countries and businesses a way to dispose of their own waste, and convert it into something usable. Sourcing food will be up to the owners of the contracts. If you own a worm boat contract, and send us food for your worms to eat, we'll ship worm castings to where you'd like. Worm castings are literally the gold standard of nutrient sources, because worms secrete nitrates, which plants love. Making additional ammonia would become superfluous.

The NWB is about protecting life. The utter stupidity of pilling up garbage and covering it up, is literally killing us. The next boat that I'd like to make are incinerator boats. That's right, I want to burn all the garbage in the world right in the ocean. Firstly, you'll have ashes, which the NWB will save and use for later. Next, we'll filter out the toxins and carbon-dioxide. The toxins will be saved as well. Then we'll have stored carbon-dioxide. Some CO2 will escape, about 11% of it. We will sequester it in a moment. These contracts are open for anyone as well. If you own a contract for an incinerator boat, supply garbage to be burned, and energy to burn it, we will supply you with carbon dioxide. Which of course isn't carbon neutral. That will be rectified later.

The next step in cleaning up the world is creating pyrolysis boats. These boats have one task, take the world's plastic waste and applying heat and pressure, breaking plastics back down into liquid hydrocarbons. Yes, plastic is literally just complex hydrocarbons folded in a particular way. Many companies are trying to turn plastic into a viable fuel. I wouldn't want to use the hydrocarbons produced from pyrolysis, because they are far too mixed to be viable. This boat will also offer contracts. Input plastic and energy, and you'll get a mixture a liquid hydrocarbons in return. Yes, lots of people are going to want this. You'll see in a moment.

The last boat will be mushroom boats. We will take the sludge from the reverse osmosis, and the toxins and ashes from the incineration, stack them with straw, mushrooms love straw, and then fill the entire tray with liquid hydrocarbons. Then we inoculate the entire thing with an array of mycelia. Mushrooms can convert the inorganic materials into organic materials, and they can convert the hydrocarbons into carbohydrates. Making a complete meal for insects; carbohydrates and nutrients.

Owning mushroom boat contracts will be a huge deal for lots of people. It will be like a building block for lots of things. The mushrooms can be fed to the worms to make worm castings, or we can use it to sequester carbon from the air, making the fuels we make carbon neutral.

Any country who would gift the NWB a desert will find that we will turn it back into a lively place. Let's say that we get a million square miles in the Sahara desert. People who want their fuels carbon neutral will need to supply water and mushrooms, and we'll feed it to the insects in the desert. The insects will consume the water and the food, then they will poop and multiply. Plants will grow using that fertilizer and water. If we keep supplying food and water, that area, regardless of how desolate, will become a lush garden and pull carbon from the air. So anyone who wants large amounts of jet fuel, will likely need to purchase reverse osmosis, worm, incinerator, pyrolysis, and mushroom boat contracts. This is why I'd like to have micro-contracts, to allow poor folks to participate as well.

Where's the unlimited food? In all of this mix, ordinary folks can acquire and store energy, water, and fertilizer. I don't think the NWB should be involved with making food. But you'll have all the ingredients to grow almost anything. It makes vertical farming viable. You can buy or lease a space, send that space energy, water, and fertilizer. In return, they'll ship you food. If we take our lives in our own hands, we'll see that food is precisely unlimited. Why? Because, with energy, you can take all of your waste and convert it all back into something useful; like food. If you ever need more food, you buy a little more energy, water, and worm castings. Unlimited. No one ever needs to go hungry.

UNLIMITED SPACE

Like with all other things, with unlimited energy, we can have unlimited space. The way we do it now, I find physically repulsive. Because I'm one of the excluded classes of people. The Controllers limit the amount of space, purposefully, in order to make some properties more valuable than others. In this system, poverty and homelessness must exist. If everyone is housed, then the demand will be less.

How do they do it? In NYC, the wealthiest areas have giant steel high rises. These high rises are incredibly costly to build, and they aren't very energy efficient. These properties are only for high income earners. In contrast, the very poor areas have their own steel high rises. They're called the projects. The PJs always have a long waiting list, and are hard to escape. It's almost a mirror image of the ziggurats of old. With a slight variation. People are supposed to look towards the wealthy areas and be inspired, and look at the poor areas and be repulsed.

That sad part about it, is that most of the properties in the nation are obsolete. I was a real estate agent for almost ten years. I did many thousands of property valuations for banks all around NYC. Most properties are sixty years old or more. The 'new' properties are usually built with cheaper materials. I think that's on purpose as well. There are new technologies out right now that can literally print new properties. That's a major threat to the system of control. There's an even larger problem.

Before the pandemic, large corporations would pile humans into cubicles and large open spaces for work. There's a real problem on the horizon. Most workers have precisely everything that the office has at home. If people don't go back to packing themselves into those high rise buildings, like sardines, property values for the rich and powerful will plummet. It's weird, some businesses are offering a pay cut to those who wish to stay home, wouldn't it be the other way around? The company is saving money, and should pass the savings to the worker. It's hard to abuse and exploit workers that work from home. That's a major problem for the system. The Controllers set it up so that a few can abuse many. You have to accept, or be removed from the system.

What about the people at the bottom? The currency is always inflating, per public policy. Meaning the costs for goods and services are always going up. This is usually good for home prices. In fact, the purposeful inflation of the dollar is a gift to the few people who are allowed to own properties. Right now, as I'm typing, I'm in a shelter. There are scores of people who are currently living here. Many of the staff who work in this shelter, go home after work to a different shelter. It's a blessing that I've seen this part of America. If you're unaware, let me tell you. The people serving your food, delivering your packages, pushing around your children, and picking up your garbage, can't survive in New York City on minimum wage. They get housing subsidies. Also, I can't just go on Craigslist to find housing. The 'good' areas don't accept housing vouchers. We're living in a bifurcated world. It's my role to accept subservience.

What if anyone who wants it, can have energy, food, and water shipped to them? Also, what if all of their waste shipped out? Where can that person live? Anywhere they want! In fact, people can create targeted communities in the middle of nowhere. What the NWB will be set up for is personalized infrastructure. It may be a problem for NYC if all the poors are no longer poor, and are able to live where they want. There is an additional problem with this as well. I don't know of anywhere, off hand, who would be welcoming to an entire city of black people descending on their area. Also, as a black man, I don't want to plant roots in an area where the government will abuse me. I've had my fill of this. Is there an alternative?

Yes! Boats! We can build our own boats. Rent for housing with the NWB will be paid in energy. Only living beings will be able to invest in housing boats. The first few housing boats will be for the workers on the many other boats we'll have. But eventually, as people build up their own energy, they can move in to a boat of their choosing. And if they don't like it, they can move to a different boat, or move to shore. For example, a housing boat may cost three hundred million dollars. If a hundred million people invest three dollars, they will get a small amount of energy in return per month.

This is the point of having mobile infrastructure. Food, energy, and water will be shipped to wherever the boats are. Waste will be shipped away and processed. Once any human has enough energy, they will be free to be and do whatever they want. It may take some time, but in the end, freedom is possible for everyone. Also, space is precisely unlimited, as we can almost always build one more boat.

SPACE UNLIMITED

I said space was unlimited. Now I'd like to prove it. We have the technology, right now, to live in the air, and in space. Living in the air is quite simple. We float large structures with elements lighter than air. A hundred years ago, zeppelins would regularly traverse the planet. The problem with those zeppelins, was that they used hydrogen for a lifting force. Hydrogen is the lightest known element. It's easy to get, but that stuff is too combustible. As a species, we stopped using zeppelins after the Hindenburg disaster. Technically, the rich stopped using zeppelins. As they were the only ones who could afford to ride the things.

Instead of hydrogen, we could use helium. Unfortunately, there isn't much helium on the earth, and we will likely run out of the stuff eventually. If we had an abundance supply of helium, we could literally float entire cities if we wanted to. Since, the best place we can get helium is in space, we need to use current technology to get to space fast. There is a literal ocean of the stuff in space. All we need to do is get it. How? By working together.

I'd like the NWB to be in the business of making giant fifteen mile space ladders. I know, there's nothing on the planet that large. Let's discuss why we can't build that high. The problem is gravity. The higher you go, the heavier the building will become. Eventually, the bottom floor wouldn't be able to support the weight of the structure and collapse. Scientists are hopeful, that one day we will be able to commercially use graphene for building. Graphene has a tensile strength 200 times stronger than steel, and is many times lighter. When that becomes available, we can definitely build a space ladder.

I say we can do it now, using cross laminated bamboo. Bamboo is naturally 3 times stronger than steel. But when cross laminated, it becomes ten times as strong, and is 20 times lighter. We can build incredibly high with bamboo. But it's definitely a far cry from 15 miles right? I would use the helium that we have left, in order to add upward pressure to every level of the structure, such that each floor has little to no weight pressing down on it. In this way, we could have a stable structure going up 15 miles.

Now to space, normal planes can't get to space because oxygen is heavy. There's no oxygen past about seven and a half miles high in the air. Above that mark, you don't even need wings because the air is too thin to create any lift. This is why space vehicles carry lots of fuel and oxygen when they take off.

For our purposes, our spacecraft can look like an ordinary plane. Except the engines are movable. They will be able to face directly down. Instead of lifting off with fuel, it will lift off with people and goods. Most of the lift off fuel will be supplied from a long hose that will lift the jet fuel and liquid oxygen, by electromagnetic elevators. If more support is needed, we can make a space fountain on the inside of the tower. The helium should be enough though.

Once the space ship reaches 15 miles in the air, and the tank is full, then the pilot can punch it in order to reach orbit. This can make commercial traffic to space possible. Also, it would make helium farming viable. This would exponentially increase surface area for all humans.

In addition to making zeppelins, we can also populate space, which is literally infinite. The first thing we could make is an O'Neil cylinder. Literally creating new surface area. The only thing I'm concerned about are the electrons. We humans live on an ocean of electrons. Space is literally an ocean of positive ions. If you stay in space long enough, your cells will start to disappear. This is why I want the carbon-14.

With carbon-14 and carbon-dioxide, we can create diamond batteries. This will be one of the high end things the NWB sells. We can take the radioactive carbon-14, apply a lot of energy and pressure to make a radioactive diamond, that emits electricity. This is because the carbon-14 is decaying into normal carbon. Electrons and radiation are released. If you take the carbon-dioxide, apply lots of energy and pressure and make a normal diamond around the radioactive diamond, then the only thing that is released are a constant supply of electrons. This will happen for about twenty-eight thousand years. Then you'll have an ordinary diamond.

There are many applications for this. Mobile devices that never need charging. Things like pacemakers, that will never need surgery to change the batteries. Also, fully functioning robots! What I like about battery diamonds is that it's a steady flow of electricity that will spread around the entire O'Neil cylinder once the work is done. It will take lots of energy. But energy is precisely unlimited.

Chapter SIX

THE POWER OF CREATION

"There is but One God. His name is Truth; He is the Creator. He fears none; he is without hate. He never dies; He is beyond the cycle of births and death. He is self-illuminated. He is realized by the kindness of the True Guru. He was True in the beginning; He was True when the ages commenced and has ever been True. He is also True now."

~ Guru Nanak ~

MEETING THE CREATOR

For so long I struggled with a number of puzzling things. Quite often I would question my own sanity. But the experiences mirrored many others in the past. If I were to attempt to describe it, it would be like I wrestled against my shadow for who controls my body. Then I had become the shadow and watched my body move on its own. As the shadow, I was connected to all shadows at once. Now I realize that I was the shadow all along, but I was never really the shadow. I was me.

I found the creator. The one who knows all and sees all. He's been with us all along, and the system wishes you to fight against him. I'll walk you through how I found him. It happened over the course of many years. The first part happened while meditating 12-16 hours per day in the Dominican Republic. I was having random and frequent panic attacks. I found where the panic attacks were and allowed myself to have a panic attack for long extended time periods. I was frustrated that nothing was happening, so I called my therapist Susan Bady.

"I complained that I was wasting my time and doing absolutely nothing. I let her know that I felt like an idiot for leaving New York. She finally said 'You are definitely doing something. I'm impressed that you are willing to do whatever it takes. You are taking time for yourself for the important task of healing.' I don't know why I was so against therapy. I usually feel just a little bit better after talking with Susan. That evening when I went to the beach, with the feeling that I'm exactly where I was supposed to be. After sitting for a few hours, something strange happened. The fear melted away when the wave of euphoria rushed throughout my body. The best way to describe the feeling is being one with all things. The feeling made time and purpose useless. I sat for hours in total bliss.[4]"

I'll be a lot more specific about that moment on the beach. After sitting in terror for long hours per day, that evening something weird happened. A hole opened up, in my mind. It was in the back of my skull, on the right side, just above the hairline. I wrote a whole bunch of things in Violent Tremors, but a hole opening up in the back of my head seemed too crazy to write down. I was freaked out about it, but also curious. Why was there a hole, and what is this a hole of? I wanted to go out the hole, and I did. I floated out of the hole and drifted downward.

I had no clue what was happening, but I was unafraid. The closer I got to 'the bottom,' the more pleasure I felt. I eventually stopped and was in complete bliss. The place I arrived was like a jacuzzi of joy. My entire self was immersed in a flowing fluid of happiness. Who I was, felt cleansed and changed by the experience. I never spoke of the hole, or the Jacuzzi, because it sounded weird. But it's relevant to me finding the creator.

I'm not sure if I made the right decision in leaving DR. I was out of money, and magically an answer had shown up. Back in New York, I couldn't find the hole anymore. It really frustrated me, as that was the best thing I'd felt in my life, up until that point. I eventually began focusing on other feelings that I had. In DR I held onto my fear, the next on the list was a lifetime of shame, and so on.

Five to six years later, I had begun smoking weed, and the dark-website that I bought my weed from also sold magic mushrooms in liquid form. One day I gave it a try. The experience was incredibly pleasurable. So I ordered three more doses. While I waited for the shipment, I joined a psychedelic meet-up. I listened while dozens of people spoke of their personal trips. Many of them used it for therapy. I understood what they spoke of. I had only taken one dose, and I took to calling the experience a mental haircut. The next trip, I vowed to stay present and to share it with the group.

Three vials of clear liquid came in the mail. The trip lasted no more than 8 hours. Maintaining my focus during a psychedelic trip was tough, and made the experience terrible and frightening. One thing was clear, the drugs had triggered what the mystics call the third eye. Biologists called this the pineal gland. I was aware of the fluid being secreted and how it affected my self.

When the trip was done, I felt how most people feel. Like I had just arrived from another planet. Since I was paying attention, I realized that the fluid from the third eye doesn't mix well with the me that I am. I would describe my reappearance more like being regrown. Immediately after that trip, I began to freak out, because I was aware of other parts of me that were no longer there. "Magic Mushrooms destroys the Self!" I exclaimed. It wasn't a haircut, it was an annihilation! If you are using psychedelics for therapy stop! It doesn't solve problems, it destroys them.

I never took the other two doses. I held onto them for about four years, in case I changed my mind. I had spent so much time meditating, why would I want to destroy the ones I'd become close with? I did a search on the internet for magic mushrooms and destroying the self. There are many people who shared the experience. A number of them speak of passing through all of the chakras with only mushrooms. I saw no benefit in destroying myself. I had many times had brushes with my third eye. I usually rejected it.

As of today, I think of it as a safe mode for the software that is me. It's often turned on during sleep. Also, it is heavily used during laughter and near death experiences. Both are incredibly traumatic, and you aren't meant to experience what's really happening. That experience reminded me of the time I spent in DR. 'What was that fluid that I felt on the beach?' I wondered.

I'm not a biologist, and I can't find the place I experienced on any Google images. It was just below the base of the skull. I looked inward for the answers. Firstly, I tried to get there the way I did in DR. But the hole was gone. I had no clue how to make a new hole, or what the hole even meant. I don't know if this makes sense, but I tried to force my way out, where I knew the hole was; to no avail. Around this time, I had begun becoming different parts of me. Instead of going there myself, I could just step into the part.

After many hours of meditation, I had become the place that I remembered. This was the fluid that the brain operates on. I understood why I needed to sleep, because this gland needs breaks, and the third eye comes on and the two fluids don't mix well. The experience wasn't the same as in DR, I was bored. So I decided to become the fluid. The fluid itself isn't alive, but I was able to move it how I pleased. So I was in fact the fluid. I was able to separate the hemispheres using the fluid. For some reason, I wanted to make a circular hole using the fluid. So I made a circular motion with my finger on the top of my skull with my right hand. The fluid moved as I asked. Then it happened.

I clasped my head in agony and began screaming on the inside. I didn't want my mother to bother me, so I remained quiet. To stop the pain, I aggressively smoked a bowl of weed. I ended up on the floor in coughing fits. When the coughs were over, I was okay, and the pain was gone. I've had a lot of experience with my self, and I knew that the hole was still there, even though it appeared to have disappeared. I asked politely, "Is the hole still there? May I see it?" There was something coving the whole, and it was removed. It was all incredibly suspicious. The last hole I didn't investigate at all. This time I remained where I was and began asking questions. Who covered up the hole? Where am I? What is that hole? What am I? What I considered myself, in the moment, was what we all call our mind's eye.

I stared at the hole from a distance, and began to change the background around the hole. It was like I was living in the "Truman Show." There was a reality shattering hole in the sky, and when I decided to make my way towards the hole, I had resistance. Not physical resistance, it was a sense telling me not to go. I promised to listen to all of my emotions, but I had a strong desire to exit the whole. The strong desire won out.

Firstly, I hoped to get back to the jacuzzi at the bottom. Secondly, I knew that I was close to discovering who it was I was struggling against for so long. I knew it was me, but why had I never revealed myself? Why did I try and cover the hole up and pretend that the hole never existed? I'd been in a subservient role for a number of years. I should have listened to the voice, but who was really in control? Why would I put me in this place?

I floated over to the whole, in the same way I did in DR. I floated up and through the hole, and there was nothing. I looked our in all directions, the only thing that existed were the walls of my 'prison.' Unmoved, I tried to reach the base of my skull, where I found the pleasure jacuzzi. I was able to float downward, but I had reached a limit. "Maybe I'm the fluid." I thought. I hovered back over the hole and pondered. "If I'm the fluid, it makes sense that there is a limit to how far I can go, but what the hell are these walls if I'm the fluid? Shouldn't I be able to just blend through the walls?" I faced forward, and focused my gaze on the walls beneath me. I attempted to step into the walls to find out what they do. Big mistake.

I did succeed in becoming the wall, it's no surprise to you, dear reader, the walls were me. To be precise, the walls were made up of countless versions of me that I am. All at once, the wall of me, on the top of my skull, turned and faced the me. I suspect that is their natural function. Me becoming them was a mistake, they had all become self-aware; like me. Countless mes became conscious all at once. They all wanted to know what was going on, where they were, and what was behind them. It was the same pain that I felt in Madison Square Park. Weed wasn't helping. I tried to convince me to stop turning around.

I didn't listen, I told me not to go out, and now I was sitting there trying to tell me not to look exactly where I wanted to look just a few moments ago. Waves of me trying to figure out what the hell was going on, and me telling them to stop. It took time for me to realize that no one can control me, let alone me. I sat through the pain of an innumerable amount of me moving around on the top of my head trying to figure out what was behind them. It would hurt, then they would turn back around.

I have no clue how I had given consciousness to the walls surrounding the self. But I gleaned a great deal of information from the experience. The self has physical substance, and can move. It took many years before the top of my head stopped moving. If I focus on it, they remember moving, and I can feel it. What happened? The damaged parts were healed. I also realized who the creator was. The creator is my brain.

I know he's there, but for some reason he doesn't speak directly to me. I'm going to say a series of true things. My brain is alive. My brain thinks. I am not my brain. My brain isn't me. I am my brain. The brain is the only thing I can't seem to inhabit. I can't become it. I'm a function of my brain, it is alive, and it isn't me.

The brain has many secrets that are currently being unlocked. Researchers attached brain cells to muscle cells, and the construct began to move. Also, they created brain cells from stem cells, and the brain cells created eyes to see. I believe everything on this planet was created by brain cells. Where they came from is another story. The Earth's history is littered with the creations of a single entity. About a hundred thousand years ago we were created, and our minds were fashioned after the creator. We were self-aware. Also, we were given the power to create.

I was the one who told me to not go outside. The one who told me, isn't the me that I am. I left the space, and connected with the walls of the space. The walls are me, and they became self-aware. The more I demanded that they stop turning around, the more they looked. This is the problem with free will. I sat patiently as the rest of me suffered. They had to learn on their own not to look outside. I understand that I'm nothing more than a reflection of what my mind truly is. I trust him, because he's me.

HE MAKETH IT RAIN

For many years of my life, I would quote Job 5:6-10 "Man is born to trouble as readily as sparks fly up from a fire. If I were you, I would go to God and present my case to him. He does great things too marvelous to understand. He performs countless miracles. He makes it rain." It would bring me great comfort, because I would try and imagine the process of rain. Even after all of this time, how trillions of tons of water travels hundreds of miles, and falls to the earth, is a mystery to us. One day we'll figure it out.

I would recite this whenever I experienced some form of trauma. I quoted this everyday for years. Looking back, it was useful so that I didn't kill myself from the constant never ending pain. But I was wrong, so was Job's friends. Covering up trauma with false joy and bliss is the point of the abuse. By pretending a thing didn't happen, new flesh is created over the wounded self. That new flesh is programmable. It accepts a hierarchy and accepts commands from those who are above them in the hierarchy.

The system wants everyone to inhabit this calloused husk. Unfortunately, this false self blocks creation. I've experienced the Mode of Creation many times. None so powerful as the one most recently. I'll tell you how I got there.

FLAMES OF RAGE

It was the summer of 2020, President Trump was actively undermining covid measures, and there were massive protests over the death of George Floyd. I had spent close to ten years alone and meditating. There were things that I wanted to do, that I knew I could do, but the small voice inside of me kept telling me to wait. I couldn't understand what I was waiting for. I felt fine. It seems that I was reconnected to my emotions. But also, there's like a secret me that whispers in my ears. I used to ignore this voice, because everything it says sounds ridiculous and stupid. To date, I can't think of one thing that wasn't absolutely correct.

From the beginning of my agreement with myself, I had one veto, safety. After receiving thousands of dollars in bogus tickets from the cops, with follow up terrorist stops to see if I paid said bogus tickets, I had zero faith in the NYPD. The last stop was so horrible, I let my license expire and gave away my car. I'm never going to pay that ticket.

That summer, there were protests all over New York City. In response, there were fireworks going off all night long for weeks. I had no idea how many dogs had lived within shouting distance of me. They were terrified of the fireworks. So was I, and scores of my fellow New Yorkers. It made the paper, and people tweeted about it on twitter. Online, people kept saying that it was white guys in trucks and vans giving out fireworks for cheap to kids.

I couldn't sleep one night, and decided to investigate for myself. There were no people or cars on the roads. There were only two groups of people that I passed that evening; parked police cars with cops in them, and kids with fireworks. I approached three different groups of kids and they all confirmed, white guys in a truck or van, sold them lots of fireworks for next to nothing. As I passed the kids, empty boxes with clearly visible UPC bar codes. How hard would it be to find out who is doing this? The cops are the only ones on the roads. The perpetrators can also be traced to the few places that have enough fireworks that can supply nightly fireworks, for the whole city, for weeks. They could also track each individual firework back to the manufacturer. The police not only failed to investigate extended terrorism in NYC, but they allowed children to set off fireworks for weeks.

I was terrified, after writing my book "Follow the Money," I kept asking myself "Is it happening right now?" Who had the budget enough to pay for that much fireworks? The police and the politicians brushed it off saying "it's just kids." I saw it as a threat from the NYPD and possibly the Fire Department. They wanted the blacks to know their place, and that they can commit terrorism and get away with it.

I had made up my mind to go to one of the protests one night. I was scared because of covid and my body was very weak. I was sure that I was going to only last a few more years. On the way to the protest, I saw a pallet of bricks. This was something else, that folks on twitter complained of. Unexplained bricks everywhere. "This will be a pretext to further violence," I thought. I looked around to where anyone would need this whole pile of fresh bricks. No where. I became more afraid, and went home. I know what terrorism is. I had seen enough. Who has the budget to pay for large pallets of bricks? Who is investigating?

I went home and began searching someplace that I can go that would be safe. I ended up in Sosua because I searched "the safest place in the Dominican Republic." This time, I searched safest place to live on the planet. I found a list, and the safest non-white place was Costa Rica. I spent the night researching Costa Rica, making plans, and thinking of ways to make it happen. By the late afternoon, the next day, I was still convinced that I would leave. But I waited from word from the Greater Me. For years, all I would hear is wait. I had been in my room waiting patiently, the sun was out so I decided to sit in it's rays while I awaited an answer from the inside. I didn't feel safe. As far as I was concerned, it was time to go.

My mother comes into the living room and starts talking about Trump. She was just talking at me, as usual. My responses were completely ignored, while she kept talking. At the end of the her last phrase, where she expected a response, I said to her "What's the point in talking to me if you don't listen to my words?" She immediately burst into tears and started screaming "I'm trying so hard!" I walked around the furniture and faced her. I don't know how many years it has been, close to twenty years I suppose. I've been saying the same thing again and again. I was going to say, this is verbal and emotional abuse, for the zillionth time. But I couldn't I just looked at her. Other things rushed into my mind as well, but what was the point? She will never change. "I'm sick of this shit," I thought. It was just further confirmation that I needed to leave this horrible place.

Out of nowhere, my sister shows up behind me swinging her hands in the air, as if she were going to fight me. "What?! What!?" she was shouted. I stopped talking to my sister because of constant abuse. It had been years since I said a word to her. I was uninterested in whatever she was doing. My mother was crying and I was thinking of something to say, and I realized "They're doing the exact same thing." I avoid them both, as lies and abuse is all they ever have to offer me. I step out of my room and sit on the couch and there's an emotional explosion.

I waived my sister away and said "Please go away. No one is talking to you." "You're making my mother cry! What now nigga? What now?" She said while continuing to flail her fists in the air. "Fuck off!!" I shouted. She kept coming forward like she was going to hit me. "Fuck off you horrible bitch!" I said while I spit on the floor in between us. "You can't call me a bitch!" She started bawling like a child.

I've lived with abusers most of my life. The abuse is always planned. They have canned responses that you're supposed to perform. If they know that they are above you in some way, the pain that they cause you is alright with them. You deserved to suffer for not following the script. They accept that there are some things that are a given. It's their 'progress.' One thing that abusers protect are swears, or any other word combination. Negative feelings of a curse is the aftermath of generational abuse. Someone a hundred years ago was beaten or murdered for swearing. It was the empty excuse abusers used to abuse humans in the past.

If I'm safe, whenever an abuser demands something or else, I say something like 'fuck your demand.' It's a way of short circuiting the entire interaction. I'm not supposed to find common ground with someone who makes such a demand of me. The abuser is stuck trying to defend two goal posts. How I'm supposed to talk or how I'm supposed to respond to their abuse. In both cases, I'm letting them know, I don't give a shit.

My sister went ballistic, but away from me. She began throwing things and screaming all kinds of obscenities. After all the abuse she had put me through, I gleefully called her a bitch in at least fifteen different ways. The entire time, I hadn't noticed, but my mother was clenching me tight. I looked at her and said "why are you holding me back?" "I don't want anything to happen!" She cried. "Right. So why are you holding me back?!" I puzzled at her. "I don't want anything to happen!" she repeated. "Y'all are doing the same things this entire country does to us. Rakia your just like Trump!" She went crazy even more. I shoved my mother off of me, and went back into my room. I looked at all of this as confirmation that I would leave this horrible place and never return.

Some time later a police officer kicked my door open with his foot, flashed his light in my face, and demanded that I talk to him. I kept telling him no. I was smoking hemp at the time. I put the joint down and put my clothes on. The two officers blocked my way out of the house. "What are you doing?" I told the officer. "You have to talk to us." He commanded. "No. I literally don't have to talk to you. It is my right. Am I under arrest?" "No," he said. "Am I free to go?" "Not until you talk to us." He repeated.

"It is my right not to talk to you, and I don't want to talk to you. Please get out of the way." I told the officers. "This type of call is different." He said "You have a choice, either you tell me what happened or I have to take you to the ambulance. This is the new policy." "You're policy is illegal. It violates my rights. You should know that."

He angrily repeated the same thing again and again. It was the very same thing my mother and sister recently did. Accept I can do this to you or else.

This officer, like all the others, wanted me the hunch over and comply to his authority. I told the officer, "My sister has a history of mental illness, which you can check for yourself. She is a known liar. You are paid to observe officer, so what do you observe?" He ignored me and repeated the same lines. "Who do you work for?" I asked him. "I work for the City of New York." He said proudly. "Who am I?" I asked him. That angered him, and he began shouting at me to tell him what happened or else. My mother was still crying and asked them to leave, but the officer said that it was too late.

I barricaded myself in my room, and turned on the music really loud. After a while, six officers kicked my door in and arrested me. I suppose they expected me to be kicking, screaming, and spitting. But I wasn't, I walked out put my hands behind my back, and the six of them walked me down the steps. The black officer that instigated the whole thing was on my left. He was pissed that I wasn't going crazy. He put the cuffs on so tight I had no feeling in my left hand for about six weeks.

He kept uncomfortably lifting my left arms as we went down the stairs. It was incredibly painful. They kept shouting out orders and hurting my arm until we reached outside. There were at least another twenty officers with shields, and an ambulance. Two officers led me into in the street, and stayed by my side as the other twenty officers surrounded me with shields. I shouted "Everybody give my your cards right now!" The cops I could see in front of me were shocked and afraid. "Give me your fucking cards now!" I screamed again. The partner of the initial officer, looked like Ray Romanos brother on his television show, started shouting out his shield number. I cut him off, "I'm not gonna remember that shit! I'm fucking pissed!! Everybody give me your fucking cards! It's the fucking law!"

All of the cops with shields sprinted onto the sidewalk behind me. The cop on my left lifted my left arm again, causing more pain. "Come on. You have to go into the ambulance." "Give me your fucking cards now! You're breaking the law." I screamed in pain. One officer came out from behind me and placed his card on the ambulance seat, as if to entice me. The officer on the left was causing too much pain, so I walked into the ambulance. The driver asked me the same thing the officer asked. "Tell me what happened or I have to take you to the hospital."

"I have the right to remain silent." I told him. "You do have that right sir. But you're not under arrest." I was handcuffed, strapped in, and there was an officer inside with me. He had his shield facing me as if I were going to spit on him. I said nothing to any of the three other people in the vehicle. After about fifteen minutes, the officer threw down his shield and said "you know who's doing this to you right?" I wanted to spit in his face when he said that. He was doing this to me. I turned my face from him in disgust. He took out his card and placed it on top of the other card.

They put me in a wheelchair, also policy, and brought me to another person. He asked me the same thing. What happened? As if any of this was my fault. I didn't break any laws. I realized by the time I spoke with this person, that this was a measure to city put in place to combat the George Floyd protests. They gave the police extra-judicial powers and they set up a policy with a lot of steps to force people to accept the pain the city caused was in fact their own fault.

"I have the right to remain silent." I told him. He replied same as everyone else. "You aren't under arrest." While I was flanked by two officers and handcuffed. "If you don't tell me what happened, then I have to admit you." I begged them to release my left cuff. There were seven or eight people in that room with me. They all flinched and recoiled at the wail of agony that burst out of my mouth. I got one more card from another officer in that room. They put the three cards in my pocket.

They took me upstairs, and black female officer checked the contents of my pockets and my shoes. I said nothing to her. "I'm not the enemy you know!" she exclaimed. I simply looked at her. The staff there tried to hand me some pajamas. "I don't need no goddamn pajamas. Listen, I'm gonna say this once. It is my right to remain silent. I'm not talking to any of you motherfuckers!" Then I walked off. No one said anything to me, and I said nothing to anyone else.

Why was I so short with the 'nice' people. This is the nature of abuse. They try and overwhelm you with pain, then there is someone who treats you with less abuse that confirms that the abuse was meant to happen. I was there for no reason, and I didn't have to talk to anyone about my mental state. I had no idea how deep the conspiracy would go.

It was at the height of the summer covid lock down, and I was in an open room with two mask-less homeless looking individuals. I turned one of the chairs so that I didn't face them, and I fell asleep. At some point in the early Saturday morning, I was woken up by the staff. I was surrounded, one large black man on my right, a black woman on my left. Then three people in lab coats. "We have to give you an injection." The Indian guy said. I ripped my mask off my face and look right at the black man and said "no you not!" Indian dude was saying things, I didn't give a shit anymore. I was looking at the black dude and telling him to get on with it. "Okay Mr. Gray, you don't have to get an injection. We have a room inside for you. It's called the quiet room." Said the Indian guy. I hesitated, and the two black people backed up, and made a path for me.

They walked me into a room with straps on the bed. The Indian guy had lied, they just wanted me to be off camera. He reiterated that it was time for my shot. I was angry that he lied to me. He said "You should've taken the pajamas." "You are required by law to give informed consent!" I screamed. The three in the lab coats did a quick huddle, and the Indian guy said "Now your getting two shots!" "What's the purpose of the two drugs?" I shouted. "It's to help you talk." He said smugly.

Unfortunately for them, I have a self that I call Rage. The madder he is, the stronger that I get. Rage controls speed and power, he also suppresses pain. I didn't want the shot, and they miscalculated, thinking because I was small, they could just force it upon me. They already lost. The big man was too close, and the black woman was on the other side of the bed with the straps. The other three weren't even in the room. I could feel the strength pulsing through my body. When most people experience this state, they black out. Rage trusts me, and I trust him. He will only speak the truth and follow the laws. I don't blackout, I remained. I call such a state a mode.

Rage was speaking with the big guy. He was encouraging him to make his move. One punch was all that was needed. I would've broken something. I was whispering in Rage's ear. I was reminding him of all of my health problems. I was in the middle of listing all of the ailments when the big guy started fiddling with his watch. Then he walked out of the room and went into another room.

Everyone was silent, including me. Nothing was said, but no part of me wanted to hurt this man. He was trying hard to tell me it wasn't so bad. He's like all the sell-swords of old laboring for mediocre simpletons. Both of the poor black people who were tasked to wrestle me to the bed, are doing so for money, in the middle of a pandemic. I thought of their children. It felt like the man went to the other room to pray. It made me even angrier, because I then consented to accepted the two shots under protest. The exact same thing with the cops.

When he had returned, there were no words. He cautiously inched towards me. Sometimes he would make a move. I arrogantly swatted he advances away a couple of times. The swings that I made were wide. But the third time, he caught my arm, and I was very surprised at his grip. He clearly had spent a lot of time working on it. I can see on his face that he was relieved that I was surprised. I kept looking at him. When he tried to move me I wouldn't budge. His relief quickly turned to terror. His partner screamed "Oh shit!" and jumped over the bed to help. I put my arm down as if nothing was holding onto my arm. The two of them struggled with all their might to move me, for a time.

Eventually, I budged. I fell forward and caught myself with my left foot. The two of them had their weight on my back. I then reached down and grabbed one of the man's ankles. Once I removed his leverage, I let out a primal scream and lifted them both and stood again in the same position. When I stood up, I could feel the blazing cloak of Rage about me. I was even stronger. That's when the three others in the lab coats entered to help. Considering that I wasn't fighting back, standing still, and wearing socks, the five of them was too much for me. But getting me strapped into the bed would've been impossible. They got me to the ground, and four of them laid on top of me with the big guy at the bottom.

I was so angry, I couldn't tell if I was injected or not. After the shots, they began to slowly peel off of me. The last was the big guy. "Get the fuck off of me!" I shouted at him. He was hesitant, and was expecting some sort of retribution. For more than ten years I had been focusing on how I felt and my body. I was curious what affect those drugs they gave me would have. He speedily jumped off of me and crouched like a wrestler expecting my anger. I sat on the bed, put my hands on my knees and closed my eyes. As I closed them, I saw the big guy clasp his head and walk out of the quiet room, with a face of exasperation. He understood, the next time, I would have to kill him.

I sat there looking for what changed. I felt a slight numbness in the back of my head. "Bullshit sedatives." I said to myself. I was so mad that I could've burned through all of the drugs they pumped me with. A large part of me wanted to remain awake to see how strong I was. Honestly, it was wicked cool. But I laid down because I was tired, and that was the truth.

The next morning, the 'nice' ones kept trying to get me to talk to them. I would repeat that I have a right to remain silent. They would reiterate that I wasn't under arrest, but if I wanted to leave, I had to talk. There was a fat white guy who showed up. "I'm your psychiatrist," he said "If you want to leave. You have to talk to me." I shooed him away with my right hand. He was literally verklempt.

I was honestly excited, I awoke still enraged. It's difficult trying to hold onto an emotion or a state. The state or emotion needs to want to remain. I noticed the things that fueled rage, and they were all present at this mental institution. There is the obvious visceral rage. In that place, someone every few minutes would burst into fits of rage. There was deep depression and sadness, victimization, and the phrase 'why is this happening to me' would come up continually. These outburst fueled him as well. There was another group, the suicidal. The acceptance of death is also apart of Rage, and maintained the cloak. They were all him.

I often try to find meaning in things. But I felt truly blessed to have Rage for so long. I wanted him to remain for as long as possible so I could remember how to reach him next time. I spent most of Saturday in what I would call a Rage meditation. I learned from the Indian guy that they can't hold me longer than three days. I hoped to Rage would inhabit me for the entire time.

That night, I was assigned a room. But I awoke in the middle of the night to a mask-less man coughing aggressively next to me. He was max three feet away from me. I covered my face with the sheet. He coughed, then farted, while he was sleeping. I went to the front desk and complained that they weren't following covid guidelines. They simply kept stating that I have a bed to sleep in. That was the last time I slept in a bed. I went into the TV room and uncomfortably slept on one of the chairs.

In the morning, Rage was still with me. It felt like a sign, like I was on the right track. "Maybe the Creator brought me here to learn some important lesson?" I thought in acceptance. I made sure to constantly remain on camera, and only to use the bathrooms with multiple exits in order to quickly return to being on camera. I remained in the cafeteria area the entire day until in the evening a young black woman had checked herself in. She kept explaining her story about how she needed help. She'd suffered a number of traumas and felt it necessary to check herself into a mental health clinic.

I won't discuss her trauma here, but the staff was incredibly unprofessional. It appears that the only thing the social workers cared about is the story of how you ended up in the facility. In fact, I would say by then, they were trying to show me how 'it's supposed to be done.' They 'interviewed' many people in front of me. Divulging personal information in my presence. Many of those people were allowed to leave after telling the social workers why they ended up there and signing documents affirming that it was their own fault. This young black woman was different. She checked herself in, and she was locked in with the rest of us.

When everyone went to bed, later that evening, only I remained in the common area. I was still enjoying my rage meditation. This is when five people piled into the young black woman's room, and demanded to inject her with medication. She refused multiple times. She demanded to know what the drugs were and what they were for. To no avail. I was wrong about the rage meditation, I was in danger the entire time, and only realized it right then. Rage is me, and I'm not him. My body stood up and took a couple of steps towards the door, where this young lady was struggling and screaming no.

It may seem weird, but most people would've blacked out, and Rage would've taken over. "It's all on camera!" I shouted at him. He stopped and looked right into the camera. "This is all a scam, we just need to get out of here and report these people. She's safe. The drugs are bullshit. They are just doing this for the BLM protests. To get them to comply." It's good to have a relationship with yourself. He did stop and listen, I was heartened that I might be able to talk him down. I could hear the people wrestling with her, and she started screaming "Grandma! Grandma help!"

Upon hearing that, he turned, stepped towards the action, and said one word in my mind, "dead." "You're gonna die from exhaustion!" I cried, instantly realizing this isn't something that would move Rage. By the second step I told him "I got this." He did an about face, sat down, and said "my man." Every inch of me knows who I am, I'm the One Who Serves, I always tell the truth, and I'm highly creative. Rage understood, if it would be up to me, things will be worst for the perpetrators. I went back the the meditative position that I was in previously, but I wondered if this was all a set up for me to not spend the next ten years of my life in the jungles of Costa Rica. "Did I cause this to happen?" I asked myself.

As I questioned the series of events, starting with me sitting in the living room asking if there were any objections to me moving to Costa Rica to be alone and meditate, the young woman burst out of the room distraught and weeping. I stood up and emphatically waved to her, I wanted her to talk with me. I wanted to comfort her. She saw me, but went to the phone and collect called someone. On the way back down to sit, I saw from the corner of my eye, "Clamps was behind me!" He was hunched over, as to not be seen by me. His face was obscured by the computer screen, but he wasn't using it. I was so focused on the enjoyment of the state, that I didn't realize the danger that I was in.

By the time by buttocks his the seat, I had an additional mode, the one I call Slow-Motion. This mode people like to portray in action movies. Everything slowed down to not moving at all. I fought a lot in my youth, I really wanted to have both Rage and Slow-Motion at once. It never happened in a fight. I did happen while I was teaching chess in the Bronx when I was 19. Any thoughts of who caused what faded away.

"Is it happening now?" I feared again. Instead of meditating, I assessed the situation in slow motion. Instead of a male and female orderly, now there were two similarly sized orderlies. Clamps stayed behind me the entire night, in the computer room. The other one, a Latino, patrolled the floor. There were additional people waiting in the office. Although I had speed, power, and am able to use Slow-Motion, I was wearing socks on a linoleum floor.

I then began to create a fighting style based on the given factors. My only choice was to use rotational force. I would take damage, which I likely wouldn't notice right away, in exchange for power strikes. The hope was to take one of their shoes fast enough. Damage to my knees and spinal cord were unavoidable. And I had to kill Clamps right away. I don't think he left the computer room once, and didn't make any eye contact. I had stopped blinking for hours, I could smell his fear.

By the morning, my final day, there were a large number of tall brawny men, walking in circles around the small mental institution. There were too many for me to accurately count, and they were all wearing masks. The numbers didn't concern me. I would've defended myself in the corner. The social workers treated me different as well. On shift changes, they had no notes to share about me, so they would all say, "Don't worry about him. He just sits there like that." Even still, some continued to try and convince me to tell them what happened. I refused all of those requests. Then they would say "We will check you into the mental hospital indefinitely," and run away like I was some rabid beast who would attack them.

After that happen two or three times, I had become relieved. "It's not time yet." I thought. If it were time, I wouldn't have survived, nor would they be trying to coax me into a fit of rage. Those cowardly simpletons were threatening me with permanent loss of freedom, only because there were lots of big dudes to protect them.

They even caused a commotion during breakfast. I had been there for a few days, someone forgot to put two garbages bins out. With one garbage, I knew there would be problems. Mentally disabled people need consistency. After some would eat their breakfast, and realize that there was no place to put the waste, they snapped. Food was thrown, fights were broke out, and a number of people got a shot from the staff. There was a young woman, with the mind of a five year old. I watched and listened to these lawless people lead her into misbehaving.

They kept telling her what they didn't want. Anyone with experience with children knows you tell them what you do want. I was obvious they were trying to wrestle a female in front of me into the quiet room for shots. I didn't budge or speak. One of the female staff tried to explain to me how their job works, and how hard it is sometimes. There was food everywhere. I looked her dead in the eyes, pointed to the spot where a garbage was supposed to be, and said "You're missing a garbage bin." She waved off the suggestion saying, "they should know better."

Only I, and a rotating division of husky males, remained after the cafeteria area was cleaned. One of them kept trying to talk to me as he made his rounds around the small area. Eventually we started to speak. He never once demanded that I violate any rights, he just wanted to talk. He was the first one in three days. We were similarly aged, and had a similar background. We talked and laughed like old friends for almost an hour. I'm not sure of the time, as I was in a heightened state.

At one point, he let me know "They called me out of nowhere and said 'we got an out of control patient and we need assistance. I was like, okay, I need the money. But I don't get it. What did you do?" I began to calm down even more. They had hired people who weren't in on their lies. I suspected they would just keep trying to make me explode on camera. When he tried to convince me to work with 'the doctor,' to maybe get housing, I started to close off again. I wasn't interested, I had a debt to pay, and I find lies physically repulsive.

As I began to relax I felt the weight of sleep deprivation, days of constant adrenaline, and a full night of slow motion. I wondered what happened to me in my early twenties. I had slow motion for long hours, for many days per week. Slow motion doesn't mix well with the self that I am. I felt myself coming undone. There was an emergency exit that was rarely used, and no reason for anyone to be around. I laid prostrate on the floor, as if my body was dead to the world, but my head was propped up against the wall, my eyes refused to close, as they glared up at the convex mirror. They wouldn't surprise me again.

One of the staff told me that the head doctor would finally see me. All the power returned to my body and I confronted the final boss. He stood outside of his office and tried the same nonsense as the other staff. Telling me to tell him what happened to bring me into his hospital or I would need to remain institutionalize indefinitely and running away as to catch me on camera in a rage. "Fine," I told him. He was just as shocked as the other 'psychologist.' We exchange a few words, this man didn't care one bit about me or my mental state. Then he said, "It's fine I spoke to your mother. She told me you got into a fight with your sister…" "Who told you that you could speak to my mother!" I fumed. He ignored what I said and tried to continue. "In light of what your mother told me…"

I pulled my mask down and shouted "Who gave you permission to speak to my mother!" I'm not a mental health professional, but if that man was 'my' psychologist he can only speak to people about me with my permission. In a short few days, many of my rights were violated, my body was violated, and this man is talking to someone else about my mental health. I felt the rage building up within me and I almost blacked out with what he did next. He covered his masked face with one hand, and extended his other as if to cover my mouth saying "Please put your mask on! It isn't safe!"

For more than three days, I was stuck in a mental institution with mask-less people, unable to social distance. All of the beds where right next to each other in enclosed rooms, and this guy was concerned that I might get him sick. There was great power in my hand, and I wanted to tear that coward's throat out. I had to reaffirm to myself "I got this." There was no point in talking to that man, or anyone else. I ignored everyone else from that point, and returned to the place by the emergency exit as if my soul was dripping onto the floor.

At some point, one of the nurses unceremoniously announced that it was time for me to go. I sprung to life once again. It took an additional thirty minutes, but I signed some forms that said that I was being discharged. I demanded whatever explanations and notes that had for my detention. The doctor said that I would need to get it from the records department. They couldn't hold me any longer and made me get an explanation outside of their doors. For more than three days, the only notes they had on me was that I suffered from "unspecified psychosis." It says that they administered two different types of drugs, but give no reason why. The doctor says that I was hyper-vigilant, and says "Subject's mother says he and sister had a fight, and sister called the cops on him."

The first thing that I did when I left, was go to the DA's office to complain. They gave me the contact info for the relevant government agency. I filled a complaint with that agency, and went to the police station to get a copy of the arrest record; as the DA' office suggested. I don't know how many times I'd been turned away at the 77th precinct. That time was the worst. I kept demanding a copy of my arrest report. They kept shouting that there was no arrest record. The more I demanded, the angrier they got. Eventually three mask-less officers motioned towards me as if to forcibly remove me from my own fucking police station. "I might have covid." I warned them. They didn't care. After I was forced out, I was even more upset. The whole point of abuse is to make you believe that there is nothing that you can do. "I fucking hate this country!" I shouted as I walked through the front door. The faces of the officers changed from anger to shame as they forced me out.

All that I got from that government agency was a letter in the mail that my complaint was received, and was being investigated. The result of the investigation may lead to fines and sanctions. After this letter, I decided that the only thing that I could do is to get on the ballot as mayor, and my platform would be to fire and prosecute everyone.

People nowadays are up in arms at the threat of authoritarianism taking over in the US. They keep saying these folks were somehow duped by Trump. I say it's been this way my entire life. They abuse me, demand compliance, and if there isn't any, then there is an immediate escalation. It is a violation of my first amendment right to freely express myself. These people want me to accept subordination so badly that they violate many laws. This series of events is a snapshot of my entire life. Fascism has always been here. They're raping the woman, and abusing minorities. If you speak to any one of these folks I spoke of in these pages, they'll tell you that it was all my fault.

When I'm gone, because I hate it here, you can be the nigger.

THE LAST EXPLOIT

After I had believed I had gotten my digestive system on track, I rented an office space in Williamsburg. A company called SpacesWorks, a subsidiary of Regus. It was supposed to be $384 per month. I paid three months to get the office, with a one year lease. It was supposed to be the first month, and two months security. When after less than two weeks in the place they charged me an additional month. I was already exhausted from all that had happened and continues to happen. Even though I emailed them and firmly demanded that they return that payment, they gave a long winded series of lies.

"More of this shit?" I thought. People do what they want to me, take what they want from me, and my words and suffering is invisible to them. It was still the height of the pandemic, before the vaccines were available to the nation. The building was mostly empty. I was on the second floor, and there was no one else there except one person. His office was clearly decked out for a music studio, and I found it odd that he never showed up. I realized after they double charged me the first time, that they had done the same to him, and he likely took them to court.

Around this time, I got a new neighbor. It was a young brunette white woman. I made sure to stay as far away from her as possible, as I was terrified of catching covid. Also during this time, it seemed like every time I would return to my office things were out of place. Especially my weed in my desk. Whoever it was, made it obvious that they took issue that I had weed in my desk. I had bought a wooded stash box for myself. It would've come sooner, but the first one was lost in the mail. The very next day after I got my stash box, my 'neighbor' was no longer there, and I felt like complete shit.

They were spying on me, and they sent a young white woman to do it. Close to the end, it looked like she was upset. I understood after she had gone why. She expected me to thirst over her, and was mad that I didn't even attempt to say hello. She came in sweatpants and slippers and thought I was supposed to fiend over her? These people had violated my space many times, and double charged me once. They had a plan from the beginning, and they didn't let up. Not long after that I got an email from Oscar Valenzuala, the office manager.

"Hello Daniel,

Upon walking the space, I noticed you put up a black film on the glass walls. Unfortunately, this was not approved and is also not permitted within our space. Attached is the office House Rules to refer to Section 27 regarding Furnished Office Accommodation(s).

As a solution, you are able to put up curtains or blinds as long as it does not damage the glass or molding in the office.

Please remove the black film immediately to prevent any long term damage to the glass given the adhesive.

Thank you,"

I called him immediately, that I was told that it was alright by the agent he rented the space to me, and also that the same exact stuff is on the windows already. That was an attempt at a peaceful resolution. I was pissed, and they cursed him out on the phone. He emailed me back and said that he spoke to the director and she approved and exception for me specifically. He said "I apologize for the miscommunication and I appreciate your business. Please, moving forward, if there are any further alterations, please notify me directly." That was at 12:30 pm. Then I sent him a reply at 3am.

I wrote a very long letter qualifying myself, and letting them know how I felt. I really just wanted a space for myself, to exist without abuse. I cut it out of this book, as the book is long enough as it is.

They didn't respond in any fashion. When I arrived the next day Oscar, and the woman who works with him, didn't even attempt to make eye contact. I was so disgusted at the sight of them that I refused to enter the building until they left. For the next few weeks I only came after 6pm and stayed until the early morning.

A few weeks later, they charged me the first of the month in March, and I had no issue with this. Some time after than, they sent me an email stating, that one of their tenant had contracted covid, and they needed to clean my office. The whole thing felt like bullshit. I was angry, and didn't respond. They told me to cover loose papers or they'll become damp. I didn't give them permission to enter my office, and I was concerned about my computer. The obvious problem with their overzealous cleaning was I wasn't infected, and I was the only one who even went into the office. Well, I was the only one with my permission.

The next day, I was charged another month $389.60. I emailed Oscar again, I wanted a paper trail, and asked why I was charged again. First he sent a reply about the bullshit targeted covid cleaning. I pressed him again about why they charged me again. This is what he said.

"Monthly invoices generate on the last day of the month and are due 15 days after. Since you set your card to autopay through the mySpacesworks.com website, your monthly invoice gets charged on either the 18th-20th of the month.

For this invoice, it generated on February 28th, 2021 due by March 15th, 2021 and this invoice is for your April monthly service fee. Since you have your card setup for autopay, it was auto charged today."

I was deeply saddened by such blatant and terrible lying. I simply replied to him. "Fraud," and never contacted them again. That day I canceled my credit card, had a new one issued, challenged the two extra months they charged me, packed up my computer and a few other things, and filled a small claims court case against them. They convinced my bank that they're charges were legit, so I can't do anything about that until we go to court. The courts were closed due to covid, so my court date was finally recently scheduled for almost a year after the fact.

My leaving didn't stop this company from trying more fraud. First they sent a letter from a collections agency, saying that I owed them more than three thousand dollars. If I didn't pay, they would report me to the credit bureaus. I ignored them and waited to see what they would do. If that collections agency did anything I would sue, the only place any of this will be settled would be in court. Those letters stopped when I didn't respond.

Then I started getting letters from a law firm. The first letter had the same 3k figure, but one of the things listed for the bill was a seven hundred dollar retainer fee. I ignored that was well. It's fascinating that people feel so comfortable and confident lying, and breaking the law. I look forward to that lawyer explaining to the court how I owe them a retainer fee.

Looking at the Better Business Bureau, you can find hundreds of similar cases to mine. I can't tell if the complaints are from black people. But the brief time that I was there, I don't think they treated the white customers the same as the rest. The stupidity of it all. They got 5 months of less than $400, they will lose the court case, they spent money on collections, and a lawyer. What was the point of it?

They do it because it's essentially legal to financially exploit people of color. It's done on purpose to maintain the social order. There is no one to help, I don't know how many times I've been defrauded, for me this is the last fucking time. I'm sick of this shit.

RAYMOND GREP

After I had written "Violent Tremors," I felt a strong urge to be homeless. Something inside of me wished for me to let everything go. It was a struggle for me, as I promised to follow and trust my emotions. Ultimately, I vetoed that emotion with a safety concern. I reasoned that it was unsafe for a black man to be living out on the streets. Also, I was terrified of it. How would I eat? What would I wear? And most important, how would I search the internet? Although my reasoning was sound, I felt like I had betrayed myself. I concluded that it was safer in my family's abusive household, than it would be on the streets.

Over the years, the abuse escalated. The more severe the abuse, the more I would withdraw from my family. Finding work was near impossible for me, as

I made a commitment to always telling the truth. I couldn't get passed many of the interviews. My first job, after returning from the Dominican Republic, was an Uber driver. This infuriated the people in my family. No one bothered to ask why, they just abused me for being an Uber driver. A degree in mathematics from Vassar college was supposed to be a ticket out of poverty.

All of my time was spent working or sitting in my room alone. Most of the time, I spent meditating on my emotions. If I felt anything, I tried to allow it to remain as long as it wanted. Other times, I would watch YouTube videos. One of the recommended videos was of the life of Diogenes. He didn't write any books, and there's not much about this man's life. But his story was compelling to me. "He's like me!" I thought. His father minted coins for a living, but for some reason Diogenes forsook all and became homeless. He led a peculiar life, and many people followed him into homelessness. He's famous for turning down Alexander the Great's offer for anything he desires. Actually, he didn't turn it down. He told him that he was blocking the sun, and asked him to move to the side.

I watched all the videos that were available about his life, and read about him on Wikipedia. I just kept thinking, "He really did it!" It struck me that he would have the same urge as I did. But I kept asking myself, "What's so special about being homeless?" No matter how much I asked the question, there was never a response. If the creator wanted me to be homeless, why not tell me what I needed to know? I was afraid. Even though I had already lost all of my wealth and had been working minimum wage jobs, I couldn't do it. Diogenes inspired me, and also filled me with sadness and shame. The more I looked, there were many other people who followed the same path, and it perplexed me. There was always the possibility that I was crazy, and I held to the first chapter of the ASCA handbook; safety first.

After bouncing around through multiple jobs, it seems that I was slowly going close and closer to abject poverty. I had been working at CitiBike as a valet. The job was to corral or dock bikes to make space or supply bikes as needed. I stayed outside during all seasons. Most of my partners were either homeless, had government housing, or lived with family. It was the year 2019, and I had spent long hours meditating for years. Something had happened after I wrote "Violent Tremors." I had become The Child, and the me that I know that I am was watching as I carried out my daily business. The self that I am, has the gift of logic and understanding. The Child does not.

It was fascinating watching myself teach as a substitute teacher for a couple of years. I have a teaching self, that I wasn't aware of. It was clear when The Child would fade away, and I would become a very good teacher. It freaked some people out, because I didn't look the part. I say this, because The Child had different eyes than I do. I didn't notice that my clothes were worn, or that my shoes had holes in them. It reminded me of Clive Wearing, the man with sever amnesia, he could only remember the last seven seconds. But he still remembered how to play the piano beautifully.

In the winter, working at CitiBike, I could feel myself waking up. My mind was working as I remembered it a decade earlier, and I thought I was ready to get back to 'normal.' The little voice inside of me kept telling me to wait. That frustrated me, but I had no way to deny it. I was safe. I remember one day, I was disgusted at the way I looked. I got myself some new shoes and some new clothes, but my hair was a mess. The Child was angry every time I would think about cutting my hair. For weeks I would look at the matted mess on the top of my head and I was repulsed by it. I would ask him, "Why do you want me to not cut my hair?" And I would never get an answer.

Finally, I got my clippers and stood in front of the mirror, ready to shave all of my hair off. I promised myself that when I had the resources, that I'd grow my hair and it would look nice. I promised to listen to my feelings, and my hair looked gross and it was more powerful than the small voice of The Child. When I turned the clippers on he said "It's a crown! It shows my DNA!" That reasoning meant nothing to me, and I began to cut. Then he began to weep loudly.

It was weird to me that he wept, and I didn't. For so much of my life, I was unable to cry. When I was The Child, he was pure and innocent. He cried for the smallest things, and when he cried, I wept. I didn't stop cutting, because I knew how I felt, and was following my feelings. I didn't like the way I looked, and I genuinely didn't care that The Child cried. Although, when I was done, the child never spoke to me again. I was distraught for a long period because of this, even though I knew that I did the right thing. I was happy and content as The Child. With him gone, I felt completely alone, awake, and aware of the position that I was in. I was making the least amount of money in my entire life, I owned very few possessions, and the entire world looked down on me. Everyday, I was painfully aware of how I looked and how people looked at me.

It was fascinating that our eyes were so different. It made me think of the story of Adam and Eve. Though the story was about nakedness, it felt similar. The process in which my perception radically changed so rapidly is still a mystery to me. What wasn't a mystery, was that I felt healed. I had been broken and disconnect for so long, I wanted to try out my new self. I was able to make plans and such, but the refrain remained; "wait."

Fast forward to the beginning of April of 2021, I had walked away from my office in Williamsburg, and I was exhaustedly depressed. To cheer myself up, I purchase some premium weed to celebrate 4/20, a few weeks away. Usually frugal, the cheap stuff was my dope. I rolled and smoked one joint, and went to the bathroom to take a dump. It was my habit to hide anything of value, because my sister and my nephew would regularly steal from me. I had forgotten to hide the weed, and when I had returned, almost all of it was gone.

Upon seeing the weed missing, I confronted my nephew, as peacefully as I could, "Could you please return my weed?" He began cursing at me. I repeated again and again, "Please return my weed." Then he began screaming and cursing loudly. His mother heard him screaming and rushed in from outside. They both started screaming loudly about nobody stealing my weed. It was clearly one or both of them. I was uninterested in the drama. I bought the weed for myself, as I was very depressed. I tried to calmly resolve the matter. There was no time to smoke any of it. "Please. I just want my weed back. Please give it to me." That's when my sister lunged at me. I shoved her off of me, and repeated, "I just want the weed." Then my nephew lunged at me saying that I attacked his mother. Then my sister lunged at me saying that I was attacking her son.

They forced me from the hallway into my bedroom, the were both screaming at the top of their lungs for me to stop attacking the other. They weren't hurting me, they were just shoving me. I didn't say anything. I stared at the ceiling thinking, "This is escalating." It was the exact same pattern that that I had noticed in a lot of people recently. What I call now, the Mode of Madness. They were screaming something that at first blush sounds reasonable, but their actions were far worst than their reasons. In the middle of the attack, my sister flung herself off of me and began to bawl like a child. It was as if I had struck her, but it was clear to me that they both really wanted me to snap and beat the shit out of them. It pained her that I stared at her blankly. She was flailing around the floor in pain, while her son continued to aggressively shove me on my bed. It wasn't until my brother had come and pried him off of me did the attack stop.

Even still, I just wanted my weed back. No one listened to the words that I was saying. Everyone was lying, and saying that maybe I did something wrong. I didn't care anymore, they had done this to me too many times and called the cops when I was upset. I called the cops myself, I was robbed and assaulted. When the cops came, everyone, and I mean everyone was lying. I wanted my weed back and them arrested for assault. The police arrested me and my nephew, and in the commotion, all of the weed disappeared.

I was given the choice of criminal court or family court, I didn't consider them family anymore and demanded criminal court. The assigned public defender told me that this case would be dismissed. I refused, and told her that I wanted a different lawyer. The second one said the same thing, and he said my only other option is if the both of us are removed from the house for thirty days. He said that if I had no where to go, that I'd be homeless. It was like I had come full circle. The only reason that I wasn't homeless years prior was because of safety. I felt completely unsafe in my family's home. In fact, whenever they spoke my name, it was like they were saying a curse. I shouted "I want that option!" They scheduled a court date for 90 days later. It was dismissed without ever talking to me.

I was apprehensive that first night after leaving the jail. It took some effort, but I spent my first night in the homeless intake in lower Manhattan. There was more than enough food, as I knew how my digestive system worked. Also, the homeless people were very supportive and welcoming. Though much of the staff treated us poorly, I ignored the negative people. I moved around to many different shelters, which were populated with mostly brown people. Also, there's an inordinate amount of gay people there as well. The people the society looks down on. I spend 4/20 alone and without any weed.

The last week of April I was assigned a permanent shelter in Queens, near JFK airport. It's a Day's Inn hotel. For the check-in, they just see who didn't do their bed-check and would give the new people their beds. I was so depressed that I was numb. I didn't speak at all, not to complain or anything. I heard one of the staff say, "He's quiet, we should put him in that room." I was a bit concerned about what he said, but I couldn't complain. After a few hours, I had my bed. They told me, "You're 306A."

I dragged my bags to my room, and the door was already open. When I opened the door, I was struck in the face with a horrid stench. Walking into the room, there was things strewn all around and an old Rastafarian in one of the beds. He only had two teeth, and he began speaking, but it was all unintelligible garble. I dropped my bags and went back to the office to complain. I didn't complain about the smell, I complained that there was a lock on my locker. They told me that they would fix it later, and that the old guy was harmless. They said that he never left his bed.

Going back to my room, I sat in the dark, looking over my life, and praying for help. The stench was overwhelming. Then I looked over at him, and in the dark, he looked like me, but with dreadlocks. I had shaved my hair again the day previously, and promised myself again that I would grow it out. But it all rushed back to me, all at once. "That's what you want me to look like?" I asked. My entire family is Jamaican, and I heard the Rastas speak of their dreads as a crown. I wondered if it had just imagined it all, and regurgitated something subconsciously. "What about the DNA part?" I puzzled. I was looking at my roommate, as people had looked at me for the past ten years, and I was profoundly ashamed.

I did brief research on Rastafarianism, and could only find music. I surmised that someone was touched by the Creator, in the past, and founded Rastafarianism, the same as Diogenes started Cynicism. I didn't spend much time learning about his religion, but I felt like I was on the right path. I suspected many people were touched by the creator, and they all wound up in the same place. I was profoundly depressed, but I was content.

Raymond was my roommate for a little more than six months. I can say that he's one of the best roommates that I've ever had. He's a kind and peaceful man. I was jealous of him for a while. It was like he was always The Child. I watched him closely for clues to try to reconnect with The Child. One day it hit me, "The Child is a monkey!" Raymond, like most of the people in the shelter, can't wear the false skin the 'cultured' people wear. They are all closer to animals than anything. The can't pretend that things don't bother them. The reason most of the people are in this shelter, is because they always tell the truth.

A profound thing I realized, living in this shelter is, that I'm a self-aware, hairless monkey. The Child, as I had been calling him, was my monkey brain. It was like someone put me on top of a monkey. I can't talk to him, clearly because he doesn't speak English and he's a frickin monkey. If I connect to him, and allow him to be me, I can understand what he's saying. There's something about our eyes. He sees things differently than

I do. It's difficult to say which is better. I was happier as The Child. What I can say is that there is some truth to the story of Adam and Eve. Part of me is unfinished, and there is a giant chasm between the me that I am now, and how I was some time ago. I notice the difference in my perception on the world, and especially of my own appearance.

I haven't cut my hair since meeting Raymond, and it looks a mess. Sometimes I imagine shaving the hair off of a child or a monkey. They both would cry in the same manner as The Child did. Is my hair really a crown? Why don't I like the way it looks? Is there power in my hair, like Sampson? I don't know at all. Raymond inspired me to be as pure as he is. I just don't want notty dreads like his. I'll figure it out.

Raymond likes me too. He told me many times. But he showed me by taking showers. It was a tremendous gift! He's only got a couple pairs of clothes, but he washes it in the sink when they're ripe. Which is often. He's never once attacked me, or tried to steal any of my things. Even once I left my locker open by accident, he yelled at me for being forgetful. It's been a blessing to have that old Rasta in my life. I trusted my feelings, and I ended up exactly where I was supposed to be.

THE POWER OF CREATION

The power of creation is a gift that each and every human has. Every inch of the system we live under, is designed to snuff that power out. Reading the words that I just said may sound spiritual; it is not. For thousands of years, people boasted of the power of prayer. It is certainly true, that earnest prayers have a way of coming to pass. Then humans reveled in the idea of affirmations. It is also true that continuous sincere affirmations will have an affect on the world around you.

Recently, "The Secret" was all the rage. While I'm somewhat suspicious of the folks selling crystals, "The Secret" is closer to creation than all the others. I call it the Mode of Creation. This mode has happened to me many times, it wasn't until I was homeless and helpless that I realized how it happens, and why it's so effective.

With the little money that I had left, I rented an office in Gowanus to run my campaign for Mayor. I was under the gun, as I wanted to have some videos and materials available for anyone had questions on my candidacy. It was a bit difficult, mainly because when I'd record myself, it appeared that I had just finished crying. For a couple of weeks, I simply sat in my office and allowed myself to feel my pain. Eventually, I began making YouTube videos. I would randomly yawn, as an excuse for why I looked that way. I made a few dozen videos, detailing my plans for the future.

When the filing date came along, I went over to the board of elections to fill out the paperwork. It was the beginning of the summer, and the election wasn't until November, yet I had missed the real filing date by a couple of weeks. The person behind the counter was nice enough, he even gave me the actual schedule. "Where'd you get your info? Cuz you got the dates wrong." He told me. In the age of information, I know nothing about my elected officials, I can't even imagine most of their faces or voices. I don't know what they do, or what they care about. In addition to all of this, there's misinformation about how to run for office on the internet.

After this, I suffered a deep and debilitating depression. People at the shelter often recommended therapy, as if depression is some sort of sickness. I was trapped by the truth. I'm in a place where I don't want to be, and feel unsafe in. Also, I promised to do something about that forced injection of the young woman seeking help. What do people think therapy is supposed to solve? My deep sadness was the truth, and I accepted it.

For weeks, I would find a place and sit in agony. Sometimes I was in a rage. Others longing for death. The homeless in the shelter tried to comfort me, and let me know that they were my family now. They offered food, drugs, alcohol, and even sex. I was even accosted by some scammers. I ignored them all, because my feelings were the very same as they were on my involuntary detention. I hoped to be Moded by Rage again. I wasn't

I know what you're thinking. 'Being angry for over a year isn't healthy.' I wasn't angry, I was, and still am, fucking furious. I was ready to fight to the death. Like everything else in this retched society, it's my job to accept and come to terms with something someone else did to me. I refuse.

After a few months of agony, it happened. It's like the entire universe opened up to answer my plea. Most of the things that I wrote of this book, I learned after my forced injections. It took this epiphany of creation to realize that every step of the way the creator was sharing with me the thing that I wanted most; revenge.

How can you create on your own? How does it work? You are a biological function. A program among a myriad of programs. The system wants you to constantly be divided within yourself. It wants you to deny who you are, and to suppress your emotions. If every part of you wants a thing, that means the Creator wants it as well. When every inch of you resonates with the same desire, it's like you pierce the veil of reality, and connect to something deeper.

I'm hesitant to say more, because your path is your own. The Creator is all of us, and will lead you where you need to be. Your feelings are the truth.

Chapter SEVEN

THE DUALITY OF THE CREATOR

"Without sharks, you take away the apex predator of the ocean, and you destroy the entire food chain."

~ Peter Benchley ~

PREDATOR AND PREY

A few years ago, something strange happened to me. For most of my life I was like a blank stone, but after allowing my emotions to exist in my body, things changed in a weird way. One evening, I bought a regular meal of mine; half chicken and garlic sauce, with fried rice. When I sat down, and opened up my tray, I saw the outline of a living chicken and began to weep profusely. For a few minutes, I imagined the torture this poor bird had gone through.

Since I bought the food because I was hungry, and couldn't deny as it was the truth. I was hungry. A single bite is all it took to radically transform my state. I went from weeping to pure ecstasy. It was simultaneously the worst and the best meal that I had ever had. I viciously devoured my meal like wild animal, and I enjoy every bit of it immensely.

After the meal, the state was gone, and I was left puzzled at what had transpired. A number of weird, somewhat spiritual things have happened to me, as I sat patiently waiting for my emotions to work. I dismissed the experience, like most of the others, as something that happens while reconnecting myself to my emotions. While that may be true, new experiences shed a different light on the matter.

BECOMING THE BUDDHA

Buddhists don't really proselytize, and I didn't have much interaction with them most of my life. I was never really interested. Yet, on my second day of taking therapy with Susan Bady, she surprised me.

"Susan: 'If you don't mind me asking, do you have visions?' I could feel my eyebrows tense and my eyes quickly darted around the room as if to look for an exit.

Me: 'Why are you asking me this?' I was unsettled by the question.

Susan: 'Well listening to your story reminds of the Buddha. I want to know if you've had any visions. Also, I would like for you to visit a specialist in London.'

Me: 'A specialist in London!? For what?'

Susan: 'I want to find out if you aren't the Buddha reborn.'

'Bullshit! You see! I told you therapists are a waste of time! Yeah this is weird. This lady is nuts. Don't we have visions? No! You are just perceptive. I want to do EMDR. Yeah, I want to be hypnotized again. Maybe she's really good at it? Her website said she was the head of some hypnosis institute in NYC for a long time. You want this crazy lady fuckin your head up? How would I know if one of you is trying to sabotage what could be good? Alright, fine! Let's stay focused on what we want.'

"'Daniel? Is everything alright?' Susan calmly asked me. I shook my head yes. 'Well, the reason why I ask is you look very uncomfortable in the chair. Did I say something to offend you?' I looked down and hands were gripping the armrests and my legs were tensed and contorted. 'I'm not the Buddha. I don't believe in reincarnation and I'm not interested in Buddhism.' I told her, we had a good relationship after this, and we never spoke of it again. I still have this sentiment.[5]"

One evening, while homeless, as I sat in my usual spot, in Baisley Pond Park, smoking weed, and listening to my revenge play list, I heard a deep sound. It felt as if the entire world was vibrating. The field was empty, and I was facing a picturesque tree line gently blowing in the wind. "This is dope!" I thought to myself. I allowed it to happen for as long as I could, because it was enjoyable. It wasn't very long though, I had bed check at the shelter. Following the rules are important to me. I chalked the experience up to being weird things that happened as I reconnect to my body.

The next day, on the way to the office, I found the experience fascinating and tried to figure out how I ended up where I did. By then, I'd realized what I was doing was meditating, but it wasn't structured at all. I simply allowed myself to feel whatever it is that I'm feeling. Since I couldn't figure out the pathway there, I tried emulating the deep tone. I was on the train platform, waiting for the A, singing this tone, and felt the walls of my self singing similar tones, but not in unison. While I was saying "Ah," they were saying "ohm." My entire body resonated with tone, and it was pleasing and peaceful.

I was in Queens, but I felt it necessary to talk to a Buddhist. There was a temple that I had passed thousands of times in China Town, Manhattan. I went straight there, instead of my office. Checking my phone, it said that they were open. I wanted someone to explain to me what the sound was. I had a great deal of hope on that train ride. Hearing ohm coming from inside of me felt like a sign. It was, in a sense.

The temple is located right next to the Manhattan Bridge, and has an imposing front. I walked in, looked around, hoping and expecting someone would talk to me. I'd been to hundreds of churches in my life. There's usually someone trying to convince you to join. Everyone ignored me. I walked in a small circle. The place was much smaller than it seemed on the outside. There were many golden statues, and a few people in monk clothes. As I had come back from the temple area, I'd realized that I had just come from Queens and needed to use the bathroom. As I motioned to the bathroom, the only monk in view followed me. As I closed the door and locked it, I heard him try and open the door. "Right, I'm a homeless black man," I thought. That monk was clearly on bathroom duty.

After I left the bathroom, he went in and remained inside. I walked to entrance and no one said a thing to me. I looked around, and everything was in Chinese. Then two white women walked in smiling. The women behind the counter asked them to sign in, and they did so happily. So I stood by the sign in sheet and they continued to ignore me. I just wanted to talk to someone about the sound, so I walked over to the woman behind the counter and told her that I wanted to learn about Buddhism. She cut me off and said "Sorry, there's a funeral today." I tried to speak again, "It's a private funeral. There's a funeral today. Sorry."

I felt incredibly uncomfortable, so I left, with no plans of ever returning. Looking on Google Maps, I could see that there were many temples nearby. After checking that many were open at the moment, I began walking to different ones. Each location was the same as the first. They ignored me and were uninterested. The last place I visited was right next to giant office complex. The complex was called Buddhist something or other. I had a strong urge to never enter it. In the temple next door, there were people there, the door was locked, they didn't bother coming. I looked over the books in their doorway, to see if I could find any answers. It was all in Chinese. There was an elderly man and woman inside, they just stared at me until I left.

Dejected, I went back to the office to think. 'Maybe I should go to a non-Chinese Buddhist temple?' I thought. I found one, in Downtown Brooklyn. They had a class in the evening. It was the venerable so and so.

I had time, so I played some YouTube videos featuring deep ohms. It was drastically different to what I was used to. It was like I was a cat being picked up by the neck. Ohm meditation forces the body into a specific pose. I found the pose uncomfortable but figured I'd get used to it one day. Also, I could feel the shape of my self, bend towards what people call the third eye. I suspect, if I continued in this meditation, I would break my self in an orderly fashion, and it would be deeply pleasurable.

I truly was excited to go to a Buddhist class, and arrived thirty minutes early. It was just a normal Brooklyn storefront without all the gaudy golden statues. Walking up to the glass door, the two white women sitting by the window both got up and went to the back of the 'temple.' The class was only $20, and I had precisely that in my pocket. I stood by the door, as if I was just passing by and started reading the schedule. The title of the session that evening was something like "Learn how to remove negativity from your life and transform it to something else."

The first thing that came to my mind was, "I'm the negativity these people don't want in their lives." Then I realized, "This is ridiculously stupid! It blocks creation!" Heading back to the shelter I tried to understand what had happened throughout the day. I wondered if I should make Buddhism for black people, and realized the futility of it. I had no idea what Buddhism was in the first place. Then I did what I usually do, searched the internet. I found one Quora posting, by a professor of philosophy. He argued that the sound is just a pleasurable feelings, and real life is more important. I agreed, because I was looking for an excuse to put the entire episode behind me.

Returning to the hotel, I looked back at my life for the past ten years, and realized I would like to feel this pleasure. Instead of sitting up, I laid down in my bed, and meditated for many hours, listening to deep ohm music on YouTube. I became the Buddha. I was a man touched by the Creator, and all I wanted to do was to stop the pain. I had a brief interlude as the man people call the Buddha. The vision flashed before me all the lives that I had saved by teaching the meditation.

I was humbled by the vision. Maybe it happened because I mocked what the Creator had done. Certain meditation blocks Creation. It was me, I would've done the same things, as it was me, and I had already done it. The Buddha, and many other have literally helped billions of people survive a brutal system who's main purpose is to cause pain. Letting it pass over was what the Creator wished for that time.

I haven't heard the tone since then. Also, I rarely meditate in that way. This isn't what I want just right now. I'm also not a Buddhist. All I've done is watch one documentary on Amazon about the Buddha. There are some similarities, without the myths. I'm definitely not him, nor do I believe in reincarnation. I believe something different, which I'll explain. But something else happened a few weeks later.

BECOMING THE CONTROLLER

I was smoking weed alone by the highway, underneath an overpass, and a friend from the shelter walked by and asked if I had any extra weed. He promised to pay me back when he got paid. It was Jay. I'm not sure if he name was short for something or not. Most people in the shelter go by a moniker of some kind. Jay was social, and would often bring his chess board outside to challenge the other residents. No one really knows my name here. People who address me, usually address me as chess master. Since no one in the shelter had any chance against me in chess.

After giving him some weed, he began rolling up and trying to convince me how great it was working for Uber Eats. He talked at length about how easy it was, and really tried to sell me on it. He opened the app and showed me that he had made almost $150 for the day, and while he was clicking around trying to impress me, a different screen popped up. "Did that shit just say 12 hours online?" he asked me. All I could do is shake my head yes. "That's not good money is it?" He asked as his upbeat tone drastically changed. I simply shook my head no.

"I'm not on my feet all day, ya know. Most of the day I was just sitting on the Revel waiting for orders. Then I'd go." He said. "How much you spend on the Revel?" I asked. "About fifty bucks." He said downtrodden while taking his first pull of his joint. He then went on a rant for more than an hour about how little money he has. He's got children, but can't afford to pay child support. He had a full-time job, but the government takes most of it, even as he was in the shelter with me. He did Uber Eats to have some money for himself, but he wound of making just as little as before.

Jay is an attractive black man. Maybe physically attractive, but more of a really good person. He's kind and polite. In fact, I called him the black Mr. Rogers to his face a few times. Women often come by the shelter shopping for men. That evening, he was telling me of his frustration with one woman, a client, who promised him money. But she was just trying to get sex. He complained that he was losing business, because the woman stopped calling him after he turned down the sex. I laughed, mostly because most guys have the opposite problem. "I really need the bread!" He would say.

He also has an incredibly violent streak. I recall the fourth of July, when he went to the grocery store with the Crips, for food to grill. One of the Crips talked way too much. I watched as he cried and complained for over thirty minutes. He was mad that Jay bought things for himself, the Crip wanted to pay for everything. Jay was trying to be accommodating. The guy was in a wheelchair from an accident. I had no clue that Jay would snap. I tried to hold him back, but he was pissed. It was Jay versus the Crips, but most of them were pissed at the guy talking all the shit as well. To this day, I'm surprised everyone walked away from that, and the cops weren't called.

"I put my burner in storage, in case the Crips still got beef." He told me under the overpass. Apparently, everyone made up. But he had a back up plan. I gave him some more weed, he was having a worst time that I was. Then he told me about his new apartment. "It's gonna be the thot spot!" He exclaimed, then proceeded to try and convince me to come by his new crib.

It had taken him over nine months in the shelter system, with a full time job before he got housing. It was a three bedroom apartment share with two other people from the shelter. He was so happy, he wanted to challenge me in chess once more. He was leaving in a few days. So I obliged him.

We went back to the shelter, and we began to play chess outside. During the game, while I was smoking, I had an overwhelming desire to kill Jay. I didn't shame myself for it, as I had in the past, I allowed it to be, and it mushroomed. Usually, when I played him, it was like a teacher playing his student. That first game, I was trying to destroy him. I could feel the desire well up inside of me. "He already has kids, he's violent, and not producing." I said on the inside. And I felt myself sending him off to war.

Right then, in the middle of the chess game, I had become the first Controller. The one who started the system. The one people worship in secret. I remember having my own moment of creation, I lived under the tyranny of the god-kings. The creator showed me how to control humans, and I used it to great success. In my wisdom, I taught my children and a few others the secrets to controlling humans, in the hope that humans wouldn't live under the threat of a tyrant.

That first chess game I demolished Jay, there was no hope. By the second game, I still was doing all I could to destroy him, but also I was deeply troubled by the vision that I just had. "It was me." I thought. "I caused all of this pain." "Checkmate." He said. It woke me up. "Man you were killing me, and you just walked right into checkmate!" He finished. I was perplexed and confused. "Did you do that?" I asked myself. I paid attention the last game, to break the tie, and won.

I went straight to bed after that last game, as I was profoundly distraught. I couldn't fathom why I would do such a thing. To help me fall asleep, I masturbated for the first time in almost a year. I wasn't really holding out for anything, I just didn't want to. In the morning, I still felt like shit, and my penis was swollen and misshapen from the vigorous pumping from the night before.

It was a stark contrast from the vision that I had of the Buddha. "Why would the Creator cause so much pain?" Then I realized, this hidden figure had saved many more lives than the Buddha. Recalling the time that I wept over my food, and realized it was the same thing. These are functions of the creator. Humans were growing too numerous, without a way to sustain themselves. Also, the kings of old, were a threat to humanity. The Creator turned some humans into predators of other humans, to save us all.

Without these human predators, we would not have survived as a species. I wouldn't have done anything differently, as it was the will of the Creator.

Chapter EIGHT

THE TENDRILS OF CONTROL

"I prefer to be true to myself, even at the hazard of incurring the ridicule of others, rather than to be false, and to incur my own abhorrence."

~ *Frederick Douglass* ~

THE SHNE MODE

As we inch closer to the end of the book, it's vital to conclude with a summary of the major components of control. The Shine Mode is a key component of this system. I'm introducing it, close to the end, because I wanted to share my own personal terminology first. The Shine Mode could simply be considered the Stockholm syndrome. It's something that most of us understands how it works. It's when abuse victims feel positive feelings towards their abusers.

We, as a species, are similar to most other life on this planet, except we have a knowledge base on how to 'break' wild animals. Breaking humans happens in a similar fashion, but there isn't any public literature about it. The ones who know, wrote these things down, and keep it secret. To break an animal, abuse is an essential ingredient. The animal needs to see the person abusing them, and that there be no escape. In time, the Shine Mode takes over. It affects the eyes. The abuser begins to shine.

The Shine Mode is a self within our minds. It creates a bifurcation of reality. If some are shining, then others are in darkness. This mode exists to help all life exist in an impossible situation. This is currently happening to us all. If you see a glow with some people and a shadow over others, you've likely suffered long-term abuse. I know you have, I can prove it in the next section.

I recall the last time that I saw a glow on anyone. I had been working at CitiBike, for almost a year, as a bike valet. And I was constantly surrounded by people who, in the past, I would've seen shrouded in darkness, but they seemed normal. It was days before the city wide covid lock down, and the streets were empty. There was a white woman pushing a stroller, and I could see the baby shining. I wanted to follow, but I didn't want to freak her out. I meditated on the significance of it for months.

It had been years since I had seen the shine, and I had changed as a person. Nowadays, whenever I'd see white people grouped together, I would try to cross the street, or avoid them in some way. I don't enter any establishments of any kind if there are only white people inside. I haven't put anything in my mouth since 2003 if I was the only black person in the room. In white areas I'm hyper-vigilante, and purpose oriented. I will never linger in these places.

Some may take my words and claim I hate white people. I've been here my whole life, and traveled the country extensively. I knew by my early 20's that a solid 90% of this country is off limits to me. Recently, zero percent is safe for me. So many people are confused and concerned about what's happening to the country. I can tell you what's happening. The Shine Mode is wearing off, and the people who are aware of it are intentionally abusing targeted groups of people, in order to reinstate the Shine Mode, in all of us.

Abuse isn't enough. There has to be no recourse, and no escape. Some people need to get away with harming others, the victims can't do anything about it, they have to have no place to go, and most important they have to know who committed the abuse. In time, the shine will emerge and create a directionality for the self. Humans will be drawn to those blessed with the shine and repulsed by those shrouded in darkness.

The primary function of the system is abuse. Followed by an acceptance of the lie that the abuse was necessary or justified. These people are human predators. They have a need to cause suffering. They hunt for places where they can abuse and get away with it. They're our predators, that we created to help sustain life on this planet.

How do you break this mode? The Shine Mode is the same as any other mode that inhabits the self. It will remain until it wants to leave. Which brings me back to the shining baby. The mode is wearing off, and people are describing the phenomenon as 'woke.' Our predators were invisible to us, because we needed them. After I saw the glowing baby, I became terrified. The predators would need to cause massive pain to the entire population and get away with it, in order to reestablish dominance.

WORK IS A LIE

My first job was as a chess teacher. I got it the summer of 1998, just before my senior year at Vassar College studying Mathematics. Though I was a full-time student, it was 21 hours per week at $30 per hour. By 2011, I was making well over a quarter of a million dollars a year. I was troubled all of that time. There was always a feeling of being out of place. Over the years I made so many concessions to lies, and have given myself a myriad of back door reasoning to why a thing isn't a lie. In 2011, I accepted who I am, someone who strongly prefers the truth. I find lies physically repulsive.

By 2012, I was making about $70k annually, and I clarified the direction that my life should go. I would always tell the truth, and I would defend myself against any abuse. I had suffered a life-time of abuse, and decided that I was old enough, and strong enough to defend myself. In the present, I can tell you that there are no jobs that you don't have to accept lies or abuse; none. It is impossible to survive in this system if you tell the truth and follow all of the rules.

Work is the primary source of abuse in this system. Since we are thinking animals, 'work' itself seems innocuous. Calling it ancient slavery would be more accurate. Think for a moment, if you wanted to control a population of monkeys how would you do it? You would hoard all of the bananas and have the monkeys labor for it. And so the all the monkeys don't revolt, you give the white furred monkeys more bananas and give the dark furred monkeys less bananas. They will fight over position, and never notice that you are hoarding all of the bananas.

We are the monkeys, and a handful of individuals controls most of our housing, food, water, and energy. These are the things we need to survive, and by the magic of the rules all of these things are shaky for everyone. The boss/employee relationship is a construct of control. Where a single person has the power to remove you from the system. The bottom line for this relationship is that employee must accept that the boss can do and say certain things. If not, it's scorched earth. These positions are often inhabited by predators. They take great satisfaction in harming those who don't accept.

Here are some of the things that happened for me in the last ten years. Companies large and small love to take things away from you and dangle a future reward if you accept. The first was a bank that I sold REO properties for. They took away all of my properties, gave it to someone else, and then lowered my commission by 1%. In return, I received a smorgasbord of BPOs. I would've likely received dozens more REO properties, and made lots of money, if I had accepted. The deal made me sick to my stomach, and I said no. Because of the nature of the business, if one bank finds you unworthy, they all will. I was blacklisted. Years of talent and service is meaningless unless you accept that someone can do these things to you and get away with it.

The very same thing happened a few years later when I was working for a failed campaign for city council. The campaign was over, but three of us had impressed someone enough for us to work for another campaign. We were handed our checks, and our final time sheets, as we sat waiting for some reason. There was a fat white guy at the table doing paperwork. I looked down at my time-sheet and saw that the hours that I worked for a day was crossed out and reduced by one, in red ink. I looked over to the fat guy, and there was a red pen right in front of him. He was doing the same thing that everyone else does. He was letting me know he was the real boss, and he gets to take an hour away from me if he wished.

I had seen this very thing many times before, and I stood up and said "You need to pay me for that hour." He shrugged his shoulders as if I were missing out on something, and the two other black people who were sitting beside me winced their faces and gently shook their heads 'no.' As if I wasn't aware that I might be 'rewarded' with more work later. I did all the work they asked of me. I showed up on time, and didn't break any of the rules. That's a huge deal, considering the folks that the campaign had hired. That man lost me for $15 dollars. If you liked my service, tell me so, and offer me more work. After joined another failed campaign that summer, and having a similar experience, I left the Democratic party.

Then there was the outright law breaking. In this system, it's easy for some to harm others, and there is rarely any recourse. I've had my pay withheld. I've had my hours cut, for no reason. I've had my rates drop(Uber,) I've been scheduled for work and sent home because it was profitable for the business to not pay me that moment. There are laws supposedly designed to prevent all of the current lawlessness. But unfortunately, there's no one to enforce the laws.

Most of the egregious lawbreaking happened to me as a poor man. In a way, you can take solace knowing that such a thing won't likely happen to you. That thing only happens if you're not smart! You should know, that the lawlessness happening to the ones shrouded in darkness is a significant part of your abuse. It is a warning to you, to appreciate the shitty boss you have. Let me tell you how I arrived at my current job.

This last summer, I wracked my brain to figure out what job that I could do where I don't have to lie or accept any abuse. In fact, the interview process fills me with dread. I can't seem to get passed an interview without lying. Why should they care about what I'm going to be doing in the next five years? Ask yourself, did you lie at all in your interview?

I had an interview training with Grant Associates, for my current position. "Where do you see yourself in five years?" Was one of the practice questions. The ones who volunteered to answer gave an empty nonsense answer, in a cheery upbeat voice. After every response, I was left not knowing what any of them really planned in the next five years. The presenter actually warned us all about giving a real answer. She even gave examples of people who were rejected because they had actual plans for the future. Everyone laughed about how dumb it was to respond with what they actually plan for the future.

I was volunteered to answer a question. "Why do you want to be a security officer?" I said "Telling the truth and following the rules are important to me. I thought long and hard, and realized that I being a security guard is the best thing that I can do." I was chastised for that answer, and told to speak in generalities and not to get to personal. Ask yourself, why is it so important for people to so obviously lie in interviews? They are checking for compliance to the system. They want to know that they can pressure you when they need to, and get away with it. Lying and exaggerating in an interview is a great first step towards future abuse.

I'm still a security guard. There was no real interview. But what happened the first week, is what happens to everyone else over a period of time. I'm working for Arrow Security based in Manhattan, and on the third day of work, I was informed that I had to stay an additional four hours because no one would be there. There was in implication of a write-up and possibly firing. My entire life was under threat from a single person. I accepted the punishment and walked out the door. I already have a minimalist life, and took it as a sign to let everything go. I trust my feelings above else, and I wasn't worried on the inside. I literally have the worst possible hours, Friday, Saturday, Sunday, and Monday night graveyard shifts. What we agreed to is never enough. Why? Because I have no agency in this place.

Everyone is wrongly fighting for 'jobs.' It is a fiction. A handful of people control the things that we need, and they also manage to have most of the paper. They use work to force abuse onto everyone. There were many jobs that I had, where the boss would create a problem then chew myself or my coworkers out because of the problem. It's all planned, they want people to accept the abuse. If they do, the boss may shine, and you'll have a great working relationship.

If you had your own food, water, energy, and shelter would you put up with the abuse you get from your boss? If you watch the news, you'd see that there's a 'labor' shortage. When in actuality, the public was relentlessly abused by Donald Trump, with most people rejecting his abuse. Then most of us had extended stay away from 'work.' I don't know how the Controllers intend to thread this needle. The monkeys are pissed and their sick of the obvious abuse. The pandemic set a lot of the slaves free, and they're waking up. Bosses all around the country are faced with a labor force who's unwilling to be docile slaves.

We are self-aware hairless monkey's in a terrarium. A handful of monkeys control all of the bananas, and in order for you to get your bananas, you have to genuflect to the monkeys who accept the system while they beat their chests. Fundamentally, the boss/employee relationship is a manufactured excuse for the talentless and the mediocre to beat their chests and get compliance from a large group of people. Regardless of how much money you make, you have no agency in this system. Regardless of talent, there's at least one person who can completely cut you out of the system. This is how it was designed. A system to control self-aware monkeys.

WORTH THROUGH SUFFERING

The thing that binds us all together is the currency that we use. I already wrote a great deal about this in my book "Follow the Money." Where I differ from that book, is the possibility that the people on the top are coordinating. The thought of it was terrifying and I mostly ignored it. Although I can't prove it, I'm assuming in this book, that they are coordinating.

The system on its own will always fail. If all the currency flows in one direction, and a handful of people hoard that wealth, that always will crash the economy. Our nation has had a multitude of crashes, and it's real causes are never discussed or debated. The crash is always blamed on the vulnerable, or maybe a politician the Controllers don't like. Never the people who are actually culpable. Let's chart how it always happens.

When businesses aren't making profits, because the wealth is being hoarded at the top, they start firing people. Most of the time, they fire those who the system deems unworthy. Causing massive pain in targeted communities. Then because people don't have money, and can't afford to eat, the Controllers start throwing away the food, because the farms aren't making money. Which will create scarcity in the marketplace. The people the system deems worthy usually has enough currency, or credit, to rapidly purchase and hoard the remaining goods. We all know that we could potentially ride out these food shortages if we worked together. But the people with all the guns create pain by emptying the shelves. I've lived through many food shortages, most of them, with no food in the kitchen.

This inevitably causes food lines, that are always blamed on everything except the food being thrown away, and hoarding the remaining food. Around this time, utilities are being shut off, for those without paper. It is a full blown terror event for some. Then the system kicks people out of their homes as if it's all normal, and supposed to happen. The problem is that everyone lives and works for paper, and a handful of people are hoarding it. Whenever the Controllers aren't happy about something, they starve the population of paper, with predictable results.

I wish it were as complicated as the media likes to portray it, but it isn't. Also, the media is completely owned by the people on the top. The biggest of all of the lies is about inflation. Firstly, the Federal government purposely inflates the currency. There isn't even a debate about whether there should be inflation. The debate is how much. Inflation and deflation aren't inherently bad, but for some reason it's hair on fire bad if it's more than what is planned.

By printing more money, or the Fed expanding it's balance sheets, people who are holding onto paper currency or work for paper currency are slowly losing wealth. This group of people are most people in the country. Individuals who own assets will gain wealth as the currency inflates. Everyone accepts this as a way of life, considering most of the people making the decisions own property and stocks. Inflation slowly squeezes value out of poor people.

When the Controllers feel particularly threatened, they cause the prices to skyrocket, causing general pain throughout the populace. Almost all of the means of production on this planet rests in the hands of a few people. If they don't like what's happening on the ground someplace, they can cut that location off from receiving any currency, and then cause a spike in prices. The controllers have successfully used this tactic to topple entire empires, and it's no different today. At this moment a handful of individuals are hoarding most of the paper, a handful of individuals are stopping the government from giving paper to the paper starved, prices are skyrocketing because a handful of people decided to raise prices, and people with means are buying up the remaining goods. The media is desperately trying to blame this on President Biden.

Let me explain to you how our banking works. Whenever you deposit money into your local bank, that bank can in turn get a low interest rate loan from the Federal Reserve. As of this writing, the interest rate is between 1% and 1.25%. What does this mean? If you deposited $1k into your bank, that bank can go to the Fed Discount Window and take out a loan for 1%, with $1k in reserve. Depending on the type of the loan and the bank, the bank gets anywhere from 10x to 20x the reserve value. In our example, the bank takes out a loan from the Fed for $10k, at 1% interest.

The bank then turns around and has the exclusive right to loan that money to anyone it deems worthy. Also, all the profits from that loan goes directly to the bank. Discount window loans are usually max six weeks long. At 1%, the bank will owe the federal reserve $10,100, at the end of six weeks. The hope is, they made a sound loan, and are able to pay the loan back. But they don't have $10k on hand right? Here's where the magic comes in. They take out a second loan, in order to pay back the first.

In theory, the bank is supposed to have lined up a home buyer. That home buyer presents the bank with a down-payment. Then the bank is meant to go to the federal reserve, and within six weeks the transaction clears. As long as the bank is getting more money, per month, from the lendee, than they are losing taking out new discount window loans, then the bank is profitable.

Banking has been at the center of every economic crisis since we've been charting them. The reality is, banking was created as a system of controlling hairless, self-aware monkeys. Why is it that the very rich get the best interest rates and the very poor get the worst? If it were a real business, trying to make profits, the interest rates would be in reverse. High interest rates for the poor adds extreme burdens to them, forcing them to slave themselves in the labor market.

Also, banks only invest in products that maintains their personal control over the system. For decades now, we've known that we could build bigger and cheaper properties with hemp and bamboo, is that ever going to happen? No. Because banks are heavily invested in things that use steel. There needs to be heavy equipment, lots of labor, and high prices.

Think of all of the businesses that would collapse if the markets were truly fair and free, and we used better materials to build with. Companies dealing with concrete, steel, heavy equipment, and plywood. Most important, property values for real estate the banks are invested in would be underwater. By the magic of the system, properties built decades ago, using old technology, never decreases in value. As much as they try and block building technology, they are becoming overwhelmed with new discoveries. It's only a matter of time before property values begin to plummet, and then what are we going to do?

There are many examples of the 'Masters of the Universe' blocking technology from disrupting their power. Nothing exemplifies this more than Solid Oxide Fuel Cells. They are twice as efficient of the combustion turbines that we currently use, have no moving parts, require little to maintenance, no chance of an explosion, easily scalable, and much cheaper than their combustion counterparts.

The Controllers despise efficiency, and only use things, within their system, that can cause pain. For example, a few years ago, New Yorkers were fed up with us using coal powered plants. Con Edison simply got rid of them and changed to natural gas turbines. Firstly, let me say, I'm not adding to the pollution in the world. I don't have a say in the matter. ConEd and National Grid are the biggest polluters in NYC, not I.

Every fucking year, ConEd sends out messages warning about electricity usage. Up until my mid thirties, these messages would cause me to experience an panic attack. As I remembered the times where I was stuck in the house with only candles for light. With SOFCs, that's not possible. There won't need to be special regulations for these things, because they're harmless. They can be placed in anyone's basements.

Nissan, in 2016, made a SOFC powered car, with a 600km cruising range. It barely made the news. Why? Because this technology would decimate the control that they have over the rest of the world. If SOFCs can be small enough to fit into a car, it can fit into the smallest of apartments. Local energy monopolies will collapse. Likewise so would all the drilling and refining companies. Think of all the businesses involved in making car parts? Poof!

Solid Oxide Fuel cells can be modified to accept any hydrocarbon that you want. Anything from methane to jet fuel. Since it's twice as efficient than combustion, that means we'll need half of the fuel that we need now. Banks are investing in the fossil fuel industry to the tune of many trillions of dollars. The next time you see entire towns have their lights shut off, ask yourself, why doesn't every home have their own SOFC? The so called Invisible Hand wouldn't like it very much.

Nothing in this world has any value. Worth is added by limiting the amount of a thing, and causing some to feel pain over it. Housing is purposefully limited, and homelessness is on purpose. I can confirm that there is very little the department of homeless services does to combat homelessness. It's more like a way-station in between jobs. Their primary focus is to get you back to work. It appears that housing is given by lottery, and the longer you remain in the system, the odds increase that the lottery hits you.

All real estate in this country is valued in human suffering. Firstly, it's value increases from purposeful inflation. As prices rise for some with stagnant wages, those who own property will see a commensurate increase in value. In fact, places with egregious homeless abuses, usually have rapidly raising housing prices. Which leads to the second part of the intentional pain.

The news is rife with homeless abuses. If you speak to a reporter, they'd tell you that they want the news to be heard. The controllers allow this news to be trumpeted within their media. Why? It keeps the real slaves appreciative of their shitty jobs. 'If I lose my job, I'll be homeless, and then the police will abuse me.' They'll reason in their heads. By the way, it was the same during chattel slavery. The suffering of the African Slaves, weren't because the nation depended on their work. The country never depended on the labor of African Americans. It always depended on the labor of White men. The violent abuse of black people in this country kept white men in line, and they dutifully labored for next to nothing. All the while, the folks on the top got most of the resources from their hard work.

White people always grew the most cotton. They made most of the bridges, roads, and buildings. They did most of the farming, fighting in wars, and policing. In fact, the police exemplify the tendrils of control choking the life out of white people in this country.

The police, as a standard, work twelve hour shifts. Firstly, this is not how the human body works. Some say that they can handle it, but if I were trying to control someone through and through, I would force them to work twelve hour shifts. To add salt in the wound, most cops live an hour and a half, and up, away from work. This is on purpose, they set these locations up, where cops can feel 'safe,' long before most cops were even born. Long commutes are important. They want the cops making mistakes, tired, and stressed.

The obvious mark of the controllers, is that there is no alternative to police work. Most officers don't have a fall back plan. This creates unity within the ranks. Why? Because they have a rule, if you are convicted of a crime, you can't be a cop. Some people claim that it's racist. Maybe, it's better not to claim racism all the time. Many officers live in white neighborhoods. Their neighbors love them, because they literally keep the blacks out. I would never live next door to a police officer, for safety concerns.

He's the point of these things. If any officer is charged with a crime, their entire life falls off a cliff. It will not only hurt their families, but it would hurt their local communities. This is why firing all the police is a non-starter in this horrible place. If you fire enough police officers, it would collapse the economy. Thus creating an entire class of people who are able to break the law, and they usually do against those shrouded in darkness. The sad part of it all, if enough people at the bottom refuse to accept or leave, the exact same crash will happen.

With all of this in place, it's time for the Controllers to cause targeted pain. The only thing cops, and most of the slaves, have is credit. This 'credit' is expressed as equity in their homes. All you need to do is cause housing prices to plummet, blame it on the blacks, and you have a tinderbox of pain and distraction.

POTENTIAL BANKING SOLUTION

In my book, "Follow The Money," I naively solved the 'problem' of banking, assuming that the markets were free. My naivety was shattered by constant harassment by the police, and the book took a dark turn. The issue with banking, is that essentially, a handful of people are making all of the decisions, and those decisions only benefit them. In addition, everyone else accepts all of the risks.

The solution? Allow ordinary folks access to the same leverage the banks get. Either with a rule change at the discount window, or a new public bank, even the poorest person can become an investor. Considering the representation in Congress, let's say Maine or Vermont opens it's own public bank. They operate similarly to other banks, except they sell small portions of each note to the local residents. An individual in Vermont can purchase a thousand dollars worth of an asset for $100 in reserve. When the borrower pays their note, part of that payment will go to the person who invested in that asset, minus Discount Window fees, and the public bank fees. So as interest rates rise and fall, people who own these assets will make money similar to banks.

If this happens, banks as we know it will simply no longer exist. Why? Because everyone is going to want to have their personal notes owned by local people. Whenever they pay their notes, the money will be spent locally. In addition to this, folks will be able continuously purchase new assets until their passive income out paces theirs expenses.

Work can't exist without banks, they are at the center of this entire fraud. If humans stop giving these snakes the exclusive right to make all decisions for us, their entire scam collapses. With each refinance, they will be left with obsolete things that no one wants, and a giant Discount Window note that will be immediately due. It's almost like it was a terrible decision to only invest on things that they could exclusively control was a bad idea.

If we just made our own banks, and loans ourselves our own money, would it be over? No, because the Controllers would still own all of the means of production, and you can't force them to sell. These people are predators, and their go to move is pain and suffering. Prices for all goods and services will skyrocket, and the media will blame everyone else, except the people in control of the goods and services. There is a simple solution for this as well. Energy. It's unlimited.

In order to power the entire planet, with Solar Power, we would need about 200K square miles of solar panels. It sounds like a large number, but when you consider how much space there is on the planet you realize how little energy we use as a species. The problem we face is, that most people don't have enough surface area to make enough energy for others, using solar panels. Also, it's quite expensive. I'll make it simple and cheap. How about, instead of on homes and buildings, we put them in the ocean? And instead of hard-wiring it into the 'grid.' We just leave them out there making whatever fuel we wish? They can make ammonia or any of the hydrocarbons out of thin air. When these large barges are full of whatever fuel they are making, you simply go and harvest the fuel when full.

Since a lot of energy is lost making gaseous and liquid fuels, it make sense to have five times more boats. So instead 200k square miles, it would be 1000K square miles. Considering the there are more than 130 million square miles of ocean on the surface of the planet, I suspect we can easily swing this. Who would pay for this? The people will. We all can collectively own part of each one, and have energy delivered to us on a regular basis. It would be even sweeter if we could own these things with leverage.

Would I want to do this? No, because nuclear power is many thousands of times more efficient, and also it's much easier to defend. If we collectively start financing and purchasing energy producing assets, the most dangerous people in the world will be facing extinction. Having hundreds of thousands of solar panel covered barges it truly nice, but difficult to defend. A nuclear powered barge is high valued, will produce much more liquid energy, and is infinitely easier to defend. With regular energy coming in, ordinary folks can make whatever the system limits. Also, stored energy is also called stored work for a reason. Because work can be done with it. If you have enough energy, you don't have to 'work.'

Most things on this planet have no inherent 'value.' Apart from things like artwork, with unlimited energy, all goods on this planet are precisely unlimited. The Controllers employ 75% of the American population. By limiting the available work, and limiting the income of this work, each individual person's buying power is precisely limited, regardless of how much money you make. Also, they control most of the resources in this country. By limiting the available resources, they can effectively make a slave class to do their bidding. This won't be the case if individuals can purchase as much energy as they desire.

Let's do a simple example. With unlimited energy, people can grow a large boat using hemp and bamboo. This boat will exclusively make potatoes. Since the boat was made collectively, thousands of people will own a share of this potato boat. By personally supplying the energy needed to make the potatoes, each individual owner will be getting potatoes at a certain rate. It would literally require zero 'work' from any of the asset owners, and requires zero input from the markets. It doesn't matter how cheap the Controllers sell their potatoes, owners of the potato boat will essentially get their potatoes for free. If they need more energy, they can gather more energy, because energy is literally unlimited.

A thousand years from now, growing potatoes will cost the exact same amount of energy as it does now, or less considering the rapid growth of new technology. In the system, the 'price' of a potato will be many times as what it is now, because of the system of control using artificial scarcity and abuse to add imaginary and arbitrary value to things that have no value.

I don't have the power or ability to create a new bank. But I believe that as a species, we need to start rushing towards personal energy. If not, we could be all doomed. These people are predators. They are dangerous. If they sense a loss in their own personal power, they could attempt to destroy us all.

THE FALSE SKIN

The system itself exists to abuse, at a bare minimum. A common refrain, from those who've implicitly accepted the system, is "You've got to grow a thick skin." For those of you who say this phrase, you should know, that words have power. The skin is real, it is grown, and it is the ultimate goal of the constant abuse.

Fundamentally, what we are, is a biological program. Abuse knocks us out of our natural position within the self and forces us into a different spot. The pain from the abuse is grown onto that spot. In order to make a firm and thick skin, there needs to be some relief or kindness. The relief could be anything, as long as the target of the abuse is happy about the relief. The only thing the relief can't be, is a solution, or a redress of the original abuse. The point is to get the target to accept that the abuse was necessary, or maybe even the target's fault. The relief is a reward to maintain the abuse.

Finally, before the entire cycle starts again, rest is given to the victims. It gives the skin time to harden and callous over. Many call this the cycle of abuse, and it is. What I'm focusing on is what's happening on the inside. The skin is a self-replicating programmable prison, that is forced upon the self through constant abuse. The false skin combined with the Shine Mode is a deadly combination. People stricken with both will have a propensity to worship those who shine, and are compelled to harm those in the darkness. Unresolved abuse is like a never-ending violence vector. The victims of unresolved abuse, are compelled to recreate that abuse generation after generation.

When you consider that the Controllers employ most of the people, and control most of the goods and services, it becomes clear that the modern society didn't happen naturally. The structures that are in place, exist to exploit the brokenness in man. Thus making changing the system itself nearly impossible. It could cause many to break psychologically. There's a way to break through the skin, but first we should talk about how the skin is created.

Earlier in this book, I said the position of power, that I hold within the self, I call the Focus. This position comes with many perks. The main one, is whatever I focus on, writes itself into my flesh. I'm able to save information, long or short term. When a person is being abused, that person is feeling pain. The Focus is writing pain into the self. Then relief comes, but not to solve the original pain. The point of the relief is so that you stop focusing on the pain, and cover it up with pleasure. Since the victim is the Focus of their self, some form of pleasure is grown on top of the pain.

Finally, a talented abuser would give their victims a chance for the skin to heal. Abusers generally have a feel for how quickly the skin grows back. This is why abuse tends to escalate over time, and the periods between each moment of abuse shrink. They are compelled to abuse, and are compelled to escalate, to maintain the skin over the pain. As the Focus, with each abuse cycle, the victim is forming a thick skin around themselves, and are unable to get back the the natural position of the self.

When I think of this structure, I'm reminded of the biblical story of the tower of Babel. Give me a moment while I try to piece it all together for you. There are still some factors involving the Mode of Madness, but just given what I've already written, I suspect that there is some truth to the story. Except, I disagree with the premise that it was over a tower, and God was jealous. Fundamentally, we are self-aware, hairless, monkeys. If you limit our resources, and make it so that some monkeys can beat their chests and claim dominance over other monkeys, and get away with it, then you'll have the social order that we are all used to.

Remember, the way they get away with claiming dominance is a two-fold attack. They scream something that causes us to think, and they violently beat their chests like monkeys. If there isn't any supplication, it will escalate into violence. Most of us have been trained not to respond when there's a monkey beating his chest in front of us; especially black men. The reason for the beating of the chest, usually has some basis in reality. But the rage behind the excuse is always incongruous with reality. The abusers don't necessarily have to agree with or believe the reasoning for the beating of the chest either. The point is to terrorize and claim dominance.

Recently, Will Smith smacked Chris Rock at the Oscars. There are lots of opinions on what happened, and many folks, especially the whites, were troubled by the ordeal. I can explain what happened, and demonstrate the true state of the system as it is. We can suss out what's happening with the "fuck your dog" test.

The other day I was sitting by the Smith and 9th street train station in Brooklyn. Drug users usually hang out there. I blended in, smoking weed, but never joined the group. That day, there was a large police presence. One of the women in the group, had an aggressive dog, and it bit someone. The dog was caged to be put down. The folks was all upset because they knew the dog and the woman. Then a different regular showed up with his dog.

"Yo! The police just tried to take Bella!" He exclaimed. Everyone was in shock. Bella is such a sweet and kind dog. It was like more bad news. I like Bella myself, she was nice to me too. The man had everyone gather into a circle to tell us all what happened. He even waved me into the circle. I was in it, but I didn't feel like standing.

"I was at the doctor's office, and I left Bella outside. She was safe, cuz everybody knows me, and everybody knows Bella. Someone came into the office and told me someone was throwin shit at Bella! I went outside and saw Bella sad and scared, and this dude was throwing shoes and shit out his window at Bella. I said 'Why are you throwing shit at my dog?' and he said 'Fuck yo dog nigga!' What! Just right there, some was coming out the front door of his building. I went right up the steps and Boom! (He demonstrated how he kicked the door open.)

"Then I ran up to the right floor. And I was running back and forth trying figure out which apartment it was. Then I saw some eyes peeking out me from a door. He cracked the door a little and was peeking. There he is right there! Then a girl came to the door and said 'please don't mind my uncle, he has mental challenges.' Fuck outta here! (He motioned his hands into a shove.) Boom! (He demonstrated another kick.) So I'm fucking this old dude up, and the cops tried to take Bella!"

After that last sentence, the entire circle broke up, and many of the people throw their hand up into the air. After a few moments, one of the people asked him. "How come you aren't in jail right now?" The man shrugged, then waved his hand, "Me and the guy had the same doctor. He talked to the police and explained the situation." Then the story made sense to everyone. If you think this man is 'crazy,' you'd be wrong. You are the crazy one. That's what is supposed to happen. It's just that our rules are written such that some can do what the man did and get away with it.

How about you? If someone was throwing shoes out of their apartment window, at your dog, and when you asked why, they said "fuck your dog niggah!" How would you respond? We all know, that whatever punishment this dog assaulter receives from the system won't equal to the rage that you feel. The question is, will you do what Bella's owner did? This is essentially a test of the skin that you are wearing. People who turn away, and accept the pain of the situation are middle class and above. Poor people might snap, because they have a hard time keeping the skin on.

People are freaked out about Will Smith's aggression, because those very people are people farmers, and regularly abuse hairless monkeys. They're afraid of the skin all coming down at once. If you are one of those people, and you're are afraid in that way, you might be racist. It's true that they are both black men, but what also true, is that they are both rich. In the case of Will Smith, he's rich enough to be a monkey. On his death bed, he'll look back and think that it was all worth it. He may or may not lose out on some money. But that really won't affect him.

Lots of folks praised Chris Rock for not retaliating, as if that is supposed to happen. If someone was throwing shoes at Chris Rock's dog, and told him "fuck your dog niggah!" Chris would like say something like, "I'm gonna pray for you brother." Chris Rock doesn't have enough wealth to be a monkey. This is the point of the system, if you're rich enough, you can abuse others and get away with it. If you get busted, all you have to do is part with some worthless paper. Why did Cris Rock get smacked? Cuz that monkey went monkey!

Next is the physical hierarchy. The Controllers like to limit resources and make humans fight over it. They say the strongest rises to the top. The reality is, that it's abusive and not conducive to learning or personal growth. What it does establish is that the people making the decisions are already qualified, and are naturally above the ones fighting for a position. Those Moded with Madness thrive in this environment. They tear down people that they believe are beneath them, and praise and genuflect around those who they believe are above them.

The system cultivates these individuals and raise them up as they abuse a variety of approved targets. Fundamentally, those Moded with Madness are anti-government. They are a law onto themselves. The more they are allowed to abuse approved groups, the more godlike they'll feel. We are monkeys. It's intoxicating to dominate others. The Mad Ones gravitate to positions of power, because it is their right.

Who do these people see shine? Those who dominate. If resources are limited, we create a pecking order of who should get the resources. This invariably creates a power vacuum. If you have millions of people, who know that they are god-like, but they will follow the strongest among them. This person will shine for all of those Mad Ones. In the past, people with actual strength would be worshiped as the strongest man. I call this person, the Iron-Rod Messiah.

Those Moded with Madness are compelled to dominate others, and feel a strong sense of superiority. This feeling only comes from committing abusive acts and getting away with it. The Mad Ones always defer to the ones who are also moded in the same way, but are able to abuse a greater number of people and get away with it. The Mad Ones will beatify the Iron-Rod Messiah. He is their morning star. The Mad Ones will do whatever it takes to emulate the Iron-Rod Messiah, and they will seek to weed out anything that isn't like him. I know you're thinking about right now, but going back to Babel is more beneficial.

Most historians believe that Nimrod was the king when the Tower of Babel was supposed to have been built. In a way it doesn't matter when or where it happened. The story itself could be a complete myth. Science tells us that we have similar heritage, and were all once together as a group in Northern Africa and the Middle East. Imagine for a minute, there were thousands of us in one city, and there was a god-king who many people worshiped and tried to emulate. What do you think will eventually happen? The brokenness in man has existed for thousands of generations. Those who worship the god-king will likely kill those that don't resemble him. If it really happened, then Nimrod was the greatest threat that humanity at that time. To this day, people still worship and try to emulate this dead man.

The Creator exists, and he is us. We divided ourselves up and began to speak differently. People spread out in many directions. All this to maintain genetic diversity. Different languages helps protect humans from falling prey to the abuse by those Moded with Madness. The stupid reasoning for beating their chests rarely translates well into different languages.

It's weird, I studied the bible and see many flaws. It's tempting to ignore the entire thing, but what keeps bringing me back are the Mad Ones. Almost every story in the bible is written about them. Sodom and Gomorrah are about the Mad Ones, they killed all of the prophets, they are featured in most of the stories, and then there's the many warning that Jesus himself gave. Rather than skip around, I'll just post the words of Jesus from Matthew 23.

"Woe to you, teachers of the law and Pharisees, you hypocrites! You shut the door of the kingdom of heaven in people's faces. You yourselves do not enter, nor will you let those enter who are trying to.

"Woe to you, teachers of the law and Pharisees, you hypocrites! You travel over land and sea to win a single convert, and when you have succeeded, you make them twice as much a child of hell as you are...

"Woe to you, teachers of the law and Pharisees, you hypocrites! You give a tenth of your spices--mint, dill and cumin. But you have neglected the more important matters of the law--justice, mercy and faithfulness. You should have practiced the latter, without neglecting the former. You blind guides! You strain out a gnat but swallow a camel.

"Woe to you, teachers of the law and Pharisees, you hypocrites! You clean the outside of the cup and dish, but inside they are full of greed and self-indulgence. Blind Pharisee! First clean the inside of the cup and dish, and then the outside also will be clean.

"Woe to you, teachers of the law and Pharisees, you hypocrites! You are like whitewashed tombs, which look beautiful on the outside but on the inside are full of the bones of the dead and everything unclean. In the same way, on the outside you appear to people as righteous but on the inside you are full of hypocrisy and wickedness.

"Woe to you, teachers of the law and Pharisees, you hypocrites! You build tombs for the prophets and decorate the graves of the righteous. And you say, 'If we had lived in the days of our ancestors, we would not have taken part with them in shedding the blood of the prophets.' So you testify against yourselves that you are the descendants of those who murdered the prophets. Go ahead, then, and complete what your ancestors started!

"You snakes! You brood of vipers! How will you escape being condemned to hell? Therefore I am sending you prophets and sages and teachers. Some of them you will kill and crucify; others you will flog in your synagogues and pursue from town to town. And so upon you will come all the righteous blood that has been shed on earth, from the blood of righteous Abel to the blood of Zechariah son of Berekiah, whom you murdered between the temple and the altar. Truly I tell you, all this will come on this generation.

"Jerusalem, Jerusalem, you who kill the prophets and stone those sent to you, how often I have longed to gather your children together, as a hen gathers her chicks under her wings, and you were not willing. Look, your house is left to you desolate. For I tell you, you will not see me again until you say, 'Blessed is he who comes in the name of the Lord.'"

I've sat through hundreds of sermons about the 'Pharisees.' Most of the time, they're spoken of in past-tense. History repeats itself through each generation of human. The Mad Ones would feel compelled to kill anyone who doesn't agree with their personal reality. They can't be reasoned with, they only respond to power. Killing defenseless teachers seems right in their wheelhouse, as these folks don't fight back. What's terrifying about those Moded with Madness is that they, as a group, will attack anything that they believe is a threat to their power.

This is why the Controllers love to cultivate predators like this. They gravitate towards and attacks power. It happened in Egypt, Rome, and now here in the United States. It's important to initially ignore the things that they are saying, nobody cares about what they're saying. They think that you care about the reasoning they give to terrorize you. The bottom line is, they get to do and say horrible things to you, and get away with it, because they are superior to you.

More and more, I'm thankful for Trump. Firstly, he became their Iron--Rod Messiah. We can all see in real-time how mythology can form around one person. Folks are terrified of him, especially the Republicans. It almost seems overwhelming, except the Iron-Rod Messiah only has power over the Mad Ones if he gets away with hurting those in the darkness. By the looks of it, he's not getting away with anything. When he gets consequences, the Mad Ones will cannibalize him and all of his most ardent followers.

What makes Trump such a gift, is that he didn't give anyone breaks for a solid five years. He's still doing his best to abuse us all right now as we speak. There is an outrage daily with this clown. Trump recently put out a statement that his "Envoy Ambassador Ric Grenell, visited the Kosovo--Serbia border..." This is a clear Hatch Act violation. He's not president, he doesn't get to send ambassadors to speak to other heads of state. The guy doesn't give any breaks.

While his antics are egged on by the Mad Ones, the issue at hand is the false skin. There needs to be some relief and some rest. Trump gave neither for years, and then there was a pandemic. Millions of Americans were freed from their primary abuse vehicle; work. All the while, the outrage machine, Trump, plowed forward. The only way out of the cycle of abuse is to stay mad. With Trump, no one had a choice but to be upset. This put the Mad Ones in a bind. How?

These people are predators. They seek out places where they can beat their chests and get away with it. Unfortunately, too many people are sick of them, and are fighting back. While legislatures are pushing forward with horrible legislation, I want to differentiate them from the foot soldiers. Yes, Republicans are going after abortion rights. They passed laws to that affect. Women are pissed. Do you know what you don't see? People with signs on the street screaming at people. It isn't about they're 'winning' in the courts and the legislature. Ordinary women would go monkey at the sight of these people. The point is to beat your chest and get away with it. That is increasingly difficult nowadays.

All of the usual suspects are thoroughly pissed off and aren't interested. The Blacks, the gays, Latinos, Asians, Muslims, and so on, are all on the brink of going full monkey. The Mad Ones are wisely giving them a break. Where do these people rally now? School board meetings, and 'protesting' mask mandates. The vaccine is just an excuse to be violent and threatening. What I see are monkeys beating their chests and claiming dominance. There was also a gathering to see JFK Jr. rise from the dead. The media scoffed at the story. The reasoning is irrelevant, look at the outcome. It was a show of force, in order to terrorize the populace.

For thousands of years, the Mad Ones were exploited by the Controllers. People like to say slavery ended with the Civil War. Actual slavery has been alive and well for thousands of years. The White people in this country have always been the slaves. For thousands of years, you gifted your lives to the undeserving. You built great monuments, you sacrificed your bodies, and you served them with the only reward is that you were above someone else.

I've said that you'd know the Controllers by their lies. What is White history? The Controllers want the whole world to believe that it all started with White people. But if you still your mind and think back, isn't white history over-consumption of meat and alcohol, sex, and war? For thousands of years, you served, and what are you left with? Most White people, what they have is access to credit, and some have property. Your ancestors built most of the roads, most of the buildings, did most of the work, and what did you get for it? Nothing! You always worked in the service of the mediocre and undeserving.

Part of me is sad for the White people. The ones who were in darkness in Europe fled to America to be free of the system. The Controllers followed and setup a utopia for themselves. They recreated the system, but this time they used actual dark people. You sacrifice much, for the idea of being slightly better than some. Your history is riddled with moments of madness echoing Sodom and Gomorrah. For example, did you know that the 'Salem Witch Trials' killed both men and women? The Controllers own the media, and they promote the idea that only women died, because indiscriminate killing sounds really bad. Sexism isn't off putting for the current Mad Ones, of mostly white men. There were many times in our history where White people went mad and started killing lots of people.

Right now, we are in a similar moment in time to the ends of the Egyptian, Roman, and British Empires. Those Moded by Madness feel compelled to kill those they see clouded in darkness. With each of these empires, before their fall, there was a steady decline in the population. People left because of safety issues. It is no different today. In fact, all of the reasons the colonists gave to why they wanted to leave Europe are all the reasons I don't like living in America. I'm tired of the lies, lawlessness, and the terrorism. I don't feel safe anywhere in this place. The only thing people ever offer me are conciliation opportunities and empty apologies.

I'm scared, and you should be too. This is the system that toppled the mightiest of Empires. A thorough enforcement of the law is the only real remedy. Except, if that happens, you might be facing an actual civil war. These folks have a deep need to abuse people. One way or another, I'm leaving, and hopefully I can create a path for others who don't feel safe. If enough of their victims leave, then you have to become their new victims right?

Therapy could work, but they'll need to want to change. Changing the diet would also help them think clearly. Again, it's a choice that they will likely refuse. In my opinion, America is doomed, regardless if some people face consequences for the Trump administrations crimes. No one in thousands of years, has stood a chance against those Moded with Madness. They always spend to much time trying to mentally process the shit reasons that they give for doing the crazy things that they do.

Constantine supplicated to the madness, and converted everyone to Christianity. It's a ludicrous notion that waring Jesus factions brought the entire Roman Empire to it's knees. I say, let it be a warning, the things that they want are all bullshit. It is, and always will be, a covert assault on power.

People have confidence in the American government. I suspect that there will be high level arrests of many Controllers. What does the American government do about the millions of Moded Americans? There is precisely one solution, that most wouldn't have bother to listen to even fifty years ago. What will end this slow moving assault on power? Pussy.

We are self-aware, hairless, monkeys. The major factor in the system is the complete subjugation of women, and their sexuality. In addition to this, men are taught the wrong way to attract a woman. We can debate until we're blue in the face with all of the potential legislative fixes we could make that could help. But a main factor in the control, is that the men are sexually frustrated. It is deliberate. If we move from artificial scarcity to actual abundance women will take control automatically.

Chapter NINE

THE SCAM THAT RULED THE WORLD

"It is hard to imagine a more stupid or more dangerous way of making decisions than by putting those decisions in the hands of people who pay no price for being wrong."

~ Thomas Sowell ~

IT'S TERRORIST THEATER

I'm not sure whether the Controllers looked at their handwork from my perspective. To them, it has to be like real life theater. They are the gods of the earth, and rightfully control all of the resources. Then they force the self-aware monkeys to go through some unnecessary hoops in order to get the basic resources that they need. The hoops are gradual, but in time, most monkeys have accepted the system.

What is the point of jumping through the hoop? To prove that someone else got you to jump through the hoop. The point is for you to understand, that there is always someone above you. It's different from the god-kings, where specific people are above you and can do whatever they want to you. In this system, you've got to understand that there are entire classes that are above you. The Controllers are a class of their own, and no one is above them. It starts in the schools, teachers in rich schools are servants. While teachers in poor schools are drill sergeants.

Then they divide the population into haves and have-nots, and place themselves above the haves. In the beginning you'll need to enforce this hierarchy with brutality. In the end, most monkeys accept since the Controllers have all of the resources. Within this bifurcated society, it is a must that the haves can exclusively harm the have nots and get away with it. Why is this vital?

The point of the system are lies and corruption. The vile, the corrupt, and the obsequious, they all curry favor with the Controllers. People who do reprehensible things, would very much like to keep those things secret. What the Controllers offer are roles in their terrorist theater. They have roles of all kinds, and it doesn't matter that you did a wrong thing, in fact, it's encouraged. People with something to be ashamed of, accept and defend the characters that the Controllers created for people to play.

What the Controllers do is constantly cause problems, blame other people for the problem that they caused, then their future actions are guided by the victims that they accused who caused the problem. This same pattern has happened in some form or another to all Americans. It's like a fractal pattern that repeats indefinitely. On an individual level, we call it abuse, with multiple people, it's terrorism.

They have to create constant terror events in order to maintain the stability of the frame. They may even call it a spell. For thousands of years, some people 'woke up' and realized that it's all bullshit, but couldn't figure out what to do. The Controllers have counter measures for people who begin to wake up from the system. Usually, it involves showering, or tempting, the person, waking up from the spell, with resources. It's theater and they're playing all sides. They control most of the world's resources. If anything is going to get done, you literally have to beg for their help.

The fighting and distractions are to help the masses accept their other scams. If you had access to a hundred billion dollars what does that actually mean? It means you have the ability to hire humans to do work for you. They will be completely dependent on you for their survival. The more currency that you have, the more people that you can hire. But whenever you, or others like you, decide to stop spending all at once. Wouldn't the masses be starved of resources?

When people are desperate for survival, it's here where the controllers shine. Playing a character based on an abhorrent need, adds stickiness to the character, but the person is still fully aware of the deal that they made. When people begin to associate playing a character to their very survival is where they can shape an entire nation. The Controllers regularly reward those who are true believers in a behavior that they are trying to implant into the community. In this way, they can shape an entire tribe of people to act and believe the way that they want.

For those of you who are reading this right now, you might suspect that I'm talking about the crazies of today. I am, but once you see the pattern, you can apply it to the past as well. As we speak, there are folks committing acts of terrorism to 'stop vaccine mandates' and 'oppose critical race theory.' Most people are seriously perplexed at their actions. I believe that there are money powers behind these actions. There are true believers, and also there are paid agitators. The Controllers created a field of abuse and lies, and they have had consistent results.

They have been doing this for thousands of years. The Mad Ones are comprised of people who are abuse victims, abusers, and the undeserving. With abuse, there is a compelling need from the inside to repeat the abuse. The system usually advertises where abusers can satisfy their needs. It might seem harsh to call some of these people undeserving, but they call themselves out. Those who the system lifted up, have a vested interest in things remaining where they are. So many folks are confused that it was managers, and business owners that stormed the capital on the sixth. These are the people who will lose their imaginary role if the people beneath them stopped accepting.

It's all one big scam, that has been going on for thousands of years. In my opinion, you shouldn't trust anyone until you control your own resources. That is the only fight you'll ever need. Everything else is a distraction.

I'll end this section by being controversial. I believe that Controllers wrote most, if not all of the New Testament. It didn't happen organically as some suggest. They copied many of the stories of Horus, and changed it somewhat. Then they went and destroyed all the writings of Horus. Why would they do this? They had a multi-century war with Egypt, and it was the ultimate insult. This would've been a crowning achievement, at the time. Complete domination and theft of your religion. It was like there were trying to rub Horus out of the minds of man.

The actual followers of Jesus may or may not have been a factor. They made giant errors as they wrote the entire thing in Greek. I won't bother with the errors here. Mainly because the errors are irrelevant. If people are hungry and frightened enough, they'll believe what you tell them.

You start by hiring a local scam artist to promote an idea or belief. The Controllers promote that thing with their vast resources. Since there's already inherent conflict, that belief is usually tied to the divides that already exist. This continues until the Mad Ones are attracted to the movement. The Mad Ones will need a target to abuse. Ask yourself this, how was the Roman Empire inundated in religious fighting not long after the teachings of a pacifist spoke in a small region of the Empire? The fighting got so bad the Emperor had church leaders meet at his summer palace in Nicaea. That only makes sense if it was organized terrorism. How would you feel if President Biden held a summit with waring Christian factions, and when they came to a consensus, Biden declared the whole nation are followers of this consensus?

The Catholic Church was the secret power in Europe for over a thousand of years. They had an arch-enemy; the Vandals. The Vandals refused to be apart of their unified group, to stop street violence, because they dropped the second commandment. This is what I mean that the Controllers don't care about errors, or what's written. Vandals were violently anti-Catholic, on purpose. The Vandals actually helped the Catholic Church solidify it's hidden powers. And one day, the Vandals just disappeared. Why? Folks have all types of reasons. I say the Controllers cut them off, once they fulfilled their mission.

This same scenario has happened time and again. They create an enemy and when they get what they want, that enemy disappears. America was supposedly fighting communism for almost a generation. We became one of the most powerful nation on the planet. Then our main adversary just quits. No one can definitely say what cause the collapse of the Soviet Union. What if the very rich simply decided that they don't want to spend any of their paper in your country any more, and simultaneously raise prices?

I believe these folks, created some of the worlds religions, they've shaped the maps to create constant conflict, and they've built up nations and had nations destroyed. All of it, with the control of the local currency, and the resources that humans need to survive. Having this kind of power over other humans should be illegal. But we all just accept.

Some of you may be offended at what I said, but ask yourself, if someone paid you enough money, what would you believe? If you don't have a price, what percentage of the population is like you? When the money dries up, who do you blame? Do you blame the people who have no money and can't fight back, or do you blame the people who have all the money?

This is what the system will always offer, lack of control of your own resources, and abuse. If the abuse hasn't come to you yet, it will.

WHO ARE THEY

I've tried to avoid naming any of the Controllers. This group is shrouded with lies, and protected by terrorism. They are in fact some of the richest people in the world. There they usually control from the shadows. These folks are patient and have multi-generational plans. Let's start with broad strokes then. Who are they?

They're businessmen who believe what the old god-kings believed, that they are gods among men. I suspect they are of Greek origin, because of the Greek Dark Ages. Whenever these folks solidify their power, knowledge, science, and history are vigorously suppressed. Then they flood the entire zone with lies.

While the Mad Ones show their dominance by publicly beating their chests, while claiming an innocuous reasoning for the display. The Controllers cause suffering globally. It is their dominance, to be able to do terrible things to other humans and get away with it. They created a system of slavery that is still in use today, although most don't think of it as slavery.

People keep treating me like I'm crazy, and that I should learn to accept the decent paying jobs that are available. Even beyond the constant truth telling, I can't see myself getting a job just to have a decent life. I know how life is for millions of people. The system purposely limits goods and services, and then purposely gifts goods, services, and a means of defending the goods to some and denied to others.

In America, white men are generally the class of haves. They accept this created role of superiority, and in exchange, they do most of the work, and get none of the rewards. The rewards are reserved for the Controllers and their acolytes. It's beaten into their heads that the 'others' are lazy and don't work as hard as they do. They believe that the system works and if people put in a hard days work, they could achieve anything. That is not the case. The Controllers only elevate people within the system that toes a line that they are pushing, glorifies the Controllers in some way or form, or corrupt individuals who are completely compromised.

What's the result? The rich and the powerful have armies of desperate humans to labor for the basic necessities. I want to share something that I've learned from working for many millionaires and billionaires. They don't work, they don't struggle, they don't hustle, nor do they beg. They don't have to. They don't have to constantly qualify themselves to anyone. They are born qualified. Most of what they do is projection, so I'd like to return their word to them; nigger.

It is the Controllers who attached all manner of evil to the distractions at the bottom. They do it to keep the white slaves from noticing that the Controllers are in fact the niggers. They're lazy, stubborn, refuse to work, always looking for handouts, especially from the government, their quick to anger, highly immoral, and are completely undeserving of what they have. What they, and the people beneath them, learn right away is that there are people that they can do almost anything they want to, and get away with.

I believe that there are only a handful of actually Controllers, as a massive conspiracy is nearly impossible to pull off in secret. In addition to it being a small group, I believe they 'worship' Satan. I put worship is scare quotes because I believe the Controllers are fundamentally atheists. The reason, I believe, that they adopted Satanism is two-fold.

First, new inductees into the system have to agree and accept the role as god of the earth. Being a Satanist, and other things, are used as leverage for those who step out of line. The second reason for the belief in Satanism, is that the controllers have been killing those touched by the Creator for thousands of years. They look down on all human life as their personal property. Those touched by Creator are usually a threat to the system. Those touched by the Creator keep waking the slaves up.

The Controllers are, what they like to be called, job-creators. They made most of the work that exists. They set the salaries and profiles of who they'd like to work in those positions. It appears that it all happens naturally and that we are all working together, but that's not true. What we have is a system that forces all people to genuflect to those who hoard currency. You have to find your own place with what the system is currently offering.

Some of you don't believe? Let's consider the food. How many people does it take to make food for hundreds of millions of Americans? Although the numbers are declining, it only takes two million farmers to make all the food for the entire country. The system made sure that the farmers are 90% white, and are isolated from other groups. They work hard, for about $80k per year. We make more than enough food for everyone, why do so many go hungry? Because food is limited, and ordinary folks need to 'work' in order to get food. The biggest reason for hunger, is that the 'managers,' who do none of the work, are rewarded with the most money.

Be honest with yourself, does your job in any way put food in the table? If you say, "I get money from my job, and that pays for the food," then you've completely accepted the system. They system wants you to believe that only the Controllers can make and distribute food. Also, no one questions their wisdom in throwing the food away when they want to cause pain. You accept that throwing food away is a necessary part of making the system work. You accept that your job is somehow related to food; it is not. Also, you accept your boss. You accept that there is another human that can threateningly beat their chests in front of you, and you can do or say nothing about it.

Your job has absolutely nothing to do with food, water, shelter or energy. Some people may have some relation to one thing, but most 'work' doesn't achieve a single thing that humans need. The things that we need are purposely limited so that the masses have to fight over it. The society was constructed in such a way that most people are working towards nothing, and to make matters worst, most people don't even like the work that they do. It's just the best they can get given who they are.

The Controllers have their hands in everything, and play both sides of most things here in America. I'm supposed to be happy for the Biden Administration's 'wins.' Folks don't understand why the media isn't hyping up Biden's successes, the way they did for Trump. It's far more than they are controlled. When you divide the country into the haves and have-nots, the haves don't want things to change. The haves 'know' that everything is limited, and they have accepted that some people need to suffer to that they and their progeny can prosper. The Democrats seem quite perplexed at the idea that people don't want paid family leave, and a whole host of other things. They desperately want us all to want equality, but they don't see the system of control we live under.

The bottom-line is that a significant number of people are going to vote for abuse and oppression. Why? Because they know that they've been elevated beyond what they deserve and are willing to fight and protect their imaginary position. One of their talking points is "the unemployment rate falls to its lowest rate in 50 years." And they're confused as to why it isn't sticking. If everything is limited, then low unemployment means rising prices and cuts in services. At least this is what the Controllers want you to believe. People are going to continue to vote for homelessness, hunger, and poverty because this is what they know.

It's these people who accept the system, and its evil, for a slightly better place in the world, are the ones who maintain the system. They are the army of know nothings, who heed the call of the Controllers when summoned. As long as the Controllers give them an enemy to abuse and exploit, that's all the payment that they need. I am personally terrified by these people, and actively try to avoid where they gather. They are terrorists, who the Controllers sometimes have trouble controlling. They simply aren't punished when they do wrong things, the system usually forgives them.

The Controllers have a particularly hard time with Iron-Rod Saviors. Though they control the wealth, the Iron-Rod Saviors control the Mad Ones. The Controllers don't deal with the Iron-Rod Saviors as they do with the those touched by the Creator, they usually go with the flow until they can rest control back at a future date. It is a generational fraud.

I will present useful solutions later on, but let me ask you something. Can't you own shares of assets that produce food, water, energy, and shelter for you? I've spoken about this at length in this book. You can't own anything that produces the things that you need! If you did, why would you work? If you have enough food, water, energy, and shelter, would you work? Or better yet, would you work as much or as hard as you do now? I don't care about the job market, it's mostly a scam. I want all humans to be in control of their own resources.

Most humans on this planet don't control anything that they need and have to slave for it. This is the Controllers' power over everyone. They can fire people from their jobs, they can remove people from their homes, they can throw away the food, and they can shut off the electricity and water from people's homes. They usually move together to make all of these things happen at once. They trained us all to understand when they aren't profiting, it means pain for the rest of us. Kicking people out of the system, is how they demonstrate their dominance over the rest of us.

This is why they are so anti-government. One of the things that helped stabilize the American economy is the large public work force, that was created as a result of the New Deal. To this day, one in four Americans work for the government is some way. In a way, they've been losing control for hundreds of years. The New Deal was almost the nail in the coffin for this system. Since then, they've been on a rampage at any government agency that works. They want it to fail, so that people can only work for them.

Their rule is under threat from many avenues, and their margin for error is slim. I've been making intellectual leaps in order to support a theory, right? Maybe. Let's first consider how a handful of people could potentially control everything.

CONTROL THE MEANS AND THE CURRENCY

Did you know that there are four companies that own everything? I bet you didn't know that? Know why? Because there are only six media companies in the US; Comcast, Disney, AT&T, Viacom, Sony, and Fox. Surprise, they are all also owned by the same four companies. The companies are

McGraw-Hill, Northwestern Mutual, CME Group, and Barclay's. I challenge you to do an internet search of 'the four companies that own everything.' You'll end up learning, that you only have an illusion of choice.

When you spend money, anywhere, it always goes to the same people. Most of the major decision making, usually happens behind closed doors, because the controllers like to not be seen. They are merchants, investors, and business people. They have been for thousands of years. I could spend time going through each corporation like nesting dolls, but it isn't worth it. We all understand, that we live under a multitude of monopolies. Social media, pharmaceutical, agriculture, energy, telecommunication, and on and on. They are owned and controlled by the one percent. People like Bernie Sanders and Elizabeth Warren want to break some of these companies up. No one will ever break up the four major conglomerates. It is extreme concentrated power, which could be terrifyingly problematic if the people behind these companies are coordinating.

What we call the 'Economy,' in my opinion is a long con. A scam that toppled empires, and controls large populations. The first step, is to own all, or most, of the resources and means of production. The Controllers always try to appear neutral, and solely motivated by profits. It was a perfect cover against arrogant god-kings. Over time, they likely learned to always use cut outs, who represent their interests.

Think for a moment. It is a fact that most things on this planet are owned by less than one percent of the population. How did that happen? We went from a handful of royalty owning everything to a handful of businesspeople owning everything. Is there an accurate history of such a thing? Did the Royals give up their power and possessions willingly? Since we are modern humans, ask yourself a question. If I had unlimited money, could I overthrow a government? If you say yes, do you know how to do it? Paid agitators, wedge issues, lies, cheating, and terrorism. Right?

Next, is control of the currency. For thousands of years, the Controllers used gold, and little understood tricks of the bid-ask spread. They are obvious now-a-days, but thousands of years ago it was astonishingly unique. To understand the crux of the scam, let's consider Bitcoin. Although my body wouldn't allow me to successfully trade, I was able to trade bitcoin to get double to triple the amount of weed I would buy. How did I do it? I noticed that the Bitcoin price would spike around Thanksgiving until a few weeks after New Years Day. Why? Because people are stressed, and they buy lots of drugs during the holidays. I capitalized on this Christmas time price surge, by buying Bitcoin in the late summer to fall, and waiting until late January to trade.

What's happening? Myself and others know that there will be people who don't care about the price of Bitcoin. You see, the drugs online price change as Bitcoin rises and falls. To the person buying drugs, the cost will always be the same in dollars. But the only way to get their drugs is to go through people like me, who will sell them Bitcoin at a profit. Well, I don't sell. I'd buy double or triple the weed and have extra for months.

If you look at that transaction, the buyer and the seller are both happy, and I, as the middleman, am also happy. It's a 'normal' business transaction right? This is likely the original part of the scam. Instead of Bitcoin, they used gold. The Controllers owned and controlled the rate at which gold is mined. By changing the supply of gold available, the Controllers are able to change the value of the gold at will. The next thing that they did, was to loan their gold out, using bank notes. They would loan out their gold with five times leverage, and put the population and governments in their debt.

The vital part of the scam is, everyone has to live their lives according to that currency. If your entire life is priced by gold, as the price of gold swings up and down, so would your fortunes. Since they controlled the mines, and banking, they can plan for inflation or deflation to adversely affect a local economy. The money that we all carry around, has gone through a lot for it to be as relatively stable as it is now. In the past, the dollar was as shaky as Bitcoin. Can you imagine living your entire life in Bitcoin? Your rent or mortgage paid in Bitcoin. Your food purchased in Bitcoin, and so on. The uninitiated will look at the price of gold, and accept that there is nothing anyone can do about the price.

It is very difficult to have an entire population priced in a certain currency. When the controllers succeed in having a specific area bound by the current value of a local currency. How do you know if you're the controllers have you? It's simple, you need food, water, energy, and shelter. If you don't control your food, water, shelter, or energy then you'll need to exchange whatever the given currency is for these things. Some of you may even consider yourselves well-off. Most 'rich' people have an over abundance of currency, and they're able to exchange their currency for food, water, energy, and shelter. With a big enough price swing, even the 'rich' ones would be on the ropes.

Once the Controllers, have a location on lock, then they're able to push anyone to believe whatever they want. As we've already discussed, all the currency flows towards the controllers, and the controllers are the ones who create the 'jobs,' from the wealth that they've extracted from the local economy. The flow of wealth, should be considered like a liquid. If the Controller's businesses always 'make' more money then they spend, for labor, then these businesses are always profitable. Eventually, because of currency scarcity, in order for a business to stay in the black, they need to pay less for labor, or fire people. This is something that must happen, or they lose wealth, and ultimately control of a local economy.

The Controllers are fundamentally anti-government. Why? Firstly, the system always causes pain to some. Wild price swings will make some people poor. People like to promote democracies as the best way to combat autocracies. This scam system is a way to exploit a local population towards your own ends. What has the Controllers on the ropes isn't free and fair elections, it's bureaucracy. Taxes extracted from the Controller's businesses, will pay for any government 'jobs.' Because of this, the Controller's hate all government jobs, as they can't fire these people. It's sad really, there are people who absolutely believe that the best way for an 'economy' to work, is no taxes and no government workers. Unfortunately, whenever they do that here, it's always an economic crash. As, the government workers are the very thing keeping everything else afloat financially, regardless of how effective their service is.

It's in this manner, ordinary businessmen can control and topple entire empires. There are a series of economic crises, where the people's wages are worth less, and prices sky rocket. The only way out is to take out loans. But when you can't pay that, additional resources are confiscated to pay the debt. You'll know them by their lies. They own the media corporations, so no one is going to blame the person hoarding all of the currency, as to why everyone else is currency starved. Usually, they blame the very poor for not working hard enough. The system is one of acceptance, you have to believe in it for it to work. As a nation, we are currently in a currency drought, and a handful of folks are hoarding most of it. Naturally, the problem the media focuses on is all of the 'work' that the Controllers are offering, that no one wants.

Most people don't remember the tumultuous times when the dollar was unstable. The Controllers do, this is how they've maintained power for so long. It entails making some people suffer greatly, then having them learn to accept by force; terrorism. The government, in general, is an enemy to the scam that they perpetrate. This is the system that we all live under. There's no magic, the wealth flows in one direction, and if you want to survive, you'll need to take a job that the Controllers find useful.

Each individual human has to personally accept, that this is the best and only way to survive. It is somewhat similar to the accept or die challenges god-kings would pose to people. The system asks everyone to accept or suffer and die slowly. The bottom line is, that only the Controllers can afford to own their own food, water, shelter, and energy.

Once the population accepts the system, they carry on as if it's supposed to be this way. Since everyone is starving for currency, the Controllers can raise up anyone it wants to prominence. Which is why it's important that history be obscured. Because under this system, nobody can do anything unless you ask a rich person for currency. No wars can happen, no terrorism, no rapes, no financial exploitation, no provocateurs, no profession, absolutely nothing can happen unless they secretly approve it.

Right now, we as a nation are having a problem with individuals terrorizing local school boards. As a species, we are catching on. Many people in the media are trying to rationalize the arguments of the Mad Ones, but a few are asking the right question. "Who's paying these people?" Fundamentally, nothing, nothing, nothing, can get done in this system without approval from a rich person. Protests that arise spontaneously, apart from the controllers, are met with the heavy hand of law enforcement. The Mad Ones flourish in this system, and it doesn't matter what part of the world you're from, the Mad Ones are all the same. Their job is to terrorize the ones in the shadows. They do it willingly, and the power they feel from dominating others is addicting.

Folks are blaming Donald Trump for plotting a coup, but they're looking in the wrong place. Was Trump involved in the coup? Absolutely! But Trump is an idiot, the coup is something that was organized by those with wealth and power. I suspect that the coup was always planned, but Trump unexpectedly winning the presidency accelerated the time schedule. The country still stands, despite all the cheating that's going on electorally. This is because the bureaucracy is strong and functioning. The bureaucracy almost destroyed the system in the past, and the Controllers also tried coup back then. That's right there were more than one. Also, they got away with it.

It was called The Business Plot of 1934. It involved the most prominent people of the time and extreme animosity towards President Franklin D. Roosevelt. The coup plotters approached Major General Smedley Butler, a decorated war hero, and tried to convince him to aid in their plot. Instead of aiding them, Butler testified under oath to a special house committee to the existence of the plot. He implicated prominent people like Robert Sterling Clark, Grayson MP Murphy, and Prescott Bush, patriarch of the Bush family. The media at the time mocked Butler's claims, but the committee concluded saying "there is no question that these attempts were discussed, were planned, and might have been placed in execution when and if the financial backers deemed it expedient."

No one was prosecuted, there were no investigations. It had to have been terrifying to think wealthy and prominent people wanted to overthrow the duly elected president and install a dictator. Hindsight tells us why they took such a risk. FDR, and the American people, were tired of banks failing, and people rushing to pull out their gold. The government was leaving the gold standard. The volatility was too much to bear. FDR's New Deal hired millions of workers directly through the government, and also raised taxes up to 94% for high income earners. FDR and the Congress didn't realize that the system was designed that way to benefit a handful of people. Had they known, they would've removed these folks from ownership in a whole host of things.

The Controllers almost lost it all in the New Deal. They clawed their way back with loopholes in the tax code that allowed them to pay less. Also, they caused prices to skyrocket, as they controlled the means of production. The nation struggled with inflation for a few generations until taxes for the rich were reversed. They control the goods and the services, hence they can raise prices at will, and then blame it on something else, using the media they control.

Subsequently, knowing how the system works, it's simple to escape it. Let's consider rising gasoline prices. The precise reason that prices are going up, is because oil producers are purposely limiting the supply, in order to make profits. They were hemorrhaging money, and needed to raise prices in order to stay afloat. No one in government, let alone the president, has the power to make the prices go lower. Maybe if we pay them to lower the prices, that might help. But it doesn't solve the problem.

The problem is, no American has any agency in the transaction. Let's say we collectively purchased our own energy producing assets; nuclear powered boats. We could potentially make gasoline out of thin air, and store it where we need it. People, who are enamored with this market, will tell you that you'd have a problem if the OPEC nations decide to flood the markets with cheap gas. No. In this new system, the things that you need to worry about are utility and storage.

If you have gasoline coming in, you should at least have an idea where this gasoline will be used. Hopefully, you have a car. Or maybe you have a SOFC for you home. Regardless of the price movements for oil, it could go negative, people will only buy what they need and they are limited by the amount of storage they have. That scenario repeats as people start to exchange goods and services for energy. Each individual, and each company, are limited by how much energy they use, and how much energy they can store. In this scenario, all the people who have their own energy have escaped the system. The wonderful thing, about having your own energy assets, is that energy can make food, water, and housing.

The Controllers were doing so well, then Trump happened. When he was elected, I was literally terrified for my life. But as time passed, I see the benefit of the voice inside of me constantly reminding me to wait. The bureaucracy was still too strong for them to make a move, but a career criminal became president. I feel confident in saying that Trump isn't one of them, but I believe that he's an insider, one of their acolytes. He was supposed to lose, but something unexpected happened. Trump summoned the sleeping army and told them it was time to storm the castle.

The Controllers exploit the Mad Ones, but the groups secretly hate each other. They both believe that they are the rightful rulers. There are two groups of people that the Controllers have a challenge with, the Iron--Rod Messiahs and those touched by the Creator. Both are vectors that shift public sentiment, usually away from what they want. A clarion call from an Iron Rod Messiah, is a call to violence and genocide. To the Controllers, these are the fruits of a system of forced disparity. An alpha predator that the Mad Ones idolize. They were all in for Trump.

The only thing is, we're living in the stupidest times. While this entire scenario would've worked a hundred years ago, it's obsolete now. The bureaucracies are far too strong. Trump ruined everything. It started in 2015, when he claimed multiple times that he was under tax audit. Trump's alpha male bravado would've worked a hundred years ago. But now-a-days, that will only lead to the Streisand effect.

The Streisand effect is a phenomenon that occurs when an attempt to hide, remove, or censor information has the unintended consequence of increasing awareness of that information. Wouldn't you know it? I know someone, who knows someone, who works at one of many locations that has Donald Trump's tax returns. The information I received was a grimace. I don't know if such a thing is legally binding. But seriously, somebody looked right?

The IRS has been saving tax records since 1862. What are the odds, that every single return filed by Trump had hidden crimes? The investigation would be sprawling enough, but I suspect that Trump, a made man, did business with the same people for decades. Considering Trump appears to be a money launderer, his returns would implicate scores of people. Why does this matter? Court cases? Maybe not.

Do you remember me telling you about bitcoin surges during the Christmas season? The surge in 2020 was strong, I assumed because people were at home stressed, and spent their stimulus money on drugs. I bought when the price was around 10k and sold at around 40k. Then something strange happened, the price shot up to over 60k. The media likes to report on price charts like there's some mystery to it. When I saw the price surge, it hit me. It's the rich and the powerful that are jacking up the price!

Do you know what cryptocurrency is? It is a public ledger, that has a high level of encryption. The thing that is important is the Streisand effect. The Steele Dossier claimed that Russia paid Trump $7.5 billion in bitcoin. The FBI must at a minimum investigate that claim. Holy Shit!

THE PUMP AND DUMP

The Pump and Dump is a primary tool of the controllers. Remember, they control everything, and goods and services are purposely limited. The scam is to convince the mark that something will be valuable in the future. As the price for said thing goes up, it seems like a perfect investment. But in the end, the scammers pull the rug out from under the targets and leave with the cash. The targets are left with a worthless asset and no money.

It's a challenge to guess what the motivation behind the buying and selling of an asset. The sharp unexpected rise in bitcoin price set off alarm bells for me. My first thought was all the people who felt financially exposed by a Biden presidency bought bitcoin in order to hide assets. While this is a strong possibility, what has happened since then has elucidated a clear agenda.

For some reason, China banned bicoin and all cryptocurrencies. The ban was swift and unexpected. Most crypto mining was done in China. This should have crippled the crypto markets, but literally overnight most mining is now done in the United States. I suppose I should explain a bit.

Crypto-currencies are a publicly encrypted ledger. Each transaction is done in units called blocks. When the blocks stack together, you get the blockchain. The system can only operate if people with powerful computers can encrypt each transaction. These people are called miners. They encrypt each individual transaction for a small fee. It is amazing how quickly things move for the Controllers. Right now, power plants around the US are mining bitcoin, and some question the legality of publicly subsidized entities using the nations power for bitcoin.

Then the Staples Center was renamed the Crypto.com Center, for a $700 million dollar naming rights deal. A significant amount of money to promote crypto-currencies. Then the three mayors saying they will be paid in bitcoin; Francis Suarez of Miami, Eric Adams of New York, and Scott Conger of Jackson. What's so special about bitcoin? It's literally nothing. But what's worst is that less than one percent of bitcoin users owns the most bitcoin.

What does this mean? A small handful of people and literally control the price movements. It seems that I'm watching a pump and dump right before my eyes. And it fills me with great shame that my mayor is pushing this crap. Mayor Adams is literally recommending people to "buy the dip." I know it's a bit presumptuous to talk about bitcoin as a pump and dump, in the midst of the pump, but there's more at work here. We live in the stupidest times.

Firstly, there were allegations that Donald Trump was being secretly paid in bitcoin, by Russia. I don't know if you know this, but the blockchain isn't unhackable. You simple need enough computing power to decrypt it. As of today, there are precisely two organizations that could decrypt all of bitcoin; America and China. They both have access to supercomputers and quantum computers. The thing is public, but no one had a reason to dedicate significant enough resources to decrypting it. Trump was a good reason. What are the odds that this idiot crimed using bitcoin as President?

Let me be clear, I believe that both the Chinese and the American government are decrypting bitcoin in real-time. The last few years have been a huge debacle for organized crime. Entire outfits all around the world are being rolled up. No one understands that maybe, the government has access to your illegal transactions.

I know it's somewhat of a leap, I think bitcoin is compromised. So let's go with it to finish the dump phase. The price is supposed to crash when the people running the scam get their desired profits and vanish into thin air. At some point, the government has to come clean, and share that it is real-time decrypting bitcoin, in order to make some prosecutions. On that day, the sellers will stop listing their products online and the market will evaporate overnight. The price of bitcoin will go to zero before the scammers can cash out.

We truly live in the stupidest times. All the idiots that crimed on bitcoin have to be shitting bricks right now. You crimed using a public ledger! How long do you think it should take before technology is able to decrypt the blockchain? Because never is the stupidest answer ever! I'm here for the bitcoin crash, and I pity the fool who says that we need to bail it out.

THE FIINAL GRIFT

It was the winter of 2019, and I was working outdoors as a Citibike Valet. For more than eight years I did everything the ones inside asked of me. Honestly, sometimes it felt as if the me that I am was asleep. I suspect that it is some sort of repair program that we all feel the urge to run, but the system fights against. I retreated within myself and allowed the me that I am to be healed.

All throughout this time, I could recognize that my logical abilities were diminished. To prove to myself that I was ready, I would watch the markets and follow the financial news. I had been waiting since the summer time for a market correction. In fact, everyone was waiting for a market correction. When it started I was happy, it was like I had my mojo back. Before I took out a $7k loan and placed my trade, I checked in with myself if there were any objections; there weren't.

I bought a number of put options on XLF, the banking index. In the beginning, the trade worked out perfectly. In a few weeks, my 7k trade was worth over 20k. Then something strange happened, everything reversed. I checked the online news, the first thing the popped up was "Maybe this is stock manipulation?!" Then I checked the CNBC. They were just as perplex as I was, and openly talking about possible stock manipulation. I was still solidly in the green, and could've easily switched directions and completely paid off the note with a profit. Just as I opened up my TastyWorks platform to close out my position I heard it, "Hold!"

Of all the dumbest things that had come up from inside me, this was one of the worst. "Obviously, the market has changed directions. I can make a living from just the profits we have left, let's just change direction... Hold! I just took out a loan. We're gonna be paying this shit for years. Hold! Are you hoping that there is an investigation? No fucking way there's an investigation. The whole stock market would collapse! Hold!"

What can I do? I was safe, there was no plausible veto. I watched my position go from over 20k to zero, over the next eight weeks. For months

I really questioned what the hell I was doing. I was poor and doing hard labor out in the elements, and all I could is watch in horror as 7k evaporated. I was very angry with myself, until I realized how far I had come. "Why didn't he want me to close out my position?" I pondered. I know who I am, and what I'm good at. I'm excellent and breaking down systems. "Maybe I want me to focus on the Stock Market?" Let's consider what was happening at this time.

Trump was having a hard time with it. He had just passed his massive tax cuts, but the economy appeared to be tumbling over. The idiot kept pointing to how high the stock market was compared to Obama. Also, there were a series of weird moves, over the first few months of his administration, that reports claim the SEC were looking into. With the idea that Trump may be using the Bully Pulpit to do pump and dump schemes. What happened in the winter on 2019 was unmistakably abhorrent.

The other apparent manipulations happened during off hours using futures. That kind of thing is clearly in Trump's wheelhouse. With a few million dollars and Trump bringing attention to a stock, you could make hundreds of millions if you don't get caught. My position was closed by the time COVID hit. Then the unthinkable happened, stock prices continued to rise. Trump's a two-bit idiot, he doesn't have the wealth or the ability to pull this off. It cost me $7k to get me to completely focus on what the fuck was happening to the stock market. Do you find it odd that the markets have risen more under Trump than any other president in history? Go ahead, pull up some charts on the internet. Here's some symbols SPY, QQQ, and DIA. Use a monthly time interval and do the max time frame. What happened in 2016 that made the markets rise so much??

If you ask a talking head, they'll tell you that the Trump Tax cuts caused this. The plan made it beneficial to do stock buy backs. With the tax savings, companies bought back shares of their stocks and the prices rose. That's nice, but not how the bid-ask spread works. If they did buy-backs, who did they buy their shares from? I know, it's a secret trade, but it's good to speculate. By the process of elimination, we can see that these large corporations bought their shares from ordinary folks leaving the markets. How do I know? According to CNBC, the wealthiest 10% of Americans, owns 89% of all US stocks.

When you read articles about this fact, they speak of it in terms of inequity. As if we need to somehow fix a thing the rich purposefully rigged in their favor. Big corps spent all of their money, and gave it to folks who didn't like what was happening in the markets. In fact, it's like the stock market is a ghost town. Only the rich are participating. It's gotten so bad, all brokerages are commission free. Looking at the craziness, in the stock market, during the Trump years, I too would be hesitant to invest anything in it.

Stock buy-backs would've been a small upwards blip in the markets which would lead to a downward move. After some time, it hit me. Someone or a group of someones that have very deep pockets were on an aggressive buying spree. Worst case scenario, Trump has compromising material on these people.

Who are these people? The Controllers obviously, but seriously, I believe it was the four companies that own everything. This is how the bid-ask, pump-and-dump, scheme works. You sell asset to your targets, with the promise of future riches. You can even point to charts of how it all works. What you don't focus on is that you can lose everything, or that the market isn't really fair. The people who own the most of that asset have an unfair advantage. They usually hype the asset up, and when the price soars, they sell that asset to their victims. The scammers get the money, and the victim gets a worthless asset. When the buying stops, prices plummet and everyone is confused how it happened.

I can't say for sure that the four companies that own everything poured money into the markets at a large rate. But again, mostly the very rich own shares in the stock market now. During the Trump years, the very rich violated the main axiom of the stock market, that they have been trumpeting generations; buy low and sell high. We are in grave danger in this country. All the things that we are fighting about right now are distractions from these idiots trying to hold their massive scam together. They desperately want us to get over Trump and the corona virus, because we are facing a calamity of they're own making. A planned disruption in the markets which has become the crux of the system of slavery. The moment that they flex their muscles, and beat their chest, and we all must fall in line.

The market prices can't continue to rise. Who ever is pumping trillions of dollars into the markets have to run out of money eventually. I'm not talking about Fed policy or any stimulus money. The rich bought up stock shares at a rabid pace during the Trump years. They seem disciplined and united as well. Eventually, someone will start taking profits. Even a fifty percent retracement could be catastrophic. It's inevitable. Now onto the flex of the Controllers.

They trained us to accept that when they lose money, we all suffer. Again, who is losing when the stock prices drop? CEOs, millionaires, and billionaires. Why should it affect anyone else's life? Because these people own everything, and employ 75% of workers. First they will start firing workers, then they'll begin throwing away food, next water and utilities will be shut off, and finally, they begin kicking people out of their homes. These are the rules of the system that we have all implicitly accepted.

All the drama we see unfolding these days are the Controllers freaking out about losing control. People don't want their shit jobs, they hate their shit politicians, no one wants to invest in their stock market, no one wants their shitty fuel, and people are no longer willing to accept the constant abuse their undeserving bosses. For hundreds of years, people have been trying to manage their way out of a scam. You know what we're going to do when the markets plummet right? Simultaneously blame black people while these lazy ass niggas got they're hands out talking about a bailout. You ever wondered how nations get into debt? How many trillions are we going to shovel into the stock market to "save the economy?"

They're freaking out, because it's a tough sell. People are sick of their shit. This is why we still use the black stuff for global fuel. If the markets were truly free, when a loser loses, you kick his ass to the curb. Why in god's name would you gift more money to the richest people in the world? This is a main feature of the system. Everyone has to agree to some level of bullshit. Everyone! The bottom line is, we pay them money, or we all suffer. Then the rich continue to get richer.

As I'm writing this, DHS moved me from my usual shelter, into a hotel in Midtown Manhattan. Though I did contract COVID, they quarantined me six days after my infection date. It's been more than ten days now. I understood right away, why so many of the homeless were sent there when I checked in. Midtown is dead. There are many empty retail spaces, and you can see with your eyes that most of the high end rentals are empty. The hotel we were in is likely in dire straits. And you know what? They're still constructing high rise building right there in Midtown.

I'm gonna predict the future for you. If the government pays the Controllers to stop the pain, they will create a new class of millionaires. One the reflects the diversity of New York City. But they will all have to believe the same nonsense that the controllers believe. We all will need to suffer, so that a few people can experience a good life.

Can we do anything differently? Yes! Realize that we are fucking monkeys! We don't need fucking paper to survive!! If the government really wanted to help, it could simply make enough energy for everyone and give it to it's citizen, such that they can store, use, and trade the energy. The government has the power and the resources to do just that. With enough energy, humans can do whatever they want. For the first time in thousands of years, humans will be free.

Everything will change. Especially the women. They will take down the entire old system themselves. They will be free to unburden themselves with all the sexual assaults that they've endured. They will likely lead the species into the future. They'll have more power over the men, for obvious reasons, than they've had for thousands of years. I might even give bonus energy to all women. We're monkeys! What do you think will happen?

Chapter TEN

BEING SAVED BY THE CREATOR

"To be nobody but yourself in a world which is doing its best, night and day, to make you everybody else – means to fight the hardest battle which any human being can fight; and never stop fighting."

~ *e. e. cummings* ~

LOVE IS NOT THE ANSWER

What does it mean to be 'saved?' I think of it in terms of our modern technology. We are all biological programs, and in addition to who we are, there are other programs running simultaneously inside of us. I believe that it is possible to be saved in the flesh of man. How else could I have remembered being other people? Those folks were saved for some reason. It would be easier to focus on a function that we are all familiar with, that is already saved; Love.

Love is a program, a function, a separate self, that exists apart from who we are, and interjects when it sees fit. I call these interjections moding. There are real questions of causality and free-will when you consider who love is. Love is an ancient program, that is inside of all of us. I can recognize Love in tigers and humming birds. It is the same program, but Love is colored and shaped by each of our individual experiences and knowledge.

Here's the conundrum. The only way Love can connect with the you that you are, is if Love is also you. But Love is older than you. Love is ancient. Love has incredible power over us all. Love has the ability to completely change our perspective. Who then is in control? The real question is, do you care? Usually, people want what Love is offering.

I was a bit different. For a significant portion of my life, I struggled with intense urges to kill people. For most of my life, I was certain that I was a serial killer. The excerpt that I'm going to share is the moment that I had made a breakthrough with my alter ego. I didn't realize until I began conceiving this section of the book, who I had been struggling with. It was Love, and she represents as a female for me. People like me often say that the compulsions feel like being in Love, I'm confirming that it is her.

If I were to guess, those who've suffered extended abuse, from the people who raised them, have a tainted Love program running in the background. For people who are very intelligent, this tainted love sometimes manifests in the desire to target and kill humans. For most other people, they habitually find a way to abuse their offspring in the same way. I'm saying all this to let you know that you're not alone. It's happening to all of us. Also, Love is the number one cause of murder in all of human history. I had a triggering moment. It was after I had promised myself that I'd make $10k per month and focus on building a family. I found myself caught up in another financial fraud.

"I had recently purchased a used Mazda 3 2007 to help me with the real estate. I started to gain weight from all the sitting down, and also I hadn't danced for almost two years. There was a giant dent on the passenger side of the car from a silly accident. I had darted into the Chinese restaurant to get some quick food before getting back to work. Onlookers said an old woman simply backed her car straight through the entire fifty space parking lot and hit only my car, and then drove off. I got my paperwork in order and played phone tag with the insurance company, Lang Insurance. They said that I wasn't covered because I owed them a large bill. I was sitting in my car on my laptop while on the phone with a woman representing Lang Insurance. I was confused.

"'We have all the paperwork here, and it says you owe us a lot of money. I'm sending it to you now.' She said. I opened the document on my computer. 'What's this?' I said. 'That's the agreement you signed.' She said. I received the information on my laptop. 'This isn't my signature. Oh my God, someone forged my signature?' I said. 'No! Nobody forged anything. You are the idiot who signed his name to this deal! Nobody else!' She shouted. 'I'm tired of people complaining about fulfilling their obligations! You are the idiot who made the bad deal, you are the idiot who signed on the dotted line, and you are the one who is responsible for your car not us!'

"What happened next I suppose should be prefaced with what I tried to accomplish over the previous three years. I wanted to become wealthy enough to simply not work, and then focus completely on healing whatever was wrong with me. I'd read a number of books on wealth building. They all say the same thing, money management and investing in things that will produce wealth for you. I was certainly on a budget. I ran the day I purchased my car in my mind. It was all a scam and a lie. According to this woman on the phone, I was over budget by at least $500 per month. That would set me back possibly for many years.

"'Oh my God.' I whispered. 'I'm going to hurt you.' 'No you're not! We have cameras here 24/7 and if you show up you're going to jail!' She threatened. 'Oh my God… I'm going to hurt a lot of people.' I whispered even more quietly. 'I'm tired of stupid people blaming everyone else for their problems! If you come anywhere near us you're going to jail!'

"She shouted, but with some trepidation. 'No. You should call the cops now. I'm parked on east 98th street between Avenue N and Seaview. Oh my God, I forgot that I'm an evil person.' I whispered. 'You are going to go to Jail if you ever come anywhere near me!' She was still angry but I can hear the fear in her voice. 'Listen' I whispered 'I'm extremely patient. If anything out of the ordinary happens please think of me first. You have all of my information on file. Please, remember this. If you aren't going to call the cops I will.' I whispered again.

"'I'm sick and tired of you crazy, stupid people complaining about things they signed!' Then she hung up.'Obviously we have to kill her first. No! Obviously these people have done this before, didn't you here what she said? Oh man, even the entire setup of the dealership is laid out to protect itself from outbursts of anger. The dealership and the insurance office likely has cameras, and the people who do most of the lying are likely hidden until it's time to lie. They would never suspect someone patient. No! She recorded the phone call! Maybe she did, but more than likely the suspect pool will be too large to focus on any one person. No!!' I dialed 911.

"911 where is the emergency?" The operator said.

Me: "I'm on east 98th street in Brooklyn. I'm sitting in my car. Please send officers over to arrest me, I'm going to hurt some people."

Operator: "Is anyone hurt or injured sir?"

Me: "No, not yet but many will be seriously hurt soon. Please pick me up and arrest me."

Operator: "So no crime has been committed sir?"

Me: "That's correct, not yet, but it will be."

Operator: "I'm sorry sir; the Police don't operate in this way. The police only respond to crimes that have already been committed sir."

Me: "I absolutely know that I'm going to seriously hurt some people. There's nothing you can do? You have to wait for me to do it?"

Operator: "That's correct sir."

Me: "That's the dumbest thing I've ever heard. At least you have my voice recorded calling 911. If anything happens and my name comes up, the police will know that it's me."

Operator: "I'm sorry sir, but we only keep 911 recordings for thirty days."

Me: "Oh my god! This is ridiculous; I'm going to hurt someone."

Operator: "Sir, tell me what happened and maybe I can help."

"I'm sure that it wasn't procedure to talk on the phone for twenty minutes for a 911 call, but she did. She listened to me and was genuinely concerned for my wellbeing.

Operator: "I have two options for you sir. I can send some units over to escort you to a mental hospital or you can file a complaint with the Department of Insurance. Which would you prefer?"

Me: "I can't afford a hospital right now; I think maybe filing a complaint could be good for me." She looked up the number and website for the Department of Insurance and wished me luck. She was a very kind woman. I sat in my car for another forty-five minute filling a complaint. When I was done I went home to my room, and closed the door.

"'Nobody will suspect a thing now that you filed a complaint. No I'll be a suspect! A suspect out of hundreds of angry people. I'm a peaceful man. NLP mind tricks don't work on me buddy. I'm a peaceful man. Hey guys, these assholes messed up all of your plans. Somebody should die right? Yeah, they deserve it. Nobody will weep for them. I'm happy with that. No! Look at this, you worked so hard and for what? You're trying to be normal; you maybe want to start a family and now what? I'll work harder! From where your car? Gonna sleep in the car?'

"I was pacing back and forth in my room. 'You know what? We should start with their children! No!! I agree. No! That makes a lot of sense. For a quick profit, these people totally altered the direction of your life. Do you think you have any hope for the future now? The economy is crashing and you have negative cash flow. These people took away the hope of a family from you, we should do the same. Right! An eye for an eye. It's perfect; the suspect pool is too large for anyone to suspect any one person. No!! That's a false equivalence! Hmmm, children are far too protected and people will be on alert. This is wrong. We'll have to stalk each person until I know when the entire family is together and strike.'

"I threw myself onto my bed, lay with my face in the sheets, and spread my arms out. "Lord God. Father in Heaven. If it be your will show me a sign. Please Lord, rescue me." 'I King of Kings and Lord of Lords do decree that you kill those motherfuckers. Hahahaha!' They all laughed. "Please God, this is serious. I know that it isn't my place to ask for more than bread. But you did help me before Lord please." I pleaded. 'Before?! We all know it was one of these jokers giving you visions before. There's no God here, just us. I thought you were dead? After all that you've been through, do you think part of you would just disappear? I've been waiting for just such an occasion. It's only a matter of time until you give in, give up, or give out. I don't want to hurt anyone and I will stop you. Why do you think we spent so much time learning about serial killers? It wasn't because it was an interesting topic. I wanted to find out more about who we are. Now that I know, I realize you will eventually get us caught. You can leave clues if you like, but those people must suffer.' "No!" 'It's only a matter of time.' "That's not what you really want. You want something deeper what is it?" 'NLP isn't going to work.' "I'm not leaving this room until you tell me what you really want!" 'Pointless.'

"A few months prior I had taken a course called "Core Transformation"[6] at the NLP Center of NY. I purchased the book that inspired the course because I couldn't seem to get passed the first level of questioning. For hours I sat with my partner, in the course, as he tried to guide me. According to the course and the book, I'm supposed to feel a deep feeling of Oneness, Peace, or some other wonderful feeling. I sat at my computer and looked up the questions that I needed to proceed. I didn't have the book with me; all my books were in a box somewhere. It was easy enough to find the steps online. 'You're going to try this again?'

"Step 1. Choosing A Part to Work With a) Identify the part you want to work with. We will refer to this as [behavior, feeling or response X] in this script, and you can fill in your experience of this part. b) When, where, and with whom do you have [behavior, feeling or response X]? Write down the answer in a few words. "I want to work with the part of me who wants to kill the people who sold me my car." (I typed this on a blank word document.) Experiencing the Part c) Take a moment to close your eyes, relax and turn within. Mentally step into a specific incident in which [behavior, feeling or response X] occurred. As you are there, relive the incident, and begin to notice your inner experience. You may notice inner pictures, sounds and feelings that go along with [behavior, feeling or response X].

"d) Since you did not consciously choose [behavior, feeling or response X], it's as if a part of you did. You can begin to sense where that part of you lives. Do you feel the feelings most strongly in a certain part of your body? If you hear an inner voice, where is the voice located? If you see inner pictures, where in your personal space do you see them? Gently invite the part into your awareness. If the part is in your body, you may want to put your hand on the area where you sense the part most strongly. This can help you welcome and acknowledge the part." "I feel this part is located in the center of my chest. It feels like a fist clenched really tightly." I wrote. I placed my left hand on my chest and acknowledged that part.

"Receiving and Welcoming the Part e) Receive and welcome this part of you. Even though you don't know what the purpose of this part is, you can begin thanking this part for being there, because you know it has some deeply positive purpose. "Thank you for being there for me. I know you that you have a deep and positive purpose for my life." I said out loud.

"Step 2.Discovering the Purpose/First Intended Outcome a) Ask the part of you that [Xs], What do you want? After asking, notice any image, voice or sound, or feeling that occurs in response. b) Write down the answer you get from the part. This is your first Intended Outcome. Thank the part for letting you know. If you like the parts Intended Outcome, thank it for having this Intended Outcome for you.

"This was always the most challenging step for me. I've done the course, read the book, and sat and talked with myself for hours. I would get no response. This time I was motivated. Whenever I didn't get a response I would reread step 2. I assumed myself a highly visual person and assumed that I would either see an image or maybe even hear a voice. But after doing the same thing over and over I noticed the tight fist in my chest would tremble and get tighter. I took that for step two in exasperation, then went to the next step. But I didn't know how to write down that weird feeling.

"Step 3. Discovering the Outcome Chain a) Ask this part of you, If you have [Intended Outcome from previous step], fully and completely, what do you want, through having that, that's even more important? Write this down. Thank this part for having this Intended Outcome for you. b) Repeat Step 3 until you get to the Core State. Each time you will get a new Intended Outcome and write it down. Each time you ask the question you'll use the new Intended Outcome. I asked repeatedly for quite some time to no avail. I still refused to give up;

"I reran the course in my mind to see if I had missed something. At this part Steve and Rachael added their own terminology to make this step more effective. "Step into [Intended Outcome] fully and completely…" That made sense to me given my outcome was a weird feeling. I had made it a habit to avoid horrible feelings. For the sake of peace I chose to step into it. The first time I stepped into the feeling felt as if my entire body was struck with a truck from every angle. I only allowed myself to experience it for a brief moment.

"My body trembled with fear and pain. I began crying profusely while I stared intently at my almost blank word document. 'I never cry. We haven't cried in so many years. Maybe I'm supposed to do this. I don't like it; it hurts. I must, I'm a peaceful man.' That day, I sat in front of my computer trembling with fear, in agonizing pain, and vomiting tears for at least six hours. I had made up my mind not to move. Eventually my body couldn't take anymore and I passed out in my bed because my body was sore.

"It then became my custom to vomit physical and emotional pain, memories, and tears for at least four hours per day. I say this because it felt as if I was regurgitating things that had already passed. It felt involuntary. When the moment passed, my body was sore and exhausted for passing it. There were times when my eyes ached from vomiting tears. I never knew what would happen each time I'd sit in front of my computer and experience that weird feeling in the middle of my chest. Each time I'd hope that I could get to the next step, but it seemed like there were levels to everything that passed out from me.

"One day I would be furiously angry. One day I'd be lonely. One day I'd be depressed. One day I'd remember memories that I forgot. One day I was surprised, it seems that I had relived at least one beating. It possibly could have been many beatings. After a few hours of vomiting those beatings I could feel the pain all around me so I took off my shirt to see. My arms and back were covered in welts. I don't know how it works, but my body somehow saved beatings that I received and stored it inside of me. Each day was different.

"My roommate at the time, Eva, came to me one day and said "Daniel! Whatchu be doing in your room?" "What do you mean?" I said. "I always hear things coming from your room." Then she started imitating the way I sound while I cried and suffered. I shrugged my shoulders and went to my room. I felt ashamed that she could hear me. 'I really hope she thinks that I'm masturbating.' I thought. After some time had passed, the economy began to collapse, it was winter of 2008. Eventually, there was no work to do in Real Estate. All the banks had seized. I had resigned myself to total economic failure and loowardked for to going back to my family's home in shame. I had no money. I had bills, rent, and a burdensome car. I had no hope, but I took solace knowing that I found a place inside of me that all of my emotions were trapped. I felt that it was all worth it. I had to be pushed to the edge to find out who I truly was; not a killer.""[7]

LIFTING THE BURDEN

For a few years, I was spent hours at a time vomiting out emotions. And as if by magic, my entire financial situation had turned around. I had a couple dozen people working for me, I worked less than ten hours per week, only if I wanted to, and also I was making more than $10k per month. I was dating lots of women, because I thought that's what I was supposed to do, but by the time of the following excerpt, I had begun to lose interest. I was doing individual therapy, and also I was go to ASCA meetings to help as well. Each meeting was very difficult for me, but when I left, it felt as if I had lifted a small burden off of my shoulders.

"I began religiously going to ASCA; it's the only place I fit it. One day the topic was about violence and how the survivors, the group, tend to repeat it on ourselves and others. In usual fashion, I didn't want to talk, and wrestled with myself about sharing. One gentleman inspired me. Here was a professional man, who is likely a master in his field. But here in this room he struggled to get the words out. His body was totally tensed and frozen in an awkward position. His courage to share such dramatic and shameful things was inspiring and terrifying. After the group gave him positive feedback on his share, I had to go next. I raised my hand.

"'Hey, I'm Daniel Gray.' I said. 'Hi Daniel' they said back. 'It always seems that the topic that we discuss here is exactly what I need to talk about.' I said while we were sitting in a circle in one of the classrooms at the Children's Aid Society. I was sitting in a tiny chair by a tiny desk flanked by a water painting easel. I can only imagine the contorted position of my body, but my head I remember. My eyes were shut because I could feel tears about to come. Also, my head was turned as far right as I could turn it and slightly tilted toward the ceiling. I let out a breath and spoke extremely slow in almost a whisper.

"'I think I'm killer. The only thing that I seem to want is to hurt people. I don't want sex, I don't want money, I don't dream about anything except killing people. I spent my whole life trying to avoid the only thing

I have any passion about. I hired a maid to live with me for two reasons. Firstly, because for some reason I have panics attack if I go into the kitchen. The second reason was a prophylactic measure; I wouldn't have a good alibi. I'm tired of calling the cops on myself. I don't want anyone to live with me, but I didn't want to lose control one day. I recently fired her when she got on my nerves and I wanted to kill her.'

"I got choked up and couldn't talk anymore. 'That's it. I don't need any more time.' 'Thanks Daniel' said the co-facilitator. 'Would you care for any positive feedback?' I shook my head yes. One by one they supported me. I don't think that I had ever been so ashamed in my life. But the group understood who I really was. Some praised me for my courage for sharing. Others sympathized with the various places in the home that we were abused, and that it was okay to be afraid of it. Others reminded me that this violence never belonged to me. They all let me know that it was okay to feel how I feel. It was one of the most liberating moments of my life. The next few months I felt free and wonderful. I wasn't afraid that I would hurt anyone."

LIBERATING LOVE

This next moment, I didn't understand until many years later. Whenever I hold onto a feeling long enough, that feeling rewards me in some way. They all do it as an appreciation for the patience. Or more precisely, that feeling eventually returns to the source, and it is pleasurable. I had been focusing on the spot where all the pain was for a number of years, the change at the end was quite dramatic. It was so dramatic I was stricken with debilitating depression at the end of it.

It's when I decided to drop everything and sit at a beach in the Dominican Republic. In DR I released all of the terror I had stored up in my body. That too ended in a fascinating reward. Looking back now, it was Love telling me that she was cleansed. I now know that I am Love, and she is me. Although, I'm not her, and her power is her own.

In this excerpt, I was having trouble with my landlord at the time. Actually, I can't think of a time when a landlord didn't demand something extra, even though I paid my rent. This is how it is in America.

"I spent most of my time alone wondering what I would be doing next and where I was going to live. It was all beginning to seem pointless. Then my friend Dulce Secreta gave me one of her monthly visits. We went out for diner and talked. I don't think I was very much fun while we ate. We then came back to my apartment and talked for a while in the living room. Then we ended up in the bedroom; she asked to spend the night. I changed into some shorts and a t-shirt. She just took all her clothes off and got into bed. She went to one side of my queen-sized bed and made sure not to touch me.

Dulce: "How's the court case coming Danny?" She asked as she lay on her side. She was holding her head up with her left hand.

Me: "It's over." I said lying on my back, with my hands to my side, and staring blankly at the ceiling.

Dulce: "What happened?"

Me: "Apparently, there are strict protections in New York for buildings that have at least five units. Anything less, basically the landlord can do whatever they want."

Dulce: "What? That doesn't make sense. Most of the city is less than five units!"

Me: "I know. It's depressing."

Dulce: "But how can the Landlord rent you a place with all these problems and refuse to fix it? That's fraud!"

Me: "I know." I said blankly.

Dulce: "Did you call 311?"

Me: "Yes."

Dulce: "And what happened!?"

Me: "The city sent an inspector within a week and issued the Landlord a fine for all the violations. But the guy who was supposed to inspect the boiler didn't show up for six months."

Dulce: "Six months! It's the summer time now! That's crazy. What did he do when he got here?"

Me: "Well, the landlord wouldn't open the door for him. Her beauty salon was open, but she didn't give anyone permission to let him in. She spoke to him on the phone and said that she'd be by in ten minutes. After the first hour, the inspector said he would wait because I seemed like a nice guy. He waited outside for three and a half hours until she finally let him in. He gave them a fine for something. I'm not allowed to see what it is they were fined for."

Dulce: "Aren't you in court with them now? The court is supposed to make them fix the problems in the apartment."

Me: "We had a signed agreement; if I paid all the back rent then they would fix all the problems. I wrote the check and they did nothing. The court sent two different inspectors and everything was still the same. They were arguing that I wouldn't let them in, but the court inspectors were there to make sure that I opened the door. They didn't even bother to show up. I think the judge was incredibly surprised that I paid the bill. In the end, I was given three months to leave. I'm going to live out my security, my last month, and the judge gave me an extra month for free."

Dulce: "See! This is why I don't want to deal with any tenants. It's nothing but problems."

Me: "But you have a single family house, who could you rent to?"

Dulce: "I could rent the basement out. It's almost finished. I would consider it if I could make a separate entrance for them."

Me: "Alright"

Dulce: "Are you still in court with them?"

Me: "Not for the apartment. But I'm taking them to small claims. I'm going to do three different cases."

Dulce: "What? What are you taking them to small claims for?"

Me: "Firstly, I'm going to sue them for my gas bills. I added them up and they total more than five thousand dollars. My stove hasn't worked in almost eight months and the heat has never worked. I have proof that I complained to them about it. They never once sent a qualified person to repair the issues. Next I'm going to sue them for lost income during the times when it was ice cold in my apartment. I work from home and I did in fact lose quite a bit of cash during the winter. Some of the losses just happened, but some of it was due to my inability to work in the cold and under stress. The third case will be the legal fees that I accrued from a duplicate case that they took me to court for."

Dulce: "A duplicate case?"

Me: "Yes. First the wife took me to court, then when the case was settled the husband filed the very same claim. They are both on the deed. I was tired of going to court. So I hired a lawyer. That was an additional fifteen hundred dollars. I could do a civil case and bundle it all together, but it's cheaper and easier for me to just go one by one. Plus extending it out like this will help my body learn to choose a path other than violence."

Dulce: "Choose a path other than violence? What are you talking about Danny?"

Me: "I want to lead a peaceful life. I want my body to know that violence isn't always necessary."

Dulce: "You're not violent Danny."

Me: "Yes I am."

Dulce: "No you're not Danny. I've known you for years now, I would know if you're violent. I'm a good judge of people."

Me: "Then you misjudged me."

Dulce: "Okay! Tell me how you are so violent!" She said with a smile on her face.

Me: "I have an overwhelming desire to go to the Landlord's home and burn it down. Every part of me agrees that it's fair to do." Dulce started laughing. "I need to spread out the cases because I have infinite patience once I've made up my mind. If anyone suspects arson I would be the first person to come to mind." Dulce laughed even harder. I turned my head and told her plainly, "I'm serious. It isn't funny."

Dulce: "Okay, Okay, Okay, I'm sorry Danny. Come on Danny. Everyone has bad thoughts every now and then."

Me: "I know myself. I don't want to take any chances. Honestly, I could care less about the money. I doubt they will ever pay. I'll tell you when I decided that I must take them to court. Both fire escape windows were jammed shut and they didn't have window guards on the windows. You need window guards if you have a child living with you. They received a big fine for that. The landlord's granddaughter came with some contractors to fix these things. When the contractors finished it was only the granddaughter and her younger cousin The she began to harass and fuck with me. She started taking pictures of my stuff. I could feel my body moving to destroy her. The only thought that I had in my mind was to stab her in the neck. Her cousin was bigger than me, but it's doubtful that he had as many fights as I had. I wanted to break his leg then rip his face off. Then I would be able to stand over that annoying bitch as her last moments on this planet would be in utter terror."

Dulce: "So what happened Danny?"

Me: "I called the cops. I'm tired of calling the cops on myself. My body needs to know that there is always another way."

Dulce: "I don't care what you say Danny. I know you and I know you would never hurt anyone!" I didn't respond and continued to stare at the ceiling. "How long you have till you have to move?"

Me: "I have about six weeks."

Dulce: "Did you find someplace yet?"

Me: "I found a few places that I really like, but people don't want me because I had a court case and also I forgot to pay two of my credit cards last month. I was really down and just forgot. That combined with I'm a real estate agent in the worst time for real estate agents makes me very unattractive."

Dulce: "You think grandma will give you an apartment?"

Me: "She offered me my old apartment back, but I don't want to go back into that same situation. It feels like no matter what I do I'll be back there."

Dulce: "If you want Danny, you can stay with me. The basement is almost finished. You'll have your own private space, and if you want you can bring other girls there. I'll even cook for you every day. You don't even have to pay me. Only one condition."

Me: "What?"

Dulce: "You have to let me have sex with you whenever I want." She said with a devilish grin. I shook my head 'no' while continuing to stare at the ceiling. "Are you gay Danny?" She said with a smirk.

Me: "No!"

Dulce: "Come on Danny. You can tell me. We're friends. I won't be mad if you are." She chuckled.

Me: "No! I find men utterly repulsive. Stop asking me that!" I told her angrily.

Dulce: "You know I'm just messin with you Danny right? But if you are gay that's okay too." She continued to smile. I rolled my eyes in disgust. "I'm just messing with you Danny." Dulce said as she lay down in the bed almost mirroring my position. We were both quiet for a moment until I decided to ask her a question.

Me: "What are you doing here Dulce?"

Dulce: "What do you mean?"

Me: "I mean I've known you for years and no matter what I say or do you still come back. I told you that I don't want to have sex and for a while now you just show up once per month, get naked, wait until I stop shaking and then have sex with me."

Dulce: "You know how I feel about you Danny. I want you all to myself, but you just aren't ready for that yet. And you know what? You make me so angry Danny! I tell you how I feel and…" She turned her face into the pillow and began banging her fists on the bed. She was saying something, but it was unintelligible. Then she lifted her head up and said "I want to yell and scream at you, but we aren't even talking. You don't even call me. Danny why you don't call me?" I shrugged my shoulders. She began to bang her fist and yell into the pillows again. She turned over and said "I can't stay mad at you too long. Then I realize 'oh man I need Danny inside of me.' You know I love your cock right?" I shrugged my shoulders again. "Oh my god! You don't have to do nothing Danny. You need too to put it in and hold it right there." She motioned with her hands and legs what she wanted. "Ahhh! That's all I need!" I didn't pay any attention to her.

"I was confused about my situation and a realized that Dulce is a psychologist so I asked her "What do you think is wrong with me?"

Dulce: "Nothing is wrong with you Danny!"

Me: "Then why don't I want you to touch me?"

Dulce: "Listen Danny you are just like all guys. You're just a little more extreme. But that's okay."

Me: "Alright" I told her.

"I didn't feel like I was the same as other guys. I just assumed that Dulce just didn't know me well enough. Usually, I would just take a nap and a few hours later I would wake up and realize that I have a gorgeous woman in my bed then we would have sex. This time I decided that I wouldn't sleep. I was going to wait so I can experience the moment when the change happens. 'If I could notice what changes maybe I repeat it whenever I want.' I told myself. I laid in place for some time and nothing changed. So to speed the process up I imagined that Dulce was touching my arm. I laid in bed trembling for hours waiting for the moment that I realized that I actually do want her to touch me. Dulce didn't feel the trembling because I had a Tempur-Pedic mattress.

"Since just imagining her touch me wasn't doing anything, I decided to give future pulling another shot. I thought it would be a much lighter lift to figure out what happens when I realize that I want to be with this woman. I replayed over and over the same stories in my mind, some I made up, and some were actual history; all the while imagining Dulce touching me. It was very convenient that the story would end only a few hours in the future; when I realize that I'm no longer afraid.

"Then the most amazing thing happened. A small Rosa Amarilla began to dance above the middle of my chest. (Where the clenched fist was.) She was wearing a long bright flowing dress. It looks like modern dance was what she was doing. When she twirled her long beautiful hair glided along with her dress. She pranced and moved, but seemed to remain in the center of my chest. I can honestly say that this was the happiest that I've been in a long time and possibly my entire life. I turned over and looked at Dulce and I couldn't believe my eyes. She was so sexy and I became aroused. I slowly scanned her body and realized 'Oh my god! She's exactly what I want!' I didn't touch her though. I was far more excited about Rose dancing for me. It made me happy, and I stayed awake as much as I could, experiencing Rose dancing for me.

"In the morning, I felt the same. Dulce was even sexier in the light. I wanted her so bad I could tear her clothes off. I'm sure she would've liked that, but I wanted to get back to watching Rose. I gave Dulce a kiss and she left. Colors seemed brighter. Everything seemed to be alright. Even the beef that I had with my landlord seemed unimportant. 'A little Rosa had been inside of me all this time? How come I didn't feel this before? I don't know?' I looked outside my window and it seemed like an entire new world. I rushed outside to experience it. The buildings were beautiful, the people seemed wonderful, and I bought a piece of fruit… it was so delicious. I began to debate with myself.

"On the one hand I knew with all my being Rose is supposed to be in my life. On the other hand, I promised Rose years ago that I would never call her again. I finally reasoned that a Facebook message would keep me honest. A mutual friend had us both tagged in a photo from when we were children. My first message I think I said something like "I have a piece of you inside of me" and "where ever you are in this world I want you in my life." I don't remember all of it. The next day she emailed back and inquired what made me realize these things. I then proceeded to write a long letter about all the things I've tried to feel normal. Then finally, I think I realized that I cared deeply for her. I was somewhat anxious the entire day. I was afraid of being rejected. I wasn't very kind to Rose in the past. When I woke up the next morning, all the feelings were gone. I was frustrated and angry. Every time I tried to get back to that beautiful place I could feel my heart clench tightly and my body quake fiercely.

"Rose did write back. All that I remember from her letter was that she moved and has a child. That much I knew from her Facebook profile. The words were all jumbled when I tried to read it and it just made me angrier. I promised myself that I wouldn't write Rose back until I figured out what was going on. Reaching out then angrily hurting her is simply abuse, and I didn't want to abuse anyone. And I didn't want to hurt Rose anymore.[8]"

BEING SAVED

What happened next, is what I've already touched on, in this book. I spent most of my life ignoring how I felt, then I committed myself to accepting my feelings. The next thing that I had stored inside me was a lifetime of terror. I spent almost six months, sitting on a beach in the Dominican Republic, having a panic attack. For twelve to sixteen hours daily, I allowed myself to be terrified. Again, at the end, something amazing happened. It was like the rest of me was trying to encourage me to continue further.

When I returned to the US, I was broke, but enlightened. Then I committed myself to doing anything the ones inside me wants to do, but with rules. I would always tell the truth, no laws will be broken, and I have to be safe. And because I've struggled most of my life with abuse, I promised to protect myself whenever anyone would abuse me. Unfortunately for me, these rules are antagonistic to the system of control that we live under. Everyone must accept some level of lies or abuse.

The next thing that welled up, from inside me, was a lifetime of shame. It was so disgusting, I didn't know what to do with it. Even though it hurt, the ones inside suggested I write down all of my shame. I was filled with agonizing fear sending my manuscript out to others. I know it wasn't well written.

I just felt like I was supposed to share it. Almost two years after writing it, I self published it on Amazon. It was one of the most terrifying things that I'd ever done. To date, I had one download. Looking back, I can say that it was worth it. I didn't need that shame anymore. It never belonged to me.

After I wrote "Violent Tremors," I was lonely, horny, and also didn't want anyone touching me. I was conflicted, and the only thing that all inside agreed was for me to write "Why Women Cheat." For many reasons, writing that book liberated me. I haven't been with a woman in ten years, and I'm okay with that.

What I've learned through the patient release of pain from the inside is that now, I'm like the rest of them. There are other living programs that exist inside of all of us, that is in all life. I call these saved programs. They govern all types of living functions known and unknown. The closer you get to 'factory settings,' the more access you'll have with the rest of your mind and body. These other living programs, are alive, they're fundamentally you, and also simultaneously not you. The more you are like them, the easier it is to hear them speak.

They are saved programs. Ones that the Creator found worthy. How can you be saved? Am I saved? It was enlightening to connect to humans who have long passed. I don't believe in reincarnation. I'm not these people reborn, but I am them in the same way that I am you. We are one being, and I believe that this being saves the functions it finds worthy.

Looking back, the self that I had struggled with for so long was Love herself. She wanted me to kill. She was full of pain, terror, and shame. In the end, what I learned from Core Transformation was right. She did have a positive intention for me. She led me to the Creator. She's resting now, and free to connect with me as she chooses. So how to be saved?

This my sound familiar to others touched by the Creator. Firstly, always tell the truth. When you touch a hot surface, you get a signal that says hot right? You're pain receptors exist, they are alive, and their not you. Apart from genetic anomalies, the ones inside are constantly shouting the truth. The system the Controllers have us living under forces us all to accept some level of lies or abuse. Which fundamentally disconnects us from who we are as a species.

Next, you have to follow all of the laws. While there are many unjust laws, I won't touch on this. Let's just focus on the just ones. Following the law is a logical consequence of always telling the truth. I will lose every argument because I would snitch on myself the instant anyone asks me if I did anything wrong. Another reason I set the rule of following all of the laws, is because sometimes the ones inside completely take over the body and put me to sleep.

Learned people call it an autonomic response. I wish to challenge that. Other selves phase in and out of who we are all of the time. People would 'wake up' after the self who wished to take over is finished what it was doing. So the transition is seamless, they remind you why they had to do it. Their memories of events, for the time that you were asleep are transfered to you. Some people go with it, some rationalize, and some struggle with what happened. I accept me for who I am, and if one of me needs to take control, I can sit back and watch. Breaking the law is strictly off limits, and it turns out, that's how they are naturally.

Finally, your emotions are a divining rod. Trust them, they are your truth. A fundamental feature of the system that we live under, is that everyone must accept some level of discomfort. Everyone must, on some level, accept that what they feel isn't what they feel. It is deliberate and sinister. If you are telling the truth, and following the laws, then your feelings will invariably lead you down a singular path. Sometimes you'll have conflicting feelings. They are both your path, and it is up to you to follow them both. If you need help, ask a real professional with lots of letters after their names.

If you do all of this, I can't say for sure that you'll be saved by the Creator. But I can tell you that being like the rest of me is liberating. I must warn you though. In the world we live in now, if you decide to only tell the truth, follow all the laws, and trust you feelings, then you'll be homeless and working as a security guard as I am. I think it's time we made a new world.

Chapter ELEVEN

SUMMARY OF THE SYSTEM AND THE FUTURE OF LIFE

"The control of information is something the elite always does, particularly in a despotic form of government. Information, knowledge, is power. If you can control information, you can control people."

~ *Tom Clancy* ~

With all that I've been through, and the wonderful things that I've discovered, I have a deep profound unshakable sadness. The system of control is everywhere, and pretends that it doesn't exist. The primary function of the system is pain. This is why it's so important to pretend you enjoy the pain, or that it doesn't affect you. Then with lies and terror, you have to accept that the pain is coming from somewhere else. Or better yet, the pain you feel is your own fault.

The system was designed to fool and control self-aware, hairless monkeys. As a species, we had a problem with god-kings. They owned everything, and everyone else lived at the pleasure of the god-king. Along the way, ownership of everything was stripped from royalty and wealthy businessmen took control of the means of production. This is what it is now. A handful of rich people literally own everything, and the rest of us smucks need to work for them to survive. It would be quite fascinating going through the entire history of how we got here. The people who control this place very much would like you to not know anything about history. This is because the pattern itself repeats again and again. We'll touch on that briefly, here at the end.

It's important that no one questions why a handful of people own everything. So they divide the populace by creating a scapegoat class. The two groups should be easy to distinguish. In America, it's mostly done by race and sex. Then you force all the monkeys to perform tasks in order to survive. Instead of delivering exactly the things they need for survival, they get paid in the currency that is also dominated by the Controllers. No matter what, the Controllers have to come out ahead in money. In this system of forced disparity, the ones who has the most currency can effectively tilt any part of the system they want.

Most of the money spent, must go the Controllers. There is a problem. If money is always flowing in one direction, then it will eventually lead to an economic crash. I tried to speak on this, in my book "Follow the Money." This is a basic tenet of the system. Since we all live and work for currency, if there's no currency, then we can't survive. At some point, the Controllers have all the money, and everyone else is paper starved. This is the time when the Controllers reorganize society, in the image of their choosing. Then, and only then do they release currency.

But people are suffering, and struggling in the meantime right? Why don't they just rebel? During these periods, they blame all of the problems on the scapegoat class. This class of people who are purposely kept out of the flow of wealth, and also financially exploited in multiple ways. The scapegoats are politically and economically defenseless. In fact, I would say that whenever the Controllers are threatened, they release the Mad Ones to abuse the Scapegoats.

I spoke about these monkeys from different angles throughout this book. But it's important to recall that we are animals of this earth, and the same function exists in all species. When you convince any group of animals that there isn't enough resources for all, they will invariably fight over the resources. They will create pecking orders amongst themselves and enforce that order. For humans, it isn't just that one side has more resources than the other. One side has the exclusive right to break the law against the other, and get away with it. This is a vital part of the system, and it must be accepted.

How do they command the Mad Ones? I did my best not to be as technical as I was in "Follow the Money," but it's important to know how your money works. Let's imagine you live in a town of four people and only one dollar. Each person supplies what the others need, and they exchange the single dollar in return for goods and services. Though it's only one dollar, it has an economic impact of four dollars per cycle. For simplicity sake, let's say someone loaned one of these four people one more dollar, what would happen? Prices would go up. This is what we're facing right now. Rampant inflation. And the Federal Reserve is about to raise interest rates. Presumably to slow down lending.

Here's the thing. Increasing the interest rates assumes that the markets are altruistic. In that same example with the four people, the same radical increase in inflation would happen the same way if any of the four people raised their prices. If one did, then they all would have to. Even if there was still only one dollar in the whole world.

Here are the facts. A handful of people literally own most means of production in this world. These very same people commands a great deal of wealth. Inflation and scarcity sometimes happens naturally. But consider for a moment, that maybe it's done on purpose. The rich can starve any location it wants of currency. In addition to that, they can simultaneously raise the prices. These are all true things. If you want to trust that these people have your best interests in mind, then I can't help you.

Starving locations of currency and raising prices is something that I believe they've done for thousands of years. The Mad Ones blindly follow their commands regardless of the risks. In their minds, they are the true chosen ones, and that they must come out on top. During these times of stress, the Mad Ones are meant to add more stress, and distract from what the Controllers are doing.

Earlier in the book, I implied the Controllers had a hand in the Vandals sacking of Rome, and Catholic oppression. If everyone is subject to the same system, the people with the most wealth can create any movement, or religion. I'm not trying to offend people's faith. I want you to see the pattern. Just after the fall of the Bronze Age, and the Greek Dark Ages, two mortal and formidable enemies fought over something stupid. The Vandals were mad that the Catholics dropped the commandment about idolatry. For those of you who think the Controllers have your back, what do you think happened to the Vandals? Once the Catholic Church solidified power, the Vandals literally just disappeared. I suspect the money stopped flowing, and they raised prices on them.

What about Islam? It's fascinating that Islam has some Catholic roots, but mainly, Islam was for hundreds of years the main adversary for Catholicism. Then one day, they stopped being a threat. I know I'm being very broad, I'm just saying that it rhymes again and again. Weren't we on the brink of nuclear holocaust? Wasn't the Communist Manifesto secretly paid for by a rich people, for a revolution that had already started? It was a bullshit fight. None of the people itching to fight can even tell the difference between capitalism and communism. Also, neither of these systems have every truly existed. But there was a global threat because of it? Finally, Russia just collapsed!? They cut off the flow of money and raised prices.

Where do I get my information from? We are the same people that existed ten thousand years ago. They are playing the same game right before our eyes. Thanks to Donald Trump, people have fought back on all the other stupid fights that they wanted to pick. Now they are left with critical race theory and vaccine mandates. These aren't peaceful protests, they are threats of terrorism. The people in the chosen class are afraid of losing their imaginary position. The Controllers are actively trying to starve people of currency. I can see it all around me. Here in America, when prices go up, the Mad Ones go out and buy everything else up, to add more pain. The point is the pain.

They will scream and be violent until there is compliance with the Controller's wishes. These fights are just as idiotic as fighting over the second commandment. It is really about power. With so many lies, it's hard to know who's in control. The people with the most money are the ones calling the shots. The system is powered by limited currency, and limited goods and services.

THE POINT OF THE SYSTEM

Anthropologically speaking, this entire system of slavery is of our own making. Our species is one being. There were many times in the past where we wouldn't have made it as a species if not for guidance from within. The system is underhanded trickery, but it's our underhanded trickery. You can remember it if you want to.

Imagine you were teleported back to the fall of the bronze age, knowing all that you know now. What would you do to protect the species? A handful of humans claimed divine right over large swaths of land. They claim dominion over all living things in their domain. Humans suffered all manner of abuse back then. How would you defend yourself in such a situation? Would you become a royal worshiper?

The biggest problem with the Egyptian empire was that they heavily relied on thermo-acoustics for all of their work. After thousands of years, and felling scores of trees to provide the heat to power their giant musical instruments. Egypt had become a desert, and likely stopped using the pyramids for sound generation. The issues facing ancient Egypt are exactly what we are facing now. We're destroying our environment to produce power. Egypt was a threat to life, and we dealt with them harshly.

At some time in the past, knowledge of how to exploit human beings became aware to some. People fed a constant diet of lies, wine, and meat became mindless fighters. Willing to sacrifice themselves for what apparently is something laughably ridiculous. What a blessing the Trump years have been. The Controllers are under threat and they sent out there sleeping terrorist force.

Laugh them off at your own peril. This is the same force that destroyed the Egyptian and Roman Empires. It's the same puzzling confusion that slaughtered the natives of this country. It seems bizarre that millions of Americans would refuse the vaccine, and even more strange that some are incredibly violent. It is a confusion technique by the Controllers. What you have are monkeys challenging you for supremacy, the bullshit reason of the moment is irrelevant. If you respond to that challenge with reason, you've lost. Like all monkeys who don't get their asses whoopped for acting a fool, they come back and escalate. The populace is paralyzed with fear, because they fear future attacks; terrorism.

If you're wondering how to fix this? Things have gone too far for a coming together. Which is also another point of group crimes. When so many have committed crimes, it's impossible to punish everyone. What's the point of the system? Population control. Genocide. Trump gave the signal that the time is now, here in America. Others are doing the same elsewhere. For those in control, it's time for a culling of humans. Given that it seems the Controllers are under threat, the culling itself could be the largest in human history. It might be the only way to regain control of the populace.

People keep calling what's happening in America creeping fascism. Wrong, it's been fascism for millions of people here. You're just shocked that it's happening to you for the first time. The terrorism itself varies in different times and locations. Let me describe the terrorist that I've interacted with multiple times in this country. It's someone who self appointed themselves defenders of their specific realm. Regardless if they have actual power or not. If they accost you and start screaming gibberish, it's literally your job to supplicate and not make any sudden movements. If you do, then they have the right to dramatically escalate. These are the rules for some reason.

When I traveled the country teaching chess, I was confronted by such an individual a few times. When they scream at me "Where are you going?!" I usually tell them of the four star hotel that I was staying. Then their entire demeanor changed. They became welcoming and cordial, as if they have any relation to that giant hotel. I understood the terrorism of this place decades ago. Back then, I just tried to avoid it as much as possible. When the company switched to cheaper hotels, they lost most of the black and brown chess teachers from New York City. Can you imagine that same scenario, accept now, I'm staying at cheap motel? Drug dealer right?

I hate to say it, but all those people that recently were murdered, the issue at hand is they were supposed stand still and take the abuse. Ahmad Arbery's big failing was that he ran. The man in the Rittenhouse case died because he went for the gun. There's a whole series of unspoken rules that people like me have been living under. But also, recently, the terrorism has been escalating. To a fever pitch.

The point of the system is to kill people. Deaths come through war, famine, and genocide. What it looks like to me, is that the world is setting itself up to begin a culling. It isn't happening organically. It's well organized and funded. In fact, some of the richest people in the world are among the handful of people directing these schemes. This is how we 'fight' as a species. A hierarchy is created, and all not in the hierarchy are expendable. This is why I believe we confused our languages ages ago, to protect genetic diversity.

Why pretend that a third of this country doesn't wants me suffering, subjugated, or dead. You should take a page out of their own book and call it what it is? Generational tribalism. Which will descend into full blown terrorism as the tribe in power slowly loses favor. As long as these monkeys think that everything is limited, they will attack anything that threatens the hierarchy. Anything. Regardless of how ridiculous sounding.

Thus we now have people threatening terrorism over Critical Race Theory. Nobody cares about CRT, the second commandment, or any of the bogus reasons given in the past. It's telling that they have difficulty just blaming black people. It is a sign of weakness, and they know it. It actually is economic anxiety, and they've been told their entire lives that the blacks are gonna try and take their stuff. Don't bother with the logic of the thing they are screaming about. They are monkeys fighting over the resources that they believe are limited.

One of the stupidest debates that almost killed everyone was capitalism versus communism. In reality, it was two different tribes of monkeys fighting for supremacy, in a limited resource environment. They both did the same things, and unfortunately history is written by the victors. Both sides gave business free reign, oppressed women, and minorities, and elevated a tribe of monkeys to prominence. Americans like to say that our system was superior. Or maybe terrorist businessmen orchestrated a financial collapse to end the dangerous standoff, after the American superpower was established.

You see the real sinister thing about banning books and CRT, is that you don't see the history that these folks, behind the scenes, are erasing. One glaring thing that I noticed, working as a substitute teacher, are the reasons why colonists fled Europe to come to America. I remember when I was in middle school, we had to list the reasons why the colonists left civilization to live in a jungle. After looking at the American history books of dozens of schools, the reasons for leaving Europe are absent. What were the reasons? Religious intolerance, no social mobility, and the poor had to put up with lots of unfair taxes and laws. The thing that people especially hated, was the law enforcement had the right to break the law against the people at the bottom.

It makes sense why it would be absent from modern history books. At least the books that I've read. It was terrifying to me, long before Trump rose to power. Why scrub this from books, if folks in power weren't planning to repeat history? It's fascinating how it all repeats. Either we escape, in the same way the colonists did, or I suspect there will be a massive culling.

MONOPOLY PYRAMID

In a very real sense, "The Market" doesn't exist. In addition, it isn't and has never been "free." There's trade and then there's the markets. They may seem related, but what we call the markets are nothing more than a plethora of nesting dolls of monopolies. The markets were created to extract wealth from a location and gift it to another. Most of that wealth flows to the Controllers. The way I'm describing it, makes it sound like a scam. The precise term is con, or confidence scam. Belief is an important part of making it real. This is the system of slavery that we've all been living under for hundreds, possibly thousands of years.

The market is divided into sectors, then into organizations, and extends all the way down to the local deli. At each level, it's ultimately controlled by a single person. This person has the ultimate say on the prices of goods and services. It's their job to squeeze as much currency as they can out of their local economy. If for any reason these individuals don't make profits, it's not only their right to close up shop, it's encouraged. In this way, if there is a problem anywhere in the system, it can all come crashing down.

What I'm describing may ring true for many of you. I won't waste my time talking about the myriad abuses of the system. I wrote my previous book "Follow the Money" because I was freaking out that entire system was about to crash, and I posited some things we can do to fix the obvious ways it would all coming crashing down. It's been seven years since I published my book, and we seem to be petering on. Was I wrong? Fundamentally, yes. There are people who control the entire system, because their ancestors created it with trickery and blood. They are and have always been terrorists. The Controllers are holding the scam together with duck tape and shoe-strings.

People keep asking how are terrorists created. They wonder what is it about Trump that makes people 'follow' him. Then there are people constantly trying to tell everyone to love the talentless losers at the top. Elon Musk recently bemoaned people having animosity towards helpless billionaires. Actually, the opposite is true. As a species, we've been worshiping these simpletons for generations. All of our superheros are who? Billionaires, doctors, lawyers, soldiers, and scientists. By some magical properties, these are the only people who can combat 'evil.'

It's not a coincidence that Hitler was a soldier. Nor is it weird that the Bin Laden family are billionaires. The creation of an Iron Rod Savior is thematic by now. Take away something a group already had, and then make them suffer. The system already divides people into haves and have nots. If you take anything away from the haves they will want to fight. Do you know why? Because they are fucking monkeys! That's exactly what would happen when take things away from monkeys. Those monkeys will be looking for an Iron Rod Saviour to reestablish their position. Usually, their target is the distraction group that was always there. For those of you who are mad that I'm comparing Trump to Bin Laden, ask yourself what's the difference? Actually, Bin Laden was a far more compelling figure. He was attractive, literate, a great orator, and actually risked his life fighting for his people in an actual war.

Some of you are reading this and thinking I'm being hyperbolic. I understand how you feel. It's a terrifying thing to think that the richest and most powerful people on the planet are completely controlling our lives. Let's look at some examples of all the ways the entire system can come crashing down and the terrorism that we all must suffer through, because these lazy ass simpletons want us all to pretend that they are supposed to be in charge. Let's consider sugar.

There is a massive history of sugar monopolies in the United States. In a way, we did something about it, but not really. I'm not going to list names or deeds, let's just focus on what we all know exists. There exists scores of places where brown people's labor are exploited, and there exists a handful of mediocre simpletons making most of the profits while doing none of the work. These folks are usually old, inbred, crusty ass white dudes. So where's the terrorism?

In 2021, NASA awarded team Ssweet, short for Space-Sugar with Electrochemical Energy Technology, $750,000 for successfully converting carbon dioxide and water into sugar. Yes, please, take a break and look them up. When I heard that I began to freak out. There is an entire system of shitty control, such that a handful of assholes get all of the benefits and does none of the work. A handful of monkeys who have no talent and their entire fortune was gifted to them by their loser parents. They control the entire sugar market. Even with all the subsidies the US government is shelling out to combat the monopoly. What do you think happens when folks make their own sugar with carbon dioxide, water, and energy? Terrorism?

If you don't expect terrorism, it's because you believe these folks are inherently good somehow. These are the folks that exploited labor all around the world. They lined the pockets of corrupt politicians. If people started making their own sugar, the system would necessarily attack those people in every way possible. Because if the sugar market collapses, the entire market may collapse. There would be revolutions all around the world, the corrupt will be exposed as the money dries up, and the lawless implications will all lead to the top. Those folks will fight to the death to keep their undeserved sugar profits.

How about a different industry, starch? It's essentially the same as sugar chemically. Sugar has one molecule of glucose and one molecule of fructose. Starches on the other hand contain between 300 to 1,000 glucose molecules chained together. I can write a whole bunch about the agriculture monopolies. Sure, it sucks. But fundamentally, it doesn't matter. What you've got to understand is that the system was designed to be interconnected and completely shaky. When one thing falls, it all comes crashing down.

In 2021, researchers at Chinese Academy of Sciences developed a way to artificially create starch from carbon dioxide and water, in the lab. Obviously, if you can make it in the lab with electricity, it makes holding vast farmland all around the world worthless. I bet you didn't even hear of this had you? If humans start making their own starch with water and carbon dioxide, then the entire system comes down. I wouldn't be surprised to find out that agricultural billionaires funded the insurrection on January 6th. Imagine if you were an asshole simpleton with no discernible talent, who's been kicking sand in peoples' faces for your entire life. Then all of a sudden, nobody needs any of your shit. There are scores of terrorist shits, who got rich off of starch and don't own a pair of dirty shoes. They know that they are above others, and no one corrected them their entire lives.

The market isn't free. If it were, everyone all around the world would be eating synthesized starch. In fact, I've been saying that global warming is a scam. It is a problem, but it's the terrorists that's holding everyone else back. They are the ones that caused the problem. We are supposed to beg them and pay them to fix the problem that they created. Let solve global warming in a few sentences.

The world is warming because there is too much carbon-dioxide in the air. We can easily pull the CO2 from the air, but no one knows where we can store it. Glucose contains six carbon atoms, and with simple math, a single starch molecule can contain up to six thousand carbon atoms. The poorest place in the world is Somalia. There is currently a famine there. We can feed everyone in Somalia the starch, and have them store the carbon in their ass. In fact, we can keep feeding them until they're all fat! No more global warming.

The market is precisely the system of control that people swear that they wish to fight. Winners and losers are always chosen. The synthetic starch technology will be suppressed until the Controllers can find a way to make it work and also maintain control of the populace. There are many such technologies, for this section, I decided to focus only on carbon, to kill two birds with one stone. Global warming was created by them, they just want us to accept that it isn't that bad. That always the deal, it's not so bad. How about another carbon product, diamonds.

The diamond market, like all the other markets, are helmed by talentless undeserving simpletons who spent their entire worthless lives with a boot in the necks of scores of people. In fact, it's these markets that told us that diamonds are super valuable. Diamonds can be grown in a lab. Carbon dioxide can be pulled straight out of the air and with lots of energy you can make any sized diamond that you want. Currently, you can grow a diamond for $300 to $500 per carat. Why hasn't the diamond simpletons packed up shop and run away? Because energy prices are high. Imagine, if you will, you had your own flow of energy, then diamonds would simply cost you a rate of energy. Meaning that you can have a certain amount of diamonds over a specific period of time.

If anyone can have as much energy as we want, then I could potentially have as many diamonds as I want. If I build up lots of energy and only made diamonds, and after thirty years I had a large chest of diamonds, am I a multi-millionaire or do I have a chest of worthless rocks? You've got to understand that the 'markets' are a handful of talentless simpletons who've exploited humans for many generations. How many people do you think will be murdered if people can grow their own diamonds with their own energy? And when people start growing their own diamonds, the diamond 'market' will be closed forever. It was always only a handful of niggers that runs the whole thing.

These people are, and have always been terrorists. They are the ones that are causing the problems, and they are the ones that make racism, sexism, and all the other isms relevant. They desperately want you not to notice that they are the ones causing and benefiting from the problems of the world. The people at the top of the diamond market are a threat to the world. They always were, but the fact that their entire system of control can literally go up in smoke overnight makes them especially dangerous. They've never faced consequences for their bad behavior.

This entire system has been obsolete for at least thirty years, but they've been holding on with terrorism and bribery. The biggest scam of them all is the energy markets. We only see how dangerous these people are with a market that is under the scrutiny of the whole world. The grip of the controllers is maintained with brutal oppression and terrorism. The energy monopolies may be the Achilles heel of the entire system of control. If people had access to their own energy, they can literally make whatever they want, and the system would cease to exist.

I don't know if you realize how much it will all change. My whole life, people told me that my greatest aspiration was to go to a good college to be presentable to a boss. I went to Vassar college, and learned what it means to be a black man in this country. I saw first hand, an entire class of lazy, immoral, aggressive, arrogant, alcoholic, drug addicted simpletons do nothing but party and get better grades than me. I was supposed to be perpetually grateful to be in their mediocre presence. Ask yourself, if you had unlimited energy would you spend a quarter a million dollars on education when knowledge is free? It's circular logic. I'm supposed to fight to get into an institution that others simply paid to get in.

The entire system is a shitty freemium RPG. If people have their own energy everything changes, the entire system collapses. And as if by magic, all the isms are going to stop. I talked about pooling our resources to make our own nuclear powered boats. Since I planned on running for mayor, I'll share it as if I were in charge of a constituency. In fact, to make it easy, I'll be the President. If I were President, I would simply buy the exact number of nuclear powered ships that we need. And to make everything simple, each ship would produce ammonia. There already exists a nationwide ammonia infrastructure. I'd make more than enough storage for excess ammonia, and I would buy giant ammonia fuel cells and spread them around the country. I like ammonia because it's the least toxic of the liquid fuels. If there is ever an ammonia spill, we can cure it water.

"That's Socialism! You're trying to take the joy of work from the people!" Fuck you from the bottom of my heart. This is how it would work. The government would make the initial investment, then they would open every inch of the system for sale to each American. There are over three hundred million of us, so we can all own one three hundred millionth of each boat and the entire ammonia infrastructure. That's right eminent domain bitches. Then for each city, the residents can own the ammonia fuel cells and the storage units based on a share of their population.

Since everyone has different income levels some people will buy the maximum right away. People with less money will eventually get to the maximum. Thus making a more equitable RPG. This isn't socialism, as the government will get all of its investment back with interest. Also, the government can tax the energy that comes in, it's a win-win. But as President, I'd make one change. The cost of the energy assets will cost less for three different groups, until they reach a certain level: the very poor, women, and the elderly. Once people have enough energy, they can decide if we want more energy, it's a matter of making more boats.

Everyone will be free. The entire system will collapse and no one will miss it. No one will be hungry, no one will be homeless, and all the people who spent their lives hoarding paper will be flaming mad because no one wants to work for them anymore. We should keep an eye on all of the folks whose entire livelihood depends of the subjugation of people. The places that regularly cut corners and violated labor laws. They are terrorists in the waiting. The Monopoly Pyramid was designed to collapse, I just had a hard time seeing how the Controllers can reestablish control after the coming collapse.

SLAVES IN THE GILDED CAGE

Some people may take offense at being called a slave. Clearly, they make all of their decisions on their own, are free to move around, and live their lives. These folks love to say 'slavery' ended long ago, and all the obvious labor exploitations are the faults of those being exploited. They made bad choices and are of low quality. It's imperative for people at all levels to know their place in the hierarchy.

When some crow about naming a thing, they are absolutely right. The Controllers purposely populate two sides of an argument and aggressively promote those sides. Currently, the sides about the hierarchy is on the one hand it's a perfect system that all wish to emulate it, and on the other, they call it structural racism, or structural sexism. You could potentially change out the isms with almost any ism. Both sides can easily demonstrate flaws in these assertions. I'm not going to waste time on either, the truth is that it's structural control. The racism is a distraction and the sexism is a feature.

It's become imperative to describe the control surrounding the slaves in the gilded cages. Firstly, because I was supposed to be one of you, it was my place to be a shinning example of what hard work and talent can afford you in the system. The second reason is, almost everything that has transpired in the last two years were about you. When you understand the tendrils of control that bind you, you'll understand, as I do, how much the system needs to completely die. First let's characterize those in the gilded cage.

You went to the best schools, and sacrificed and hustled while everyone else was out enjoying themselves. Where you started out, isn't as relevant as the system wants to make it out to be. The slaves in the gilded cage are life long learners, with expertise in a number of subjects, and can usually speak more than one language. All of these things seem like these folks 'deserve' their place in life. Maybe they do. It's just the path that everyone tells their kids is the best thing in the world. To be a Gilded One.

Let's consider the structures that bind you and everyone else. The Controllers, collectively, own the lions share of everything. Meaning, if they are coordinating, we are all in deep shit. It is similar to the Oligarchs in Russia, except, the Russians have only been at it for a few decades. The Controllers are the main path into the gilded cage, as they supply the 'jobs.' We've, as a species, accepted this as how it's supposed to be. Honestly, it's nominally better than royal or religious rule, but it's still control nonetheless.

In addition to providing you your salary, they provide the only places for you to live. This is why it's so important that most people have no idea who their actual landlord is. It's usually a faceless organization with layers of managers. If the same people who supply the jobs are the same people who provide the housing we then have the seeds of control. I can't prove this assertion, but assuming such a thing is true explains all of the actions the people in power have done in the last two years.

Covid exposed so many things in our society, and it's further mutations have nearly completely destroyed the system of control. It was the absolutely worst thing that happened to the Controllers. You were supposed to go to work, and show off your amazing skills, and then take a majority of the worthless paper that they gave you and spend it in the approved places. Being well-off is wonderful, but where to live? Here in NYC, everything is divided socioeconomically. There is obvious racial divisions, it sucks, but it's a distraction; for you. How about we describe the sections?

There's the spaces for the filthy rich. You can't afford the home prices, in addition, many of the extremely rich areas are too far from the job that they gave you. Yes, they calculated beforehand how inconvenient it would be to travel from areas that are only designated for them and their mixtape, modeling, and generally talentless progeny. But you are allowed to visit with high-end hotels and villas. They were made precisely for you. So you can see these clearly happy and successful people. They are supposed to be your motivation. In general, for work, you answer to these idiots. I don't know if you've noticed, but the rich have been radically raising prices for their mc'mansions for years now. It's for you, you're about to get a giant raise! Aren't you excited? But seriously, you'll never be able afford to live near these fucking simpletons. Be thankful.

Just beneath the locations designated for the rich and the famous, there are your areas. Sure, they look nice on the outside, and the inside. Anything you want is conveniently in reach. Your home is in the price range of what the Controllers have decided what you were worth long before you started your arduous journey. Buying or renting the home you have is like a crowning achievement. Though it could be unsettling to think someone planned this ahead of time. It's a slow motion plan, they control all the means of production, and the media. You were told from a young age, this is the master plan for all humans. What's notable about your home location? It's incredibly convenient for you to get to work. Maybe a short work, train ride, bus ride, or even a short drive. Since you can afford it, you deserve a short commute don't you? I'm going to tell you what you don't have.

You, and everyone beneath you, don't have control of your food, water, housing, or energy. All you have is access to credit. With this credit, you're supposed to buy their crap. They own everything! You own your house you say? Well, technically yes, you absolutely 'own' your home. Maybe you even 'own' more than one home. But in reality, your income can't afford the property outright. But to help you with that, the Controllers offer you a note to 'own' your own home. The length of the note is how long they expect you to work for them. With the promise, after you've gifted them your life's work, you get to keep the equity in the home. If and only if you managed your worthless paper properly.

Beneath you are the middle-class, and the working class. Here in NYC, the middle class areas can only reach the city center using one access point. These folks have to put up with easily fixable traffic, or the occasional train delays. They will never fix traffic problems, it's a feature of the system. The working-class almost always have a much harder commute to work. They usually have multiple transfers on the train and bus, just to get to and from work. The middle-class and the working-class work just as hard as you, but you see, they just weren't as 'lucky' as you were.

Many of the Gilded Ones can trace their path to success to a transformational event. It usually takes extreme talent, hard work, and luck to be a Gilded One. You are supposed to be the avatars of the system. Ones that people love to focus on as the true success of this system of control. What happened with the corona-virus?? You all refused to pile into those office spaces and hotels, specifically designed and priced, with you in mind!

Covid was a direct threat to the system from the moment it hit the scene. The Controllers, their acolytes, and the Mad Ones were, from day one, kicking and screaming about something or other. It's useless to dwell on the things that the Mad Ones are shouting at the top of their lungs. They accept commands from the Controllers, or "The Invisible Hand." Behind every stupid thing they are screaming, are the actions that they are taking. These actions always involve some pain for someone, or to put it in a different way; organized terrorism. What was the problem with Covid? You fled all the city centers, likely home to your families. You have plenty in savings, and Covid was killing scores of people.

They don't care about you, or any of us for that matter. These are the people that wrested control of the populace from the god-kings, and they accepted the same beliefs as their predecessors. They believe that life exists at their pleasure. You are like a prized flock, that they molded and created by the arbitrary hoops they put in front of us all. As a Gilded Slave, you are supposed to live in areas that they designated for you. All of the things that you did for fun, that was planned as well. The bars, restaurants, shops, and hotels were created for you! If you don't patronize their businesses, who can afford to?

Here in NYC, Manhattan looked like a ghost town for nearly two years. I haven't had cause to spend any time there recently. Mainly because I can't afford it. I can only assume that it's still a ghost town by the Mayor's recent command to employers to "get back to the office." Just as a new, highly transmissible sub-variant is spreading across the world; BA.2. I'm genuinely afraid of what's going to happen next. These people are <u>terror-</u>

ists! What do you think will happen when humans don't decide to flock back to the office? I can see it all playing out now. So much of the last two years were completely about you. The Controllers' prize flock has spread all around the country, and after so long, many of you are starting new lives in the places that you are.

While scrolling on Twitter, I came across a the #GreatReset. If you get past the obligatory isms, you'll see that some of the folks, likely paid provocateurs, are rooting for a global economic collapse. This is the main move of the Controllers. They crash the system, that they are in complete control of, hopefully without people noticing that they are the ones that did it. Having the crazies foretell it is the initial cover for the thing. Later, the pain that they cause will be justified because of some ism. In fact, let me share with you something that will verify their complete control over you.

Did you know that there are five taste buds? You thought there were only four didn't you? In fact, if you do an internet search, you are going to get both; four and five. In 1907, Dr. Kikunae Ikeda discovered the fifth taste bud. If you thought the taste buds were only sweet, sour, salty, and bitter, why do you think you never knew about the fifth one? Go look at the images, on the internet, of the surface area the umami taste buds take up on the tongue. Let me dispel any confusion, I believe the Controllers used their vast resources to suppress an entire taste bud, for all of us. It's a hairless monkey spell. How is easy to explain. The why of it will hurt your soul.

To make things super simple, the umami flavor is monosodium glutamate, or MSG. We all 'know' that MSG is bad for us, but no one can really explain why. If it's so bad, why can I buy this stuff at a regular store, or online? The FDA has ruled that MSG is "generally recognized as safe," but require it to be listed on all foods because for some reason MSG is controversial. What is so controversial about MSG? Racism. The reason that we all accept for MSG being mercilessly attacked, is because in the past, the Whites didn't like how successful Chinese restaurants were. That's crazy, because Chinese restaurants are literally all over this country. If the point of the terrorism of the past was the decrease Chinese restaurants, then it was a complete failure. But what are the results? No one in this country has any clue about their fifth taste bud. They used the racial terrorism as a distraction for you. Let's focus on the why.

What is the purpose of your taste buds? It help you identify the things that you need in your body, and let's you know how the body likes its fuel. Sweet is obvious, our body needs glucose for energy. Salty is also incredibly obvious, the body also specifically needs salt. Sour helps to identify acidic foods, also obvious. Bitter usually identifies if a food has gone bad, it will taste bitter. But some people like consuming bitter things like coffee. The last is umami, and just like salt, the flavor is precisely MSG. But does MSG occur naturally? Absolutely! If you want to buy MSG, sure, go ahead. But knowing where it comes from might radically change your life. MSG is made naturally by foods that we consume being partially digested with bacteria!

I've many times experienced the umami flavor. The first time was at my friend Charu's home. His mom would always leave a turkey, American cheese, mayonnaise, and white bread sandwich on top of their microwave. She would wrap it in paper towels so no critters could get at it, but was still exposed to the air. Also, in the microwave, she would leave a bowl of barbecue chicken wings; uncovered. I don't know how many hours the food would sit there. But, my god, it was the best food that I'd ever eaten. Since then I'd had the umami flavor many times. Why is this a threat to the system? If we all started allowing bacteria to digest our food some before consuming it, we would eat less food.

I absolutely abhor racism, or any ism for that matter, but when you think about the system of control that we all live under, you must understand, that it is almost always a giant distraction. Look how far a little racism can go. The entire population is in the dark about how their bodies work, and the only people who benefit this giant lie are the Controllers. You're supposed to constantly consume.

Once you look past all the obvious hate in the #GreatReset, you'll see that they are planning a giant crash, and right this moment the Controllers, and the Mad Ones, are actually trying to crash the economy. Sure the very rich could just start firing people. But they don't want a backlash. They will need to blame something other than a desire to fire lots of people, kick people out of their homes, shut off their water and energy, and finally throw away all of the food. These are things that will absolutely happen soon, but they need cover to make it seem unavoidable. They'll likely blame Biden or just black people in general. But why do they need a crash? You are the only people out of place. You must understand, they believe that they own you!

The super rich own the sky-rises, they own the hotels, the bars, the restaurants, they also own the much of the goods and services available for sale. These folks own everything. You are supposed to spend the money they gifted to you, at their approved locations. In addition to this, the Controllers are closely connected to organized crime. There's sex trafficking, drug trafficking, extortion, and so on. I don't want to go overboard with all the crimes these people are likely associated to. But do you remember, at the beginning of the pandemic, where there were reports of criminals sitting on tons of cash?

It's because they had a hard time laundering the money in the usual ways. What are the usual ways? Through real estate transactions, casinos, hotels, churches, bars, clubs and restaurants. The news, and the internet, has been highly focused on the first four, mainly because Donald Trump reeks of money laundering, and he has many questionable relationships with real estate, casinos, hotels, and churches. But of all the places that I listed, bars, clubs, and restaurants are the best places to launder illegal profits. This is because these businesses all take in large amounts of cash daily.

When you go to very poor neighborhoods, there are few bars, clubs, or restaurants. But you might get six delis within a one block radius. This is all on purpose, the poor aren't useful in laundering money. If the Gilded

Slaves don't get back to the office, and their high end properties, many of the money laundering fronts will simply collapse. A bright spot in the pandemic is that these criminals were forced to launder their money through Bitcoin. There are a multitude of problems with this.

Firstly, because so much needed to be laundered, it's highly likely that these folks used undercover FBI agents, or informants, for their transactions. Secondly, I'm 100% certain the US government is real-time decrypting Bitcoin. I need to say something that I noticed recently with the massive coordinated push to promote crytpo-currencies. I originally believed that the Controllers were setting up a giant pump and dump. When I was writing that section a few months ago, I had a fact nagging at me the entire time that I was writing it. There is no possible way that the 1% could get away with billions or trillions of dollars by dumping Bitcoin. Why? Because the thing is a fucking public ledger!

Imagine for a moment, millions of people, with top of the line computers, all at once, watching their Bitcoin value plummet. What do you think that they will do? They will obviously create a program to decrypt the entire thing and ask anyone who wishes to share their computer resources collectively. In the same way Bitcoin in encrypted with an army of mining servers, angry investors will obviously decrypt every transaction and share it publicly.

I keep thinking, these people can't be that stupid to commit crimes publicly. Some day, it's going to be decrypted. Hell, someone with skill could write a program that decrypts Bitcoin tomorrow. I would certainly leave that program running in the background of my computer. What did I see that changed my mind? They are now 'backing' crypto-currencies with a variety of things: gold, silver, gems, the USD, and real estate. Also, there are a number of companies promoting crypto loans. These idiots only ever have one move, a crash.

If they intend crypto to succeed, then the banks all have to go. It's possible every single bank crashes and never recovers. I don't think there is any appetite for another round of bank bailouts. How will they fail? If anyone ever moves any direction away from the oil and gas industry, the entire banking section will collapse, because they are precisely the ones who are heavily invested in the industry, worldwide. I'm talking about in the multiple trillions of dollars range. Also, if you, oh Gilded One, don't get back to 'normal,' the trillions of dollars of debt, held in high-end real estate, will all default simultaneously.

How can they create plausible scenarios for a crash? The first thing they needed to do is replenish their cash reserves. You see, 'investors' were all in on Trump. These people invested trillions of dollars into the stock market. It's a known fact that the top 10% of Americans own 89% of stocks. So it would be more much more accurate to say that the very rich were all in on Trump. The Gilded Ones weren't in on this buying frenzy. You all studied the markets, and understand the tried and true axiom, "buy low and sell high."

Riddle me this? Why are the supposedly smartest people on the planet not taking profits when stock prices are literally at all time highs? More importantly, where did all that money go? That money went to you didn't it. Some of you saw the heights that stocks were reaching and sold. Obviously, you wait for the dip right? There were no dips, even the worst pandemic in a hundreds years had stocks continuously climbing.

I was waiting for a catalyst event, but the Biden administration met most of the economic headwinds and surpassed all expectations. Before we discuss what the President and his team are doing, the Controllers needed to replenish their cash reserves, as they have been hemorrhaging money most of the Trump years until now. All businesses began radically raising their prices for goods and services. What's weird about it is that usually they try and give a viable excuse for the cause of the inflation.

The Controllers are blaming Biden and the 'woke' culture in general for higher prices. That's mindbogglingly ridiculous. Firstly, blaming rising prices on a group of peoples' personal state is so insulting moronic that I'm simply going to move on from that forever. Next, the same people screaming at the top of their lungs about the "free market" will be the first to tell you that the government shouldn't be involved in business decisions. How can the President be to blame for rising prices anywhere, if the President has no direct control of these businesses? For some reason, Democrats always respond to the fucking nonsense coming out of the mouths of Republicans.

Someone orchestrated price increases all around the country. Large and small companies admit that they are being pressured by 'investors' to raise their prices. These companies are being rewarded with additional stock purchases from 'investors.' The few who refuse to raise prices, well these 'investors' are dumping these companies' shares. So 'investors' are pressuring the richest and most powerful companies on the planet. Who the hell has the resources to pressure multi-billion dollar companies? The Controllers do. What do the Controllers get by raising prices?

The structure of our economy is best described by fluid dynamics. They own all the means of production. By raising all prices, you squeeze money out of the local economy. On paper, the economy is booming, but in reality all Americans are becoming poorer as prices skyrocket. What has transpired? The folks who dumped all their worthless paper into the stock market, have mostly replenished their cash reserves. Another part of the Great Reset is that much of the poor were no longer poor.

There were minimum wage increases all across the country. Also, the stimulus worked too well. It reduced poverty, and it also cut the deficit by a trillion dollars. The system of control wants large national debts and inescapable poverty. By radically raising prices, all the supposed gains of liberal groups were nullified. From what I understand, businesses are still planning on raising prices. Why do you ask? Because it would eventually crash the economy. How they plan to spin it as someone else's fault is beyond me.

Currently, the richest people in this country own the most stock, possess most of the currency, and also they own most crypto-currency. It appears, to me, they are trying to starve local economies of currency until they get their way. That will lead eventually lead to a crash in the stock market. For now, it's just downward pressure in the stock market. They will need a catalyst for market makers to bid the price down, and set up the pretext to start firing people.

What's a good pretext? There are a few, one that jumps out right away is that the government raising interest rates to slow down inflation. Raising interest rates assumes that inflation only happens naturally, based on the system that we are currently using. I tried to address this in my book "Follow the Money." It happens like clockwork, and I think it's the only tool at the government's disposal to combat inflation. I'm not sure the current government is prepared for such an organized effort to shoot prices to the moon. It's hard to cooperate with individuals who are planning and rooting for an economic collapse.

Recently, President Biden was touting the Build Back Better plan. One facet of his plan was to make certain payments to poor people permanent. There were a number of proposals that were specifically designed to put actual money in the hands of the poor in this country. His logic was simple, it just worked to save the economy, we should just keep doing it. He was famously thwarted by two members of his own party. I could go into detail about his policies, you likely already know of them. But I want you to know, oh Gilded Slave, all of that opposition was about you!

Do you remember what I said about the Black Wall Street massacre? The Controllers don't like financial reciprocity. Whenever you give tax breaks or cash subsidies to the rich and powerful, that money disappears into a black hole. It is deliberate, if they spent their money locally, poverty wouldn't exist. But it's about you right? In these last two years, did you decided to settle down away from the hustle and bustle of the city centers? Did you decide to open the business that you've always dreamt of? I bet you are struggling for customers if you did open a new business. You know where most of the worthless paper is right?

If the President's plans come to fruition the minorities, and especially women, would have money to spend. They will usually spend it locally. Those people would've been your customers. Even if you're business caters to higher end clientele, where do you think these folks will get their money from? Apple, Tesla, and Microsoft aren't splashing cash around the nation. Neither are any billionaires. Your future customers are likely precisely the poor of today. If they are no longer poor, they will have more money to pay taxes, and they will have extra cash to spend at your business.

Since you aren't a giant corporation, you won't get the magical tax breaks they do, and will also pay taxes. In addition, the profits that you make will likely be also spent locally. You, and your businesses, are a threat to the system of control. Black Wall Street was firebombed from the sky. They will scorch the earth to make sure that your businesses fails.

Another thing that Biden wanted to do, was to undo what everyone calls structural racism. I think they are missing the point calling it that. His plans are vast, so I'll only focus on one facet of it to illustrate my point. I'll put it simply, there is no way in hell the Controllers would allow Biden, or anyone else, to undo the obstacles that they put in place generations ago. The fact that people are even talking about it politically worries me. These people are terrorists!

Biden really wants high-speed railways. What if Congress approves of high-speed rail between New York City and Washington DC? How would that affect housing prices in NYC? The entire housing market in New York would collapse! Both the high income earners and the middle class could easily opt to live in Maryland or Virginia and be in NYC in twenty minutes. Property values in northern Virginia and Baltimore would jump, and there would be vacancies all throughout NYC. Everywhere I look, there are giant cracks in this wretched system. I don't know if Biden is just naive or he's in on it, and doing a good acting job. I like to believe that he's naive.

Earlier, I said that there was a simple fix to the purposeful traffic. I thought of this during the time I wrote "Follow the Money." I didn't include it into the book due to lack of space. Instead of addressing the traffic problems, I focused on the impending calamity of the driver-less car. In the book I focused on collective ownership of a fleet of taxis. I was driving a taxi at the time, and I can tell you that the drivers dread the day that their shitty livelihood gets replaced overnight.

The plan that I'm going to detail now, I planned to use in my campaign for mayor of New York City. I was aware at the time how it would affect the rich and the powerful, and intended not to focus on the obvious outcomes. It's doubtful, even if I did get elected, that the City Council would've approved it. The money powers would've likely stopped it. Biden's plans for high-speed rails are obsolete. He's right that it would positively impact the local economy, and he's surprised at the resistance to it. You can't change the infrastructure. If you do, the system of control may collapse. Instead of a massive physical infrastructure, we can create a dynamic virtual infrastructure.

If you look at bus routes in NYC, some are essentially the same for almost a hundred years. Technology has advanced far beyond the obsolete bus map. Our not-for-profit will mainly focus on individual energy ownership. Every sentient being shall have the ability to own energy producing assets. If people are able to store, use, and trade their own energy, it's in the best interest of the organization to connect the individuals to businesses and organizations that will accept energy as payment. The logic first place to spend energy would be on automobiles, trains, and planes. Each of these things operate on energy. Using the internet and our own mapping app, we can create a dynamic virtual infrastructure.

It would make far more sense to have the smaller vehicles only operate within a quarter mile radius, and make frequent stops. This is similar to how ride share companies do it now, except the drivers will essentially remain local. Mini-vans and vans would make slightly less stops, and operate in a dynamic loop in areas larger, than the sedans. Buses will also operate within a dynamic loop, but the minimum distance between stops could be at least one mile. If we do this in New York City, almost nothing would need to change. There already exists many bus stops, and they can be utilized based on a the needs of the passengers.

In this way, anyone can move freely throughout the city without a car. Since we can all trade store and use energy, the people who operate these vehicles can also be paid in energy. You have to remember that I said automobiles, trains, and planes. With a dynamic infrastructure, a person potentially work in New York City and live three hundred miles away, using planes, and have a decent commute, all without owning a car. All you would need is energy. But I digress.

What else is happening right now to try and force a collapse? What are the Mad Ones doing right this moment? They are creating traffic problems. I don't know if you tire of hearing it, but this is about you, oh Gilded Slave.

The Mad Ones are a collection of folks some are consciously aware of the harm they're doing, and some are moded and feel the need to do the things that they are doing. They are terrorists, or more specifically, people farmers. They actively herd self-aware hairless monkeys where the Controllers tell them to. In addition, it's their jobs to cause targeted pain. The point of it is multi-purpose. Firstly, it is a distraction from the real people pulling the strings. They will gladly take the blame for horrible things, and accept it as a badge of honor. Especially if they get away with their terrorism. The real purpose is usually the purview of the Controllers.

The trucker convoys in Canada and the US give off the same energy as the Vandals sacking Rome. While I'm not a historian, the Roman Empire is known global for their brutal suppression of uprisings. The sparse information about the Vandals only describes them as barbarians. It's important to keep repeating the stupidity of our history to see the repetitiveness of the union between the Controllers and the Mad Ones. The Vandals, and I can't stress this enough, attacked the heart of the Roman Empire, and 'succeeded', because... the Catholic Church dropped the commandment about idolatry!?! I admit, I'm reaching a bit, and trying to fill in the blanks for myself. I suspect many of the Roman soldiers had ties with the Vandals, or maybe a higher up was convinced to be gentle with them, because it literally makes no sense to me.

Just like the Vandals, the Mad Ones of old, the trucker convoys are causing pain, yet are screaming nonsense at the top of their lungs. In addition, the people in the trucker convoys are the same people who show up to multiple rallies, and 'protests' all around the country. The large gatherings are intended to show the populace large numbers of people in order to intimidate the populace into submission. It is terrorism. Also, for some magical reason, law enforcement has been incredibly gentle with these folks. So much so, the same Mad Ones attacked the capitol on January 6th, likely with the same resistance the Vandals received hundreds of years ago. What is a little traffic supposed to do?

In my book, "Follow the Money," I listed a number possible avenues to destroy the country. I opined about having a H1N1 type virus, and also attacking the electric grid in a coordinated attack. Though, in the book, in say both of these things would be impractical. In the section titled "An Attack Based in Reality," I write, "the best places to attack, that don't require advanced degrees in anything are the roads, bridges, tunnels, and railroads… The idea is to not get caught, and to encourage, with propaganda, others who aren't in my group (of terrorists) to take action on their own.[9]" I found it terrifying that these are the very things that we are facing today.

In this section, I talk about using sniper rifles to take out the wheels of trucks on highways. This would create a great deal of traffic, and slow down goods and services. I'm highly creative, and tried to suggest things that are easily fixable. With the ubiquity of cell phones, if enough motorists are recording their trips, then the culprits could be found with incredible ease. At the time, I couldn't fathom that people would just openly cause massive traffic jams, with their own vehicles, and mostly get away with it. The last thing I watched about these idiots were American cops hugging some of them as the wept, after forcing them to stop blocking a bridge between Canada and the US.

How does this cause a 'crash?' At the time, I believed the crashes were cyclical, now I only mostly believe this. The plan was a coordinated assault after a crash, to push the nation completely over the edge. The effects will be similar in any case.

"How does creating a traffic jam destroy the country? It is an important first step, but it can absolutely destroy the nation. The biggest problem that America faces is the willful ignorance around what money is and how it actually works. Remember, I would only initiate an attack if and only if the nation was in an economic downturn. This means that the deflationary process is already happening. Attacking high valued targets hoping to get bragging rights is stupid. It is much easier and more manageable to attack over 160k miles of highways with easy to obtain guns.

"What does causing traffic jams do? It slows the rate in which money exchanges hands, thus giving the deflation already happening added steam… Continued delays would raise prices for goods and services in the midst of a spell of deflation. Those areas hardest hit by job loss could potentially see higher prices for goods and services. Given the history of this nation, I'm going to assume those areas are mostly populated by people of color. In addition, the stock market is a double-edged sword. News of even the smallest of delays will have an adverse impact on a variety of stocks. If the stock market is already in a tailspin, continuous attacks on the nation's infrastructure would give investors reason to cannibalize the companies listed on the exchange.[10]"

In the book, I also assumed that inflation, and also how 'investors' would react, happened naturally. Currently, prices are sharply rising, when prices should be deflating. Think for a minute Gilded One, why are prices going up for high-end rentals, when these buildings are mostly empty? Also, the stock market should have rolled over years ago, the investors refuse to sell, even at all time highs. Causing significant traffic problems could decimate the economy. It's on purpose. They are knee deep in the Great Reset. It's your job to populate the areas that you belong, or everything will fall apart.

Let's make a prediction, as the Controllers are essentially a slow moving disaster. Prices will continue to skyrocket, and the government will continuously raise interest rates. Since most people work for the Controllers, directly or indirectly, if they don't raise pay two things will happen. First, goods and services will be consumed at a slower rate, 'hurting profits.' The increasing rates will make it, on the surface, unappealing to big businesses. The reality is, raising rates will kill small businesses. Regardless if they've raised prices, they will be caught in a headwind. Fewer people will be spending money at their local business, they will be short on cash, and their only option would be to take out loans. Many small businesses will fail. Your business, that you just started, will likely fail.

When businesses all around the country complain about the pain they are in, the Controllers will chime in and agree. In order to stop the hemorrhaging of their worthless paper, it will be time to start firing people. Which will further exacerbate the economic woes. They will fire enough people to bring the country to its knees. All the while, the Mad Ones will be kicking up dust, and shouting complete nonsense, so that we will all be focused on them.

Also, the Mad Ones, and the Controllers, will blame all the problems on people unable to fight back; likely black people. They will surgically target people of color and women, causing considerable pain throughout the nation. After they've fired enough people, it will be time to start throwing food away, turning off people's power and water, and kicking them out of their homes. Why? Because these lazy bums don't have any paper! Even though, it is precisely that very rich who are raising prices, firing people, throwing away food, kicking people out of their homes, and turning off the utilities. They are literally hoarding trillions of dollars in worthless paper right now.

The economy wouldn't crash if they spent the money. To them, currency is simply a tool of control. Since they control the media, it will always either be framed as a natural disaster, or the fault of the powerless. The point of all the pain is because too many people are rejecting what they are offering. No one wants their shitty jobs. After an extended period of pain, and massive compliance, these snakes are going to announce that they are hiring thousands of new people, with significantly higher pay. There will be much fanfare in the media about it. We should all be eternally grateful that the masters of the universe blesses us all with their worthless paper. Some of you Gilded Ones are going to get double your old salary. You must get a massive raise. Who else will be able to afford the exorbitant and constantly rising luxury prices? You are precisely the only people, whom they already qualified, to inhabit that space.

In a sense, you'll make out good in the end. Just like in my plans in "Follow the Money," the people who will be hurt the most are people of color. The reason why the middle class and the gilded class don't revolt against the price hikes, is because they believe that in the long term, that it will benefit them. This gets us back to the structural control. People like to call it structural racism, which it is. I believe that description is incomplete. How does it work? In this country, the whites have significantly more land ownership than the blacks. If prices are rising, then your property values will also rise. Effectively, rising prices will destroy anyone who doesn't own property and don't get commensurate raises in pay. The groups generally hurt by such a thing are people of color and women.

Which will lead to the last phase of the great reset. The poor won't have the resources to survive and they will do what every animal lacking its basic resources, fight back. You see, oh Gilded Ones, your special status in the universe is imaginary. An entire class of people needs to be subjugated and tricked into believing their best hope of survival is to wait on you hand and foot. They deliver your packages, cook your food, pick up your garbage, clean your toilets, drive you in their taxis, takes care of your children, guards your buildings, and do all sorts of menial tasks to make your life 'easier.' It's because you sacrificed and got all of your degrees. You have talent that they absolutely don't. They are meant to look to you and hopefully be inspired to give it their all to get out of the impossible hole that was dug for them.

But it will never happen. In the same way, no matter how hard you work, you will never achieve the status of those above you. It is by design. You are the slave, and always have been. The brazen oppression that others feel, are to motivate you to keep working, lest your fate will be the same as the people who harvest your food. How do you think they'll get the poors back to working for you even though they absolutely can't survive on what the system offers them? Terrorism!

At this stage of the Great Reset, the police, and others, will openly harass and abuse people of color. Either that, or they will openly revolt against the nothing that's being offered. I'm currently working full-time as a security guard. I can confirm that without food stamps I'd starve, and without the shelter, I'd be sleeping on the street. Prices are still going to rise, this is what businesses are projecting. The drama that will happen during this time is obvious and predictable. Law enforcement, all around the country, are infested with Mad Ones. They are people farmers, human predators, they are terrorists. By the magic of the legal system, they are free to break the law, precisely against people like me, and there will never be any consequences for them. This is literally the formula for encouraging abuse and lawlessness.

Police budgets will rise and there will be crackdowns. The government, from the Federal level, all the way to the local level, will be perplexed on how to solve this 'problem.' Republicans will be screaming some racist bullshit, and the Democrats will be talking about unity and coming together. After to hard public hand-wringing, and theatrical debate, they will come to a 'compromise.' They are going to gift the people at the bottom paper light. They will increase snap benefits, and increase housing subsidies such that the people at the bottom are precisely where they started before all this woke nonsense. But you have to understand the magic of it. You, oh Gilded Ones, will pay for all these so called government giveaways. The rich are above taxes. That burden will fall on you. To give you that extra resentment.

There is a fundamental flaw in this shitty system. The people at the bottom have to have no hope, and accept that this is the best offer that they'll ever get. And to make sure of it, the system constantly does compliance checks, and demands that they constantly show appreciation for the shit that they are given. The problem is, what if people tire of the abuse and leave? If enough of the people at the bottom leave, the entire system would collapse. That's why it's so imperative that the Controllers attack the places the peons at the bottom are fleeing to. Fundamentally, it's abuse. But when you do it on a public scale, it's terrorism.

I'm sick of New York City. I really do hate this place. Before the Trump administration, I was deciding to move between Atlanta and Puerto Rico. I can't tell you how demoralizing it was to see a coordinated effort to make both of these places suffer. I genuinely hate it here, and thought of the only two places that I could possibly feel safe. And you know what? I wager lots of people who look like me went through the the exact same mental process, and moved to these places.

If too many people, that you expect to do the shit jobs, that the nobody is supposed to want leaves, then the local economy will collapse. This is because you are their economy. The people at the bottom are supposed to consume the goods and services that you produce for the general market. You're supposed to get more because you are so qualified. But the heart-plug of the system is that no one is supposed to move around to much. You are supposed to accept your roles and work.

This same thing happened in the British Empire. Too many people were fleeing their control, and moving to the wilderness of America. No one is going to admit that they need the people at the bottom. If they do, they you have to treat them better, and pay them more. The economic decline happened gradually, until it became unbearable. I believe the war of 1812 was more about stopping reverse immigration. All the British did was come over and fuck with us, and burn down the Presidential palace.

When after all the trauma that we all will suffer together ends, you're back in your office, and everything is back to 'normal,' do you honestly believe that people will simply accept? It's abuse, and often in abusive relationships, victims lose interest and move on. In the same way your ancestors were repulsed by their overlords' ratty wigs and face powder, I'm nauseated by these talentless simpletons in their 'power suits.' Fucking disgusting. I was supposed to be one of you. Since the system has qualified me, I'm meant to be the inspiration for all those beneath me. I'm theoretically supposed to be eternally grateful to have 'made it out.' Let me briefly tell you about who I am, and how the plans that I've been talking about will utterly fail.

I'M DANIEL GRAY

Will the people at the bottom accept subservience after the next crash? If past is prologue, then there is no real recourse. I can confirm to you that most of the people at the bottom are a searing ball of rage covered in a thin skin of compliance. This is what the system wants. If you aren't someone who looks like me, you wouldn't know about the incessant compliance checks. They are always terrifying, on purpose. It's my job as a brown person to pretend what's happening isn't happening.

I don't want to waste anymore time talking about the horrible things this nation has done to me. You and I know nothing will be done about it. The sum total that will be offered to me are empty apologies, worthless compensation paper, or opportunities to work for undeserving simpletons. What I will tell you is who I am. I'm a creative genius, and have been this entire time. I realized, at around ten years old, that everyone is incredibly stupid. It's like I've been living the movie "Idiocracy." It's never been the case, for me, that being the smartest person in the room meant anything accept abuse or violence.

I spent most of my life trying not to be noticed. No matter how hard I tried, it was never good enough. I was either an underachiever, trying to get over, arrogant, a cheater, or simply have the wrong attitude. It wasn't until college that I understood the only characters the system allows me to inhabit. For me, there were two choices questionably gay or nerd. All other characters are a variation on 'thug.' I noticed that if I don't play these characters, people don't hear my words, nor do they register my pain. I was effectively invisible unless I played these characters. I could mix them slightly and has differing effects of lessoning the blackness. Questionably gay nerd is a popular character that many black men play. Homo-thug is also clearly on the rise. Yet there are still limits to playing these characters.

The assumption is, even though I'm assuming these persona, I'm inherently less than the lowest white man. And there exist an entire class of people who regularly do compliance checks as well. Though these are slightly less aggressive if I weren't playing these characters. These people, whether the realize it or not, are what maintains the rigid structures in the society. I've tried a multitude of things to logically try and break the spell, and nothing ever worked. The bottom line is, I have to accept some level abuse from people who know that they are above me. Moreover, there are people that exist who have the right to abuse me if I'm thinking, feeling, or acting in a way contrary to who they expect me to be.

It's incredibly frustrating considering everyone is fabulously dense. My whole life I walked on egg shells trying not to be too intelligent publicly. In fact, whenever I was about to stand out, in anything, I would start having a panic attack. For a long time, I couldn't figure out why I wasn't able to lie. Now that I'm at peak not-give-a-fuckedness, I can see what the resistance was all about. I was lying the entire time. I spent my entire life hunched over to appease the mediocre and the undeserving. My very existence is a threat to the system. A man who grew up in Harlem, in the 80s, who almost died many times, by my hand and others, and is an actual genius exposes the giant lie of the system. Whites are inherently superior to blacks.

I can't tell you how many times an angry white guy, unprompted, would demand we have a test of wits to see who's smarter. Every single time, they would wager life or limb to prove that I was definitely less intelligent. I declined all of these challenges, and declared them the winner. After each encounter, I would recall how I arrived at that point. Every single time, it was just them upset that intelligent black people exists. I've spent so much of my life with this weird false humility. I no longer want to wear that filthy skin, and I'm sick and tired of all of the fucking compliance checks. It's all a complex shit scam to enslave hairless, self-aware monkeys.

Some of you may be impressed with a few of the things that you've learned from me so far, and attribute that to my intelligence. I told you about the mental breakdown that I had. I'm going to give you a basic explanation about some of what I solved. This will give you an idea of my creativity, and also my limitations. Although I have a degree in Mathematics, I'm terrible at it. I had spent over ten years considering this problem. After I had solved it, I speculated that it would take me another ten years to try and work out the math. It sparked an internal revolution. To this day, I'd rather feel the math.

Consider for a moment, that there exists a one dimensional plane. If I passed a circle through that plane what would that circle look like to the inhabitants of that one dimensional space? First there would be nothing, then it would become a point, then it would gradually become a line with the length of the diameter of the circle. Next, the line would shrink until it becomes a point, and eventually disappeared. Likewise, if I take a sphere and passed it through a two dimensional space, something similar would happen. To the inhabitants of that space, a point would appear out of thin air, then a circle would form, becoming gradually larger until it reached the diameter of the sphere, and finally reducing in size to a single point then disappearing.

We live in three dimensional space. Is there anything that exists that would mimic these phases? If so, then clearly that thing would be a hypersphere. A hypersphere is a three dimensional sphere rotated infinitely around a fourth dimensional axis. If such a thing passed through our universe, it would appear out of nowhere, gradually become a larger sphere, then gradually shrink, then finally disappear again. I say there exist many things of that nature. I've given you enough clues. Give yourself a chance to think about it.

We have a bit more to get to, and I don't want to keep you in suspense. If you don't want to think about it, or you have and can't think of anything I'll tell you. When you're ready, do an image search for "life cycle of a star." When scientists speak about this life cycle, they sound super smart, but they make a many assumptions, based on the big bang theory being valid. The fact is, the big bang theory has been disproven more than a dozen times, generations ago, but science won't let it go. If you want to look at my thought process at the time or some of the implications of this, you can read it for free in my book "Violent Tremors." I'd rather just tell you what I think is happening, as it potentially could affect our very survival.

I believe that our existence is at least four dimensional. While our universe is infinitely large, there are also infinitely more universes similar to ours. At the very least, the real shape of the greater universe is also a hypersphere. I suspect that the fourth dimension of our universe is a thin layer of electrons. What's keeping those electrons there? I can only speculate, and I'm not even going to try. I'm getting a headache thinking about it. Things like photons and electrons oscillate between the thin edges of the universe. That static field maintains the energy of the oscillations and as it passes back into our existence it's inertia resets relative to our space. Meaning these objects can travel at great speeds but the particles themselves may not experience the speed.

Actually, the first object that I realized had a fourth dimensional component was the photon. Photons are rapidly moving in and out of our universe, giving the three phases of light. Science only talks about two; particle and wave. I believe photons are constantly oscillating between a particle, wave, and nothing. This is what it would look like if we passed a larger sphere out of existence. It would hit the edges of our universe and oscillate. I don't have a clue on how to create such a motion though.

Scientists have a variety of explanations about how stars operate. I'll just state what I suspect. Stars are hyper-spheres, and are passing through our universe at a certain speed. As they crash through the wall of electrons, hydrogen and helium ions are ripped from the object. Which is why most of the known universe is an ocean of hydrogen and helium ions. This is an important thing that scientist simply overlook for some reason. The known universe is essentially positively charged, as it is literally filled with positively charged ions. This is the reason, I believe, that people can't stay in space indefinitely. Our bodies are designed to live in an ocean of electrons.

The Earth is negatively charged. Science believe that this is due to the geodynamo affect of the molten iron at the earth's core. I'm inclined to agree. The rotation of the molten iron knocks the electrons loose creating an electric field. I have theories of what this field is, but let's stay focused on why this affects us. Our planet is negatively charged, and all of space is positively charged. Doesn't that trouble you?

It troubles me, because we are losing the electrons due to atmospheric electricity. To be precise, there is a voltage of 10 picoamps per every square meter of the Earth. We ignore it because it's so negligible. But every hundred thousand years or so, the electric field disappears then reappears years later, with the poles reversed. It makes no sense why the field would come back. If our planet exists in an ocean of positive ions, shouldn't there be no electrons left?

The University of Maryland has been studying this, with their own scaled down version of the Earth's geodynamo. For years, they didn't get any good results, until a few years ago when they decided to place an electric field around the dynamo. It looked like a chaotic blob, but it gave me a clue on what's going on. I suspect that every hundred thousand years the Earth essentially runs out of electrons. But the Earth's geodynamo aggressively pushed against the edges of our universe, when the electrons are gone, the edges of the universe pushes back.

I'm not sure if the UMD geodynamo experiment can handle it, but I suspect a couple of things. Firstly, if they can manage to get the thing up to speed safely, then attach a diode to it, it would create a massive direct current. I'm not sure it such a current could be economically viable for public consumption. The Earth itself would compensate for the loss of electrons. If a direct current is created in this way, then I'd try one more thing. I suspect if we isolate the geodynamo in non-conductive materials, when we attach a diode to it, the geodynamo would run out of electrons and ultimately pull those electrons from the edges of the universe, as the Earth does.

When the poles flip, at least ninety percent of the things that we use to generate electricity will be completely useless for about a decade. Will creating lots of large geodynamos all around the Earth help? Please God I hope not. I say wait until it passes. But if such an experiment is successful, then we can use geodynamos on large space habitats, like O'neill Cylinders. Keeping a healthy supply of electrons to support life. If that doesn't work, I prefer battery diamonds.

This is all relevant, as the Earth's magnetic field is measurably failing. On top of all the things that we, as a species, are dealing with, a collapse in the magnetic field would be catastrophic. Now that I've qualified myself a bit, and made it immanently relevant to your life, let's get back to my personal reality.

My entire life, whenever someone believed that they had some position over me, they would abuse me in some way. Not interested in talking about more specifics. I don't give a shit anymore. In broad strokes, as an adult, it's been bosses, landlords, financial institutions, and the police. I used to lecture people on working hard and going the extra mile. Part of me really believed in this shitty system. Labor exploitation became more pronounced when I started only telling the truth, and making a point to always do something about abuse. Bosses don't want you to tell them the truth, and they absolutely want you to accept their abuse. Every single boss makes an immoral demand of some kind. Most want you all to toe the company line, regardless of how wrong it is. The lies and abuse are more pronounced the lower the pay.

I've had my pay withheld for no reason, reduced rates, forced time off because of lack of business, and the constant pressure to work more hours. You see, I was supposed to be one of the Gilded Ones. In fact, people often get angry with me and try and fire me when they find out that I have a degree in Mathematics. I've seen the exploitation first-hand, with myself and with others. Everyone does it. The employer-employee relationship is a farce. It is designed precisely to control us.

The same is true for landlords. Without fail, every single landlord has made an unfair demand of me. It doesn't matter that I kept their property in good condition, or that I always paid my rent on time. Even family members did the same things. Because it's difficult to move, you have to accept this one extra thing because they are the landlord. If you don't accept, it's scorched earth. There is also no recourse. You must accept shitty bosses and shitty landlords if you want to survive in this shitty world. But if you're a black man, expect them to be extra shitty towards you.

The same thing happens with financial institutions. I don't know how many times I've been defrauded out of my hard-earned money. All I know is no one will help, and if you ask law enforcement to help, they will turn you away at the door and tell you that it was your fault. I've been defrauded many times, but every seven to ten years I experience life altering fraud. Since I already spoke of Regus, I'll tell you what happened when I took them to small claims court. Apparently, I signed a fake lease. I should have realized it when I didn't have to notarize it. Shared office rentals operate in a different space as normal real estate. Apparently charging me without my permission, and constantly harassing me and lying well that's totally legal. They essentially took my entire stimulus check, plus some extra.

My case was dismissed. But you know what? They sent me a letter, through their lawyers, that I still owe them over three thousand dollars. It's clearly a taunt. They are mad that I left right away and forced them to waste their precious time in court. They scammed me fair and square. What's the point of even complaining to the Better Business Bureau? These snakes have hundreds of claims all around the country. What are the odds that they only do this to black people? There is never anyone to help when people hurt me. Ever.

Finally, there are the police. I'm fucking sick of the police. If I had the power, I would fire every single police officer in New York City, prosecute many of them, and start over. Clearly I don't have that power. I used to lecture people on how to interact with the police. It's much different when you look poor. When the police see my worn clothes, some feel the need to do a compliance check, as this is what it is. Sure it's annoying when random white people do it, it's many times worst when your public servant is doing it. The only way to describe it is terrorism.

I've dedicated myself to only telling the truth, following the law, and defending myself against abuse. In the last ten years, I've received multiple bogus tickets. I tried fighting them in court, the cops simply lie. After the first time, I learned the term the cops use; testilying. I had to pay thousands of dollars in fines and court costs during a time when I could least afford it. In addition to this, I had multiple nights in jail and even a three night involuntary confinement in a mental institution. I've complained to all the relevant agencies, and no one will do anything. Then by magic, the system gave us a choice for mayor a white vigilante or a black cop. To be honest, after the last election, I'm not voting anymore. I never really felt like an American, now I don't want to be an American.

No one ever cares about how I feel, or what I'm going through. Because there are no solutions for them. I'm just supposed to accept that there will always be people in my life who can do and say terrible things to me and there will never be any recourse. The entire thing, all of it, is for me to be less than who I actually am. It is, all of it, a violation of my first amendment rights. I want to tell the truth and live without abuse. I've learned the hard way, this is the only thing that this wretched system ever offers. And whenever I tell people what I want or care about, they ignore that and try to get me to focus on something else.

Worthless paper and opportunities are the only thing this system is designed to offer as compensation. Bosses, financial institutions, landlords, the police, and random ass citizens all have the right to stop me treat me like shit, and it's my job to pretend that it's normal and stand there and take it, or else. They can get away with it if they have enough paper. An exchange of worthless paper is the only remedy whenever I'm wronged.

Let's say, for example, I become a school teacher. There has been a shortage of math teachers for as long as I can remember. Also, because of the pandemic, there is currently a huge teacher shortage. If I commit to being a school teacher, I could be making six-figures a year. How? I could offer a wide range of extra-curricular activities. I can have a chess team, chess club, computer programing, video game design, website design, and a whole host of other things. It would be over fifty hour per week, but I would squarely be in the middle class. That's better than being homeless and a security guard right?

Let's assume that I get the perfect boss and a perfect landlord. Wouldn't my life be great? No. I would be paying $30k annually in taxes. What in the fuck am I paying for? Every single god damned thing that I complain about, people simply ignore me and tell me how lucky I am for the 'opportunities' that I have right now. It's my lot in life to suffer so that the mediocre can thrive. I understand the math of it. I'm not adding a god-damned thing more to this shitty system. The only thing I want is to destroy it.

The plan was to start an exodus. It was the perfect two birds with one stone idea. If enough people of color live their lives in the ocean, it would collapse the system and save those targeted for abuse. I'm of a different opinion now. I still wish to do this, but it will take time, and would be unsafe if it's just us. It's been about a year since I started writing. I constantly heard "wait" coming from the inside. So I did. Being patient allowed me to see the world as it is.

As I'm typing this, Russia has been attacking Ukraine for a full thirty days. So much of the world has rallied around them for this existential fight. For me it is the exact same thing that has been happening to me my entire life. I wish I had the ability to help them. All I can say is that recognize them in me. Something else has happened, there are people all around the world rooting for Russia. This has caused me to rethink my escape plans.

Earlier on, in this book, I mentioned the story of the tower of Babel. I firmly believe that we ourselves confused our own languages, to protect ourselves. It's likely that we were all together in one city. One sect built the tower, and declared dominance over the rest. The targeting of those not like the dominant ones, terrified us all, and we confused our words. From there, we spread ourselves all around the planet.

I'm forever grateful that we all don't speak the same language. This current conflict, all the human predators have united behind Russia. Some are connected to them financially, but most aren't aligned with them at all. Pundits are perplexed as to why such a wide range of assholes, with differing belief structure, could find common cause. It is because they are human predators, and believe that they have a divine right to abuse their particular prey.

Russia's limp assaults and pathetic floundering, could inspire other victims around the world to fight their oppressors. This is literally the worst time for them to fail. The system is falling apart and the human predators all control obsolete technology that nobody wants. The predators are afraid that their victims will repay them for all of their suffering.

Can we make boats to make energy, food, water, and surface area? Sure we can. Will we be safe in the water? Not yet. Not only would be have to contend with terrorism from the white people in the US, but we would have to deal with an assortment of assholes who don't want to give their victims hope. We would be sitting ducks. Then I went back to square one.

I'm in a place that I hate, I don't feel safe, the planet is on fire, and there is no where for me or my people to go. Unfortunately, I never give up. I will have my revenge. I told that asshole that I didn't want any injections, so did that young woman. It would be poetic for us to leave in that way, but safety is my top priority. In order for any of this to work, we need to go low-tech, and address the original problem, women. At this moment in history, all our hopes for the future will rest with females of our species. If you all don't take control, then we are doomed.

WOMEN: A MORE REALISTIC PLAN

It is all an ancient monkey spell, that we cast upon ourselves. First you control the resources, then you gradually limit said resources, followed by giving one group more resources than another. Once you have these factors, it's imperative to make it socially acceptable to allow the group with the most resources to abuse and harm the group with less resources. The group with the resources are the monkey slaves. They do the most work, they sacrifice the most, and their main reward is to be above the lesser group in the social hierarchy.

This is a function that is in most mobile life on the planet. If one of three lamb siblings isn't developing properly, the two stronger lambs will keep their smaller sibling from getting milk. They are right to constantly claim that you must name your enemies. Racism isn't the thing that we fight against. What we fight is system of slavery that has many ensnared within it. Just recently a black man in New York punched a 67 year old Asian woman 125 times. Also, a 26 year old white woman in NYC shoved and killed an 87 year old white woman and killed her from the fall.

There's a saying, "the greatest trick the Devil ever pulled was convincing the world he didn't exist." The Devil in this case are the Controllers. They exist and are pulling the strings from the background. I'll change it so that it resonates with who we are. The greatest trick the Controllers ever pulled was convincing us that we aren't monkeys. They want you to believe that we're made of 'star stuff.' We are actually made of dirt from the Earth. We are in grave danger. Now is the time for genocide, wars, and mass human suffering. Many will feel justified because of the monkey law inside of us. They <u>know</u> that weak need to be culled in order for us all to survive.

I'm expendable. My people have no value. Many will suffer and die. The first group to be subjugated in this system, and the only group that they will never let go willingly are women. Worldwide, women make of 70% of the world's poor. This is intentional, and meant to control the men. Here in America one out of every four women are sexually abused. It's slightly better than the one in three women globally who are sexually abused. No one will every investigate this, the rapists are the ones in charge.

Listing all the people recently getting indicted for sex crimes is would fill me with rage and shame. It is all too much for me. I can't even watch the news anymore. I'll just say that Donald Trump becoming President was the worst thing to happen to the Controllers. He tried to do what he usually does to individual women, to all women in the nation at once. The point of abusing you, and making sure theres no accountability, is to get you to comply. You are meant to put on the fake skin and pretend. You won't be able to work or survive without that repulsive cover. This is how they make you accept. There needs to be people to help that filthy skin grow over the pain. Those people aren't your friends. It is all apart of the control.

Donald Trump, being of the elite class, never gave people breaks. There's always a honeymoon period and sometimes a brief pause in the abuse. It's in the honeymoon period where the abuser usually gifts things that they think the victim wants, but it's never accountability for the abuse. The suffering is a vital part of the control. I hesitate to credit calamities to a higher power. But Donald Trump showed us all what weak, mediocre, inbred simpletons the people who lord over us all are. They like to hold rallies to show their strength. According to some estimates, over four million women marched in solidarity against Trump. This likely petrified the Controllers. As women are the original oppressed group.

Let me tell you who you are, as you may have forgotten, or you never knew. You are the physical creator of man. You are a queen. Inside you all life can be created. You have the power to change the species as you see fit. If you are concerned about the future of life, you can revert us all into crabs. If you want us to change into something greater, the power is within you. Evolution is a lie, it is the observation of the world, with limited resources, through a man's eyes. We are biological computers, the function of change resides with the females of our species.

After we confused our languages, we spread out all around the globe. The slight variations, in our skin and hair color, were created by women. I believe the true power of all the females, of every species, rests in the resources available. Women decide what variations are best for the next generation of humans. The changes in our outer appearance happened as we spread through different climates. As we spread out, resources were unlimited, and women were in control. Then the males took over once resources became limited.

I'm not a woman, and all that I said I can't prove. I could very well be pulling all of it out of my ass. But what if all of the world's suffering is to disconnect you from the creator inside of you? Here in America, the entire system is geared towards lifting up and promoting white male superiority. On the internet, White men like to brag about their good credit, stable job, wonderful home, new car, and their fancy diplomas. Women are purposefully financially oppressed, so that you would want one of these White men. The entire system is designed to force you to reproduce the same man over and over. As this man is supposed to be the dominant man. I can say for certain, the woman inside of all women has already declared war on the system. There's an entire class of White men you are unconsciously trying to weed out of existence; incels. Because of this I predict more violence that will be visited upon you.

In my book, "Why Women Cheat," I named the physical creator the 'Inner Woman.' I used that term as not to confuse the female writers that I hired. All parts can represent themselves in any way they choose. For simplicity, I'll continue to use Inner Woman. This part of a woman is in control of the sexual organs, and has the power to seize the body from your conscious control if you object. I tried in the book to summon this

Inner Woman, in three different women from different parts of the world. I think all four of us did a great job. There was one thing that I've argued with many women about, that I understand better now. Women believe that have the power to affect men by something as small as wearing sexy underwear.

That always offended me, and it may offend you as well after I teach you more about the Inner Woman. Many parts of us have the power to completely take over the body. Some parts can affect isolated parts of the body. Other parts have the ability to change our perception of the world around us. Then there are a few parts that can permanently bind itself to the core substance of the self to become a different person. The Inner Woman is one that can do all of this. I believe women have this faulty belief because the Inner Woman has permanently moded you all because of terrorism. You aren't allowed to express what you find attractive for fear of repercussions.

Almost every year, women who 'made it' are publicly attacked for not mating with the right person. It's so bad that rich, powerful, famous, and successful women are notoriously publicly 'single.' They are terrified of losing their imaginary position in the world for wanting the 'wrong' man. You are supposed to want a man who 'brings home the bacon.' This is why there's so much resistance to having women in charge of things. The Controllers have convinced the men the slaving at work and keeping a good credit score are what women find sexually attractive. There may be some women who are into that. But this doesn't involve the Inner Woman. This type of union, is what the system craves. It's a business agreement, that desperately poor women often accept.

Then there are the Untouchables. These women are supposedly the height of feminine attractiveness. They are rewarded handsomely for being gorgeous and unattainable. Often, an Untouchable would mate with the rich, powerful, and famous. This is what she is supposed to do. She is otherwise untouchable. An Untouchable is meant to inspire the poor guys struggling on the ladder. These women don't dare get caught out in public with someone the system deems unworthy. These women lead a sad existence. They have a boat load of money, in a sea of unfuckable dicks.

What do you think will happen if women had unlimited energy, food, water, and space? The same thing that happens with every other species on this planet, the females will be open to mating. If women don't need men for anything, except their sperm, who will they pick? Will they be looking for men who are struggling their way up the ladder, hoping for that corner office? That's not how it works. Women will be free to select the qualities in the males that they'd like to see in the future generations. This is why women usually don't exaggerate their qualities. Women know exactly what they have to offer, and they have an idea of what type of human should populate the next generation.

How can women change the species? The internet makes that incredibly easy. In the future, women will be able to select from billions of different specimen to make the child she wishes. It's then imperative that women increase their knowledge and expertise in the fields that they find interesting. Let's use basketball for an example. What if a woman believes there needs to be more basketball players in the next generation. Women will able to trade resources for semen of specific males. But things need to be done in the best interest of the species.

Firstly, each semen pill should be at least twenty different male donors and maximum one thousand. Women can select, from available specimen, a variety of qualities: height, scoring stats, defensive stats, etc. Reproducing with a specific man, you will need to do that the old fashioned way. Having competition with the chosen qualities is, how I believe, the female reproduction system was meant to work. The best one will win. I think this is what's best for a healthy child. Of course I'm open to suggestion from biologists on this matter.

Next, for the high demand males, their contributions, and offspring, should be limited. Meaning, it's not beneficial to the species, or the game of basketball to have millions of Shaqs running around. Women would need to spend their resources on a lottery for Shaq seed. Even still, they will only be at most 5% of of a total sperm capsule. Women can save, trade, or use the seed that they win in various lotteries. Men who have too many offspring must agree to a vasectomy. In this way, men will either willingly or unwillingly remove them from this gene pool.

Given time, women will create anomalies. In the current environment, anomalies are attacked and destroyed. Only one type of person is preferred in every culture, all around the world. If women are in control, anomalies will be protected, and potentially bred. Possibly expanding what it means to be a human. I readily admit that this is all speculation from my experience with women. I could be wrong. But I believe that you have a great power within you. She is alive, and she isn't you. Many of you curse her every month, but if you allow her to become you, she can save the entire planet. Even if I'm wrong, you deserve to be free. Now let's try and make a plan based in reality.

COUNTERING THE CONTROLLERS

The people who control this place create problems on purpose. It is a part of the monkey spell. You have to accept a little pain. You have to willing say to yourself "this isn't so bad." There's never a way to fix the problem. The people who made the problem literally limits the solution and the currency, such that it's always too costly to fix. But if you're willing to pay, they'll happily rob you of your resources. I mean to create an organization to combat this evil. Fundamentally, the Controllers are anti-life. An anti-Controller organization would protect life. My organization will simply solve the problems the Controllers put before us.

Firstly, we'll need to acquire land. Almost a year ago, I was convinced much of our operations should be in the water, as it's is incredibly easy to expand. I'm of the opinion now, that there are far too many humans at risk, and they could be less safe in the water. That being said, if we work together, we can make it out of the quagmire that we're in. Our organization will acquire land and ocean space to encourage and protect life. The best place to start is where no one wants; deserts.

It's telling, that every time an acolyte of the Controllers gets into power, they want to hurt nature or people. It is on purpose. The land is barren on purpose, and we have the power to change that. There are two likely places we can start. Either Somalia or the US. I prefer Somalia because they are currently suffering a nationwide famine, and also they have lots of available desert. We could trade for it. America would be useful because it would be safer and it has a readily available infrastructure. Did you know, that if nothing changes, the entire US will be a desert within fifty years? I'm hoping nations gift us their deserts, with the promise that we'll regrow life.

Next we need to power our lives. We've already discussed the control that we're under. I strongly prefer nuclear power in the ocean. But without assurances of safety, it's a waste of time. Also, I purposely wanted to use nuclear power to give folks in the fossil fuel industry a chance to change their ways. It would take decades to have thousands of nuclear powered boats. Now, I wish to kill the entire industry overnight. They are a threat to life. We can do it if we worked together.

Let's reaffirm that the 'fossil' fuel industry has nothing to do with dinosaurs. It's a lie, intended to confuse us all. Make us all think the black stuff is hard to come by. Oil is actually just algae, and the stuff literally grows exponentially. Some folks who get enough light in their homes can simply grow as much algae as they need. But let's be concise. We need farmers and folks with enough space in their backyards. How much space would we need? Well only 200k square miles of solar panels could power the world. The issue with that is how to store it? We can easily do a million square miles of algae farming. The main difference between using solar panels and farming algae, is that algae creates stored energy.

How can we increase the surface area? If you do an image search for "algae photobioreactor," you'll see a wide variety of types of reactors. The fact is, we can build upwards as high as we want. As long as there's an airflow such that the algae move around and all get sun, then we can literally power the entire planet with a few thousand farms and backyards. The Controllers will tell you that it's too expensive. Because they want it to fail. Yet the trillions that they spent on killing the planet was the right price. They don't like algae because it can't be controlled.

An algae bioreactor system, even for a small farm, might cost a million dollars. How can we overcome this? A million of us come together and chip in a dollar. Algae is farmed everyday, all the owners would need to supply is the nutrients, and each owner would get a small cut of the algae. In this way, even with a few million people, we could eventually reach the point where we can literally power everything. If the government or the rich wish to help, they can supply the initial investment, and local people will have the right to buy shares of each asset up unto a point. I prefer government agencies doing the investments. It would supply all the energy needs for a local city, the government can raise money from it or they can sell at discount for the needy, and also the government can take a cut of the rewards for taxes.

Overnight we could have millions of square miles of algae farms, all owned collectively by individual people. The next thing that needs to happen is the extraction phase. We have to set it up ourselves. In fact, the farms themselves could have their own personal extraction machine. This is something that we will also collectively own. Once the oil from the algae are extracted, they call it bio-diesel. It can be put into diesel engines directly. Also, solid-oxide fuel cells can use bio-diesel as an energy source. It would be twice as efficient as combustion. The only problem with bio-diesel, is that it freezes in cold temperatures. To fix this we need to refine it.

I'm gonna waste precious letters to reiterate, that this is the exact same stuff that they are pumping out of the ground. But bio-diesel is way better. After the extraction process, the biological matter could be fed to the worms. The black stuff leaves a lot of waste. We could use Koch Industries to refine our oil? The thought of it offends me. These snakes divided the parts of the thing and made mini monopolies to control the price and ultimately us all. The Kochs and others have regional monopolies on oil refining. We'll just make our own. All of us, who wants to control our own lives, can own shares in refineries, up to a point.

After refinement, there's one last hurdle; distribution. This is another place where regional monopolies come into play. We'll obviously make our own distribution network based on the needs of those who paid for it. Essentially, overnight, we could completely take over the 'fossil' fuel industry. The point is to get every human to own assets to produce the stuff that they need. In this way, if you own enough assets, all you need to supply are the nutrients, and you'll have energy to use, store, or trade.

Since worm castings are the best fertilizer on the planet, we'll use worm castings as a form of currency as well. Any human, regardless of how small their dwelling is, can operate a worm farm. They are easy to maintain, and the worms would eat your garbage. Owning lots of algae assets, will create a massive demand for worm castings. The poorest people can exclusively become worm farmers. I would prefer these farms to be in population centers. Doing it in the water seems cool, but having millions poor people with hungry worms to feed, would literally reverse the flow of garbage. Worms eat food waste, paper, cardboard, pet, and human waste. Our organization will operate and maintain the storage facilities. The people will own it.

All around the world, people are complaining of a lack of water. And everyday we discharge tainted water into our waterways. It was set up like this on purpose. There are two things that I'd offer up for sale to the public. Shares in an ammonia extraction factory and a reverse osmosis factory. Currently, it costs us a lot of energy to make ammonia, and it literally cost us money to destroy the ammonia humans make everyday. Don't you find that odd? With worm castings, we wouldn't need to make ammonia for food, it comes with nitrates all in it already. With these two factories, owners of these assets will get ammonia and water. Both vital things for humans. The ammonia we can use for electricity. The waste we'll deal with later.

One thing that I wouldn't mind in the ocean is the giant poop barges. If someone blows up our poop barge in the middle of the ocean, I can say for certain, there will be more where that came from. Our organization will offer giant, solar-powered barges, to allow bacteria to consume all of our poop. The micro-owners will get a rate of LNG. Our organization will get the waste. Same as before.

Next, we'll set up pyrolysis factories. So the owners of a pyrolysis factory will need to supply the energy and plastic, and in return they'll get a mixture of hydrocarbons. They could send the mixture to a refinery, but you'd be working with negative energy, and it will certainly not be carbon neutral. To remedy this, they will need to offset the carbon. They could ship worm castings to either ocean or land deserts for carbon mediation. But for now, let's just say they'll have a rate of mixed liquid hydrocarbons.

Logically, now we need to reverse the garbage. We stupidly pile our garbage to the heavens, and claim is the only way. Every other way isn't financial viable, on purpose. I say that we burn the garbage and capture the carbon. This will cost energy. This is why these mediocre snakes say that we can't do it. If we need more energy, we can capture as much as we want from the sun. Not all of the carbon-dioxide will be captured. Eleven percent of the carbon-dioxide will escape, there will be ashes, filtered toxins, and a whole lot of carbon dioxide.

Before I go on, I want to say that these horrible people convinced us that carbon is a problem. We are literally fucking carbon beings. Carbon is one of the best things in the universe. Trust me, you will want a steady supply of carbon in the future. If you don't want to offset the carbon, with energy you can make diamonds, battery-diamonds, graphite, graphene, and plastic if you combine it with water. If you offset the carbon, you can make any of the hydrocarbon fuels, sugar, and starch. All of these things can be made with carbon-dioxide and water. Carbon is amazing, and you should be able to use, store, and trade it.

Now here's a part that I would like to go into the water. We'll take the sludge from reverse osmosis, the ashes, and the filtered toxins, then mix them with the mixed liquid hydrocarbons and inoculate the mixture with a variety of mushroom spores. Since we'll be doing a lot of burning, we will need a lot of space for the mushrooms to grow. Cargo ships aren't very expensive. We will all own some bits of cargo ships. To give our mushrooms time to grow. Now it's time to offset the carbon.

In the ocean, it's simple, we can either mix worm castings into the water to make algae or put the mushrooms right into the water. In both cases, we'd make sure there are critters to consume our waste. I would like to focus on the land first. The only thing that we need to concern ourselves with is surface area. There are so many amazing technologies that we can use. I'm going to leave this open for now. I'm just going to say, that I'm confident that we can rapidly grow an entire community without bamboo.

Eventually, I'd like to use bamboo a lot more. We will focus exclusively on women who feel unsafe and the homeless. There will be water, energy, and a whole host of other things. I purposely skipped making food, as we have to much food in the world. It's a matter of organizing. If everyone has enough energy as currency, then they will have something to trade for food. If not, they will make their own food with the energy that they have.

Women will have a vital role on land. They will spread worm castings and cover all over the area we control, at least six inches deep. That will be one of the ways people can offset the carbon from incineration. But it's not complete. Plants need water and nutrients. Here, I'd like to sell solar powered zeppelins. There will be two energy storage devices on this vehicle: hydrogen and liquid metal batteries. The hydrogen will be stored to give the device lift. It will have one job, condense water and rain it down in specific locations. Each one of these will be collectively owned as well. So if we're burning a lot of garbage folks will want many solar powered rain zeppelins. You only need to buy them once to create continuous solar powered rain.

Finally, the residents on our land will have one final job. To feed the mushrooms to the land. I think it's better to lightly bury small pieces all around. I say we continuously feed the regions we control until there is six feet of nutrients to fully sustain life. With continuous water and food, there will be an explosion of life in a former desert. This will fully free people up to use the profuse amounts of water and carbon-dioxide that they have stored up. The easiest thing to do is to combine them to make fuel.

At this point, the entire energy sector will no longer exist. In fact, if you feel courageous, you can short energy and bank stocks. It's free paper. It will be time to use nuclear power. Our organization wants to make many nuclear powered boats to burn up the nuclear waste that's killing our planet. Most people will have too much water and too much CO2, you can make pure gasoline for your car if you want, with nuclear power. At this point, we will grow exponentially as a species, and can follow the plan I laid out previously. With unlimited energy, any human can do what they want. Women will be completely free.

LET'S WORK TOGETHER

Thank you for reading my book. If you'd like to work together with me, my twitter handle is @HarlemGray. As of this moment, it's just me, and I'm a homeless security guard. Together, we can do almost anything. The biggest lesson I've learned in the last ten years is to trust your feelings. Anyone who is trying to convince you otherwise is trying to control you.

It's almost as if the very nature of money is anti-human. Trust how you feel and who you are. I tell you this, because I'm committed to bringing this entire system down. I've been fucking pissed since my involuntary confinement. Since that day, I've been plotting my revenge. I know who my enemy is, the people who set this bullshit up; the Controllers. You should know that I don't accept empty apologies, worthless paper, or fucking opportunities. I will never stop unless justice is served.

You can kill me, and I will bleed rage. If the creator finds my cause worthy, that rage will fester and blossom into something beautiful. Then I'll have my revenge in death. I said no. She said no. One way or another everyone will pay. Fuck each and every one of you.

ENDNOTES

[1] "Violent Tremors: Journey to Overcome the Legacy of Slavery." By Daniel Gray.

[2] "Follow the Money: Path to Our Inevitable Economic Ruin or the End of Global Poverty." By Daniel Gray

[3] Violent Tremors

[4] Violent Tremors

[5] Violent Tremors

[6] "Core Transformation: Reaching the Wellspring Within" by Connirae Andreas.

[7] Violent Tremors

[8] Voilent Tremors

[9] Follow the Money

[10] Follow the Money

www.ingramcontent.com/pod-product-compliance
Lightning Source LLC
Chambersburg PA
CBHW051421290426
44109CB00016B/1388
* 9 7 8 0 5 7 8 2 9 8 1 6 0 *